INSIDER'S GUIDE TO MUSIC LICENSING

INSIDER'S GUIDE TO MUSIC LICENSING

Brian Tarquin

Allworth Press
NEW YORK

Allworth Press books may be purchased in bulk at special discounts for sales promotion, corporate gifts, fund-raising, or educational purposes. Special editions can also be created to specifications. For details, contact the Special Sales Department, Allworth Press, 307 West 36th Street, 11th Floor, New York, NY 10018 or info@skyhorsepublishing.com.

17 16 15 14 13   5 4 3 2 1

Published by Allworth Press, an imprint of Skyhorse Publishing, Inc.
307 West 36th Street, 11th Floor, New York, NY 10018.

Allworth Press® is a registered trademark of Skyhorse Publishing, Inc.®, a Delaware corporation.

www.allworth.com

Cover design by Mary Belibasakis

Library of Congress Cataloging-in-Publication Data is available on file.
ISBN: 978-1-62153-396-2

Printed in the United States of America

Table of Contents

Foreword

by Ben McLane, Esq.

The book you are holding in your hands is a must read for anyone that is working in—or is considering breaking into—the music business, because it explains a surefire method to get paid from music. Despite all the so-called doom and gloom associated with free downloads, paltry streaming royalties, and empty venues, the demand for music in film, TV, commercials, the Internet, radio, and other forms of media is increasing daily and globally. In TV alone there are countless channels clamoring for content, and the number of cues contained in one reality show episode can be numerous. This is great news for music creators/rights holders (both the song and master copyrights), because that means cold hard cash is being paid to the music creators/rights holders for providing the music that drive these shows. Monies can be earned either on the front-end, the back-end from performance, or often from both. Moreover, there are really no barriers to licensing music. The door is open to all ages, creeds and colors. In the licensing world—unlike the "Top 40" game—all anyone really cares about is the music; not how old someone is, what they look like, where they live, who their father is, or how many friends they have on Facebook. The link between the music creator/rights holder, the media outlet, and the compensation, is known as a "license." The basic purpose of this book is to untangle all the moving parts and teach the reader how to make it all work for them. Numerous helpful tips on maneuvering the music licensing universe and its players are sprinkled within, and well-worth applying to one's career.

Over the last twenty years, the author, Brian Tarquin, has lived, breathed and battled his way to become one of the top composers, producers, artists and executives in the entertainment business—and he has emerged as an expert on licensing along the way by really getting his hands dirty and doing it bottom-to-top (from indie films to major network shows on MTV, CBS,

ABC, and NBC). Doing it so successfully in fact, he has won three Emmy Awards and charted Top 20 in *Billboard* magazine in the process, and he has had the honor of being involved in projects that included such musical legends as Santana, Eric Clapton, Jeff Beck, BB King, Stevie Ray Vaughn, Stanley Clarke, Jimi Hendrix, Bob Marley, Steve Vai, Tommy Bolin, and ZZ Top. As a composer, artist, and music library owner, Brian has seen all sides, and his unique perspective has allowed him to master the art of the music licensing deal. Therefore, not only does his book interpret in plain English what music "licensing" really means and how to profit, it also debunks the most common mysteries, myths, and rumors associated with licensing. Simply put, the reader is getting the real "skinny" from someone who intimately knows the process, inside and out, and who, as an artist himself, actually cares about making it really work for the creator—so that person can benefit and thrive. Better yet, as a bonus Brian has included incisive interviews with several of the most important and experienced executives that operate in the area of licensing (i.e., music supervisors, composers, and many others). The reader will gain invaluable knowledge from the advice offered by the folks found within these pages. Hundreds of years of combined experience are presented here in an easy-to-digest form. All real insider stuff.

On a personal note, I have worked for and with Brian as his music lawyer for many years and have seen firsthand the dedication and professionalism he applies to the creation of his art, how he markets it, how he protects his interests, and how he respects all the participants that make the wheel go 'round. In addition, Brian has mastered the art of adapting to new media/technology—such as digital formats/platforms—and staying current with the trends, all the while maintaining mutual respect with the key decision makers. He is a model of how to persevere, adapt, and "make it" in the music business. His numerous awards speak for themselves, and his relationships with name artists and marquee, show-music supervisors are second to none.

Bottom line, Brian Tarquin has made a great living and raised his family from licensing—now you can too. Read on and find out how.

Ben McLane, Esq.
Entertainment Attorney
www.benmclane.com

Chapter 1

Introduction to Music Licensing—The Basics

The age-old question always seems to be, "How do I get my song placed on a TV show?" As you can guess, it is certainly not as easy as it looks. There is a lot of legwork, phone calls, research, and of course that certain "right timing factor."

Just because a show played a dance vocal song in a scene, does not mean that your dance vocal song will be played on the same show the following week. This might have been a rare situation that called for that particular style and may not be a reoccurring style in the next upcoming episodes. There are so many factors involved with music licensing, most importantly, building your relationships with music supervisors, editors, and television music licensing departments.

When I started in the late '80s it was much more of an open field for licensing music to TV and film, whereas, today, it is a lot more competitive out there on the street. The proverbial "best kept secret" on actually making income on your music isn't a secret anymore. Hence, through the years I've seen both sync and master fees ("sync" refers to the publishing side of a song, and "master" means the actual audio recording of a song) and the amount that PROs (Performance Royalty Organizations), like SESAC, ASCAP, and BMI, pay, go down.

As more people get into the game, the pot remains the same, so obviously with more people the supply is greater. In turn, license fees become smaller, as do performance royalties, which is good for the shows licensing the music because it makes the fees cheaper. Then there are your newcomers on the scene that offer their music for free, no sync and master fees, which can be very bad for the rest of us. As the old saying goes, "Why buy the cow, when you can get the milk for free?" Well this can easily pertain to many business models that people are using today, just out of sheer ignorance.

For instance, the Discovery Channel uses this model and insists on taking 25 percent of the publisher side of any catalog they license. Unfortunately, people jump into the pool before they realize there is no water in it! Novices think this is a surefire deal and that they will make tons of money from the back-end writer performances. Well I hate to break it to you, but the Discovery Channel performance royalties equal pennies on the dollar; absolutely laughable.

SYNC AND MASTER FEES

So let's recap this deal. You give up sync and master fees and 25 percent of your publishing just to get airplay on a channel that pays pennies for your song for a term of in perpetuity. This is because each broadcast license a network has with a PRO varies a great deal. The license fee paid to a PRO by the Discovery Channel is a fraction of what ABC-TV pays to the PRO. Why? Because these fees are measured by the size of the broadcast and the viewership is measured by the Neilsen ratings. Hence large networks such as CBS, ABC, and NBC, which have the largest numbers of viewers, have the most expensive airtime, so it's only natural they will pay the most into the pot. Cable channels like Discovery, Animal Planet, and the History Channel may only air in certain parts of the country, therefore their distribution is not as strong as the networks.

The other factor in all of this is *how* each of the PROs pay, and this varies during different parts of the viewing day. So when ABC-TV pays the licensee fee to each of the PROs, it is in a lump sum. They don't break it down by paying fees for each show they air; this is up to the PROs to do for their affiliates. Generally, the highest paying time is primetime, as opposed to daytime and overnight.

For example, SESAC uses the following "Royalty Formulas":

Station Count multiplied by Use Type Weight, multiplied by Duration, multiplied by Time of Day Weight, multiplied by Affiliate Share, equals Credits.

Station Count
Use Type Weight
Duration
Time of Day Weight
× Affiliate Share

= Credits

Television License Fees Available for Distribution divided by Total Credits, equals Value Factor.

Television License Fee
÷ Total Credits

= Value Factor

Credits multiplied by Value Factor, equals Royalty Payment.

Credits
× Value Factor

= Royalty Payment

Now back to our Discovery example, their rates are so low because the license fees they pay to the PROs are so low. Now if you did the same deal with a major network, the back-end monies would be greater. Still, I have to say the whole idea of giving away 25 percent of your publishing just to have them use your music really does not sit well with me. What's next? Pay the channel to play your music? But as we all know there is always someone out there who will do this deal.

Another broadcast company to be aware of is ESPN because they do not pay broadcast licenses to PROs, and somehow they get away with it! They do what are called "direct licenses" with music libraries and suppliers, which is a terrible practice because it lowers the value of music, and many libraries don't pass on the writers' shares to the composers. If you compose for them, they are essentially buying your writers' and publishers' performances with a one-time, work-for-hire fee with no residuals on the back-end. ESPN is owned by ABC-TV, the parent company of which is Disney, and surprisingly, they get away with not paying a license to SESAC, ASCAP, or BMI.

For twenty years I've been trying to find a definitive answer for how they can get away with this without being taken to court by the PROs, considering all of the music they play on their shows. The only answer I ever seem to get is that shrewd lawyers run ESPN and they have found a loophole. Again, no one stands up to them, not even the large music libraries or publishers that have leverage.

With this all being said, I do understand why certain people do gratis deals (waiving sync/master fees) if they are starting out in the business and need to build up a credit list. This is why music libraries are a good option for composers starting out. Good reputable libraries will split any sync/master fees with you, and although you give up your publisher performance royalties, you retain your writer's, and in some cases the underlying copyrights. I always encourage composers to contact shows directly and suggest "work-for-hire" compositions. This is a very good way to build your chops, credits, and relationships. In the beginning of my career this is how I started out, because of which, to this day, I have maintained many of the same relationships.

INDUSTRY RESOURCES

There are many shows that look for talent to keep their shows fresh, and with all of the reference guides and Internet sites, it is easier than ever to find information. Back in the day, I had to actually watch the shows and record them on VHS—slow down the ending credits to see who was licensing music for the shows. There are some great resources out there, the *Hollywood Reporter, Music Connection* magazine, and one of the most specific for the field, the *Music Registry*, run by Ritch Esra. The *Music Registry* publishes guides such as *Film & Television Music Guide, A&R Registry*, and the *Publisher Registry*, all of which are updated a few times a year. However, the *Film & Television Music Guide* is particularly good, listing actual music personnel from television networks, music supervisors, music editors, video game companies, and trailer houses from around the country. It lists specific music titles and contact information, including email addresses. It is a very resource-filled guide.

I remember back in the early '90s seeing an advertisement in the back of the *Hollywood Reporter*, in the classified section, for a small music placement company called Red Engine Music. I sent over some of my songs, and the owner, Marc Ferrari, former guitarist from the hair band Keel, contacted me and added my songs to his library. So started my longtime friendship with Marc and we have helped each other out ever since. Marc turned that library into MasterSource, which focused on vocal tracks and filled a much-needed niche in the marketplace.

Before that time no other music libraries were producing vocals, which forced productions to go to large publishers to license such music. Marc was ahead of the curve and realized the value of supplying vocals to the film and TV community at a cheaper price than what the major publishers were asking. So it's no wonder he went on to sell MasterSource to Universal Publishing years later for several million dollars. This story alone should be inspiration enough that it is possible to be very successful in the music licensing business.

The resources and the need for music are there; it's up to you to hustle your songs and get them placed, and hopefully this book will assist you.

Chapter 2

Music Production Libraries

A common question I am always asked is, "What is a music production library?" Well, I'm not going to bore you with a technical answer from Wikipedia, however I'll explain it from my twenty years of experience composing for them. Simply, they are music companies, like FirstCom, Megatrax, Sonoton, and others who hire composers to produce affordable music for all sorts of broadcast and film productions. So if a show wants a pop-vocal song and can't afford to license a track by Rihanna from Def Jam, they go to a place like Killer Tracks and license a sound-alike. Pretty straightforward and simple for productions because these libraries own both the masters and the syncs (publishing), so it's a one-stop shop.

In the new millennium there has arisen a new business model for these libraries—at places like Crucial Music, Pump Audio, and Rumble Fish—where these companies aren't hiring composers to build their catalog, but are instead licensing tracks from a plethora of musicians out there and offering the songs up for licensing. In the latter case, musicians can still own their own copyright and these deals are usually non-exclusive, because they either change the names of the songs or use specific codes in front of each song. See the Music Library Contract in Appendix C to better understand how this business model works.

The first music library model mentioned above is known as a work-for-hire deal, in which the library owns the copyright, masters, and publishing of the music composed or produced by the composer. See the sample work-for-hire contract at the end of this chapter. This has always been the most common way for libraries to do business because they control all aspects of the music, except the writer's share. They become a one-stop shop where they license everything to a particular client so that the client doesn't have to get separate approvals from various sources.

Licensing from record companies has always been a bump in the road for music supervisors, because the labels may only have control of the masters, leaving the supervisors to chase after the publishing side, commonly known as the sync side. In many cases, the sync could be split between various companies or artists stretching across the globe, making it very difficult to get approval from all parties in time to make the airdate of the broadcast. This is traditionally why music libraries came into existence, filling the void and need for music licensing in a timely manner. In turn, with such a service, the library can put itself at legal risk if the composer uses an uncleared sample, or copies another song or piece of music in the public domain without permission.

There is an additional form called a Certificate of Authorship that a composer has to sign along with any co-writers to assure the company that the music delivered is in fact original music. You can understand the company's point of view, because the music can appear anywhere in broadcast and non-broadcast, making it essential to have music that is original, free and clear to license without any additional clearances. This is similar to the indemnity clause, but extends itself to any co-writers that contribute to the work-for-hire music.

I know from experience that there can be lots of assumptions made in a contract with a composer or artist. This happened to me when I licensed a few tracks from an '80s bass player with various tracks containing famous guitar guests. He of course assured me that the defunct label that had originally released the tracks had no claim to them and that he owned everything, free and clear. This of course came back to bite me because when I released the *Guitar Master Series* on my label, BHP Music, Ltd., a large music publisher came to me and made a claim to all the songs I had licensed from the bass player. Thankfully I had the indemnity clause in the contract. It saved us from going to court because, in short, it stated that the licensee (the bass player) cleared me (the licensor) from any third party damages or claims.

Now if that was not bad enough, a couple of years later I was sucked into a lawsuit, even with the indemnity clause. I had licensed a few tracks from another indie label in Los Angeles for Volume 2 of the *Guitar Masters Series*, and a couple of months into the release all hell broke loose. It turned out that one of the tracks (a Van Halen cover song), which contained a one-time, '80s guitar hot shot, was being disputed between the guitarist and the other indie label. So even though I had legally licensed this particular track and released it through Redeye Distribution, I was still dragged into

Exhibit "C"

CERTIFICATE OF AUTHORSHIP

The undersigned, _____ (hereinafter "Contributor") residing at _____ hereby certifies that he/she has rendered writer, composer, arranger, programmer and lyricist (if applicable) services in connection with various musical compositions (the "Compositions") and master recordings embodying said Compositions (the "Masters") as listed on the attached Schedule, collectively "Musical Works", within the scope of Contributor's engagement by _____ ("Composer") in connection with the album project indicated on the attached Schedule ("Album Project").

Contributor hereby agrees that the results, proceeds and product of Contributor's services in connection with and relating to the Album Project have been solely created for Composer by Contributor as a "work made for hire" specially ordered or commissioned by Composer, or as Composer's employee for hire, for use in any and all media, with Composer being deemed the author of the Musical Works. The undersigned hereby acknowledges that Composer as author of the Musical Works, is the sole and exclusive owner of all rights of every kind or nature, whether now known or hereafter devised (including without limitation all copyrights and all extensions and renewals of copyrights) in and to the Musical Works, with the right to make all uses of the Musical Works throughout the universe and all changes in the Musical Works as Composer deems necessary or desirable. In the event that the Musical Works do not legally constitute a "work made for hire," Contributor hereby grants, sells, assigns and transfers all right, title and interest, including without limitation the copyright, in and to the Musical Works to Composer to the same extent provided herein.

Contributor hereby waives all rights of "droit moral" or "moral rights of authors" or any similar rights or principles of law which Contributor may now or later have in the Musical Works.

Contributor warrants and represents that Contributor has the right to execute this document.

Contributor agrees to execute any documents and do any other acts consistent with this Certificate of Authorship as may be reasonably required by Composer or its assignees or licensees to further evidence or effectuate Composer's rights as set forth in this Certificate of Authorship. Upon Contributor's failure to do so within ten (10) business days following our written request, Contributor hereby appoints Composer, or its successors and assigns as its limited purpose attorney-in-fact for such purposes (it being acknowledged that such appointment is irrevocable and coupled with an interest) with full power of substitution and delegation. Composer will use reasonable efforts to furnish Contributor with a copy of any documents so executed.

IN WITNESS WHEREOF, Contributor has executed this Certificate of Authorship as of this

---

this ridiculous, multi-million dollar lawsuit. Indemnity clause or not, I was caught in the middle and had to ride out the storm. The only good thing was that the other label company covered all of the legal expenses, yet I still had to seek out legal advice from my lawyer. One big mess! Anyway after two years and a deposition I gave in to the other side's lawyer and agreed to a three-hour negotiation at the Federal Court House in New York City. The other side finally settled for a fraction of what they originally wanted. That's really called making a federal case!

The newer music library business model (see Modern Library Agreement in Appendix D) is a lot more flexible and is based on licensing preexisting music from artists. Usually companies license the music from an artist on a gratis, non-exclusive basis in perpetuity. Companies can build a catalog fairly quickly and not have to pay the upfront costs for work-for-hire composers. The downside of this is that the catalog that is built will not be a custom one, rather one that depends on the sources you license. Because of today's plethora of music spurring from the digital revolution, which lets everyone record their own tracks on small computers in the corner of their living rooms, artists are producing more music than ever before. Not that long ago, less than a generation, it was a lot more costly to produce music. An artist would have to rent studio time, buy tape media, and pay for engineering costs, mastering, pressing, and artwork. This whole expense process has now streamlined into a convenient little computer; hard to believe for an old analog dog like myself. However, on the other side of the coin, the new digital age makes it a more creative process for the artist.

As for a non-exclusive agreement, the artists can shop the music themselves, or give them to another company to place. It used to be standard to just change the names of the songs for each company you licensed them to, but today the PROs (Performance Royalty Organizations) frown upon different titles for the same songs, so companies now place their own code in front of the title: for example, "TFT 001 Vitamin U." When I was supplying music to the Proctor & Gamble soap operas twenty years ago, they commonly had us change the titles of the songs so that Proctor & Gamble could receive a share of the publishing royalties from SESAC, ASCAP, and BMI. At one time a company named Verance had its own technology for watermarking each song and detecting each particular broadcast of the song through its own monitoring system. I can testify firsthand that it worked extremely well! My statements for the short, two-year period, when the system was up and running, were over a thousand pages each quarterly statement. One word . . . *incredible!* But it was too good to last. Verance had costly lawsuits as well as costly monitoring expenses and stopped the service altogether.

The most important part of the Verance years was that it detected every airplay in the local markets, even though it ranged from pennies to hundreds of dollars for the plays. This made a big impact in my accounting books, because to this day there is no system yet that detects local airplays. Why is this so important to library music? Well, my friend, it is very important when (abc) **Music Department**

Standard Cue Sheet

30 W. 67th Street

New York, NY
10023

SERIES TITLE: ALL MY CHILDREN

| EPISODE TITLE: | 8901 |
| EPISODE NO: | AIRDATE: |

Background Vocal

| AIRTIME: | 1:00 PM |
| LENGTH: | 60:00 |

Feature Instrn.

	USAGE TABLE	
	BI Background Instrn.	BV
07/26/2004		
OT Opening Theme		
CT Closing Theme	FI	
FV Feature Vocal		
MT Main Title		
ET End Title		

	TITLE	COMPOSER / PUBLISHER	SOCIETY			TIME
1	BLUE	C TARQUIN, B.	SESAC	50.00	BI	0:20
		C INGRAM, C.	SESAC	50.00		
		P PAY US 4 R MUSIC	SESAC	100.00		
2	GREENLEE THEME	C BARBER, BILLY	BMI	100.00	BI	0:46
		P ABC CIRCLE	BMI	100.00		
3	LOW DOWN	C TARQUIN, B.	SESAC	50.00	BI	0:21
		C INGRAM, C.	SESAC	50.00		
		P PAY US 4 R MUSIC	SESAC	100.00		
4	RYAN THEME	C BARBER, B.	BMI	100.00	BI	0:42
		P ABC CIRCLE	BMI	100.00		
5	AMC CATES BKRD. CUE	C CATES, RC	ASCAP	100.00	BI	0:55
		P AMERICAN BROADCASTING MUSIC	ASCAP	100.00		
6	AMC CLOSING THEME	C BARBER, BILLY	BMI	50.00	CT	0:15
		C ISRAEL, ROBERT	BMI	50.00		
		P ABC CIRCLE MUSIC	BMI	100.00		
7	AMC COMOTTO BKRD. CUE	C COMOTTO, BRIAN	ASCAP	100.00	BI	1:02
		P AMERICAN BROADCASTING MUSIC, INC.	ASCAP	100.00		
8	AMC GUNDELL BKRD. CUE	C GUNDELL, A.J.	BMI	100.00	BI	1:31
		P ABC CIRCLE MUSIC	BMI	100.00		
9	AMC GUNDELL BKRD. CUE	C GUNDELL, A.J.	BMI	100.00	BI	0:59
		P ABC CIRCLE MUSIC	BMI	100.00		
10	AMC GUNDELL BKRD. CUE	C GUNDELL, A.J.	BMI	100.00	BI	1:15
		P ABC CIRCLE MUSIC	BMI	100.00		

it comes to music libraries because this is where music is used a lot. Local broadcasters always use various libraries and rarely ever submit cue sheets.

Years ago, I heard a few of my tracks that I composed for FirstCom Music on a local Fox Sports cable channel, so I recorded it for proof. I reported it to FirstCom and sent them a VHS tape for proof and they in turn contacted Fox Sports, who just arbitrarily threw together a cue sheet with miscellaneous songs and denied ever using those FirstCom songs in question. So this is what every composer and publisher is up against, which is a really tough thing to overcome. At the end of the day, FirstCom and Fox Sports really didn't care because it was small potatoes. The Verance watermark system kept everyone honest because the detection system did not lie.

INTERVIEW WITH MARC FERRARI—MASTERSOURCE

One of the most successful music libraries I worked with in the beginning was MasterSource, which was started by an old friend of mine, Marc Ferrari. I remember back in the early '90s being a hungry guitarist-composer, answering an advertisement in the back of the *Hollywood Reporter* for a music licensing company called Red Engine Music, which later became MasterSource. I remember meeting Marc at his apartment and discussing the whole music licensing scene in L.A. and becoming one of his first composers for the library. I saw Marc form a cottage industry from scratch, first by sending music supervisors cassette recordings, then DATS, then CDRs, and finally finished, printed box sets, which took him years to achieve. The secret to MasterSource's success was that it filled a void in the licensing market, which was offering vocal tracks at competitive library prices. Before that time, there were very few vocal tracks offered by the large libraries such as Sonoton, FirstCom, and Killer Tracks. Libraries mostly offered instrumental tracks because that was what the various productions always requested. Plus, Marc generously offered to split the sync fees for each song fifty-fifty with the composers, which no other library offered to do at the time. I sat down with Marc to ask him how he did it all and to share some advice.

♫

Why did you start MasterSource, or as I remember it back in the day, Red Engine Music, considering your past experience as part of the '80s hair band Keel?

After I left Keel in 1988, I started another band, which was initially called "Ferrari" but settled on the name "Cold Sweat." That band released an album in 1990 and quickly faded into oblivion. In that timeframe was the changing of the guard where grunge became the flavor of the month and commercial hard rock was relegated to the sidelines. I saw the writing on the wall and realized it was going to be next to impossible for me to continue to have any degree of success as a recording artist. Around the same period of time, I started getting demos of mine placed in small productions. I got a few dollars and a screen credit, but more importantly, I got an idea for a business. When this all started for me back in the early '90s, there was not a music library that had commercial recordings with vocals that could be licensed with the ease and affordability of a music library, so that was my "niche" that allowed me to start MasterSource and get established very quickly in the industry as the go-to catalog for this kind of music.

In the beginning were you the main contributor to the library or did you hire composers to write for you?

In the very, very beginning I was just pitching songs that I had written or co-written with various friends, but soon I started getting requests for genres of music that I did not have, nor knew how to write (such as country, rap, big band, latin, electronica, etc.), so then I started reaching out to other writers to help develop the catalog.

Coming from the record industry, how did you find the correct contacts and make the library stand out against the other libraries?

It was a lot of researching and old-fashioned cold-calling for the most part. I read the trades voraciously to cull names. I wasn't afraid to pick up the phone and call an unknown person. . . . What did I have to lose? Back then it may have been a bit easier to make a connection as I was offering something new to the licensees. Nowadays, the market is saturated with an over-abundance of music. I should mention, I also got some help from ASCAP. . . . A few folks there made some introductory phone calls on my behalf, which really helped to open some doors.

One of the most important things I think budding composers want to know is, how did you get the placement? Especially in the beginning, did you rep the library yourself or did you have a sales team?

> For the first three or four years, it was just me . . . I was a one-man army. Placements came very quickly and the business developed rapidly. Remember, I was offering a unique service to the industry that previously did not exist before. By combining the elements of a publisher and a record company together (I controlled the copyright and the underlying master recording), I was able to simplify the licensing process into one transaction, and at the same time reduce the costs to the end user by up to 90 percent. Many people were elated to have a resource like the one I provided as it helped in so many ways.

You opened the library at a time when CDs were a very integral part of the business model. How did you deal with the distribution part of it? Were there outside companies you used for distribution or did you do it all yourself through mailing lists?

> No, it was all me on the distribution front. Every year I created a box set of new titles (usually ten to fifteen per year) and would do one massive mailing each year in early September in time for the new TV fall season. Initially I had to have the CDs shipped to my small apartment (they would take up almost the entire place!) and would have to pack them, sticker them, postage meter them myself, but in later years we were able to drop-ship them from the replicator, which saved a week of labor! Interestingly, CDs are no longer the preferred delivery mechanism for new content. . . . Nowadays it's all digital delivery via websites, hard drives, or thumb drives!

What were the critical things you looked for in composers and songs to add to the library?

> Two things: compositional skills and production value. I needed to find composers who wrote top-notch tracks and their recordings had to sound like a major label. The songs had to be authentic to the genre and the recordings had to sound like a finished record. After all, I was competing against major publishers and major label record companies. Some folks are great writers but not great producers, or vice versa. I had to have both wrapped up in the same package. My background

as a lifelong musician was the perfect springboard for me to make the jump into music production. I have a musician's ears and can tell when something is out of tune, out of time, or inauthentic, etc.

Writer Summary Statement

In Account With:

For The Period: July 1-Dec 31, 2010

Song	Production	Amount Received	% Share	Amount Due
Laurel Drive	Romantically Challenged	$166.66	25.00%	$41.66
Fast And Furious	The Loop	$750.00	50.00%	$375.00
Thunder Hill	Running EP#101	$25.00	50.00%	$12.50

Total Due: **$429.16**

How did you facilitate the sale of MasterSource, resulting in its purchase by one of the largest publishers in the world (Universal)? That must have felt unreal!

I had been using Universal to administer my catalog outside the US so I had a relationship with them to begin with. Then-president, David Renzer, was always acutely aware of the value of production music, but curiously enough Universal was the last of the major publishers to acquire a production music library. But David saw the intrinsic value in what companies like mine were offering and a deal was done. Curiously, I was twice a recording artist for MCA Records (a now-defunct division of Universal Music Group) and several Universal

Music Group senior executives worked with my bands, all those years ago, and were instrumental in seeing my acquisition happen. Soon after the acquisition of MasterSource in January 2007, Universal bought BMG Music Publishing, and with that acquisition came Killer Tracks and FirstCom (two of the industry's largest libraries). So in the span of one year, Universal went from having no production libraries to being the biggest player in the game. A new division was formed called Universal Publishing Production Music (UPPM), and MasterSource became part of a world leader. I ran MasterSource for an additional five years and recently stepped down as a full-time employee, although I continue to produce new music and assist in administrative matters. And yes, I suppose it was an "unreal" feeling initially. I am reminded of that old saying: "When one door closes (my recording career), another door opens (MasterSource)."

Finally, what advice can you give prospective licensees to be successful in getting music placed in TV and films?

These days there is a lot more competition for TV/film placements. There are literally hundreds of "libraries" out there, from the small boutique offerings to the corporate-owned monstrosities, which have hundreds of thousands of copyrights. The marketplace has become saturated and in order to stand out you have to be different and better, in order to grow and thrive. You have to research more intensely, market more aggressively, and produce material that is more outstanding in every way. There are some great resources out there such as the film/TV Music directory from Music Registry [www.musicregistry.com], organizations such as Film Music Network [www.filmmusicmag.com], California Copyright Conference [www.theccc.org], Association of Independent Music Publishers [www.aimp.org], and programs that ASCAP, BMI, and SESAC offer. You should join as many of these as possible and network. Meeting people face-to-face was key for me to develop my business. You can have success from any geographical location, but it helps to have human contact. As it would be starting any kind of new business, it may take a while for things to start happening, but cream always rises to the top!

♫

During the first years of the new millennium, large publishing companies started to take great interests in music libraries, whereas before they had always dismissed them as "mu-*zak*" companies. I believe that with the huge drop in album sales, cuts in mechanical collections, cheaper song sales from digital downloads, and with the collapse of the physical music retail market as we know it today, that publishers turned to the steady source of income from music placement. It became quite evident in 2006 when Tower Records went down for the final count, owing millions to its vendors and having no way to pay it; proving that the brick-and-mortar backbone of the record industry was crumbling quite quickly. Like the Roman Empire, it was not obvious to everyone until it was too late and the barbarians were already within the gates of Rome itself.

Luckily the collapse of music retail is not as dire as the end of Rome, but it is still a costly demise. So in 2004, when Vivendi Universal Entertainment was sold to General Electric, merging to form NBC Universal, they went on to acquire BMG, which owned FirstCom and Killer Tracks: the monsters of the library business. Founded by Jim Long in 1980, FirstCom was one of the pioneer music libraries. Its catalog has reached an uncountable number of tracks. It is worth mentioning that FirstCom is one of the few libraries that pays composers what is known as "direct music licensing royalties."

Direct music licensing royalties mean that in some foreign territories, where there aren't local PRO licenses, music libraries are paid directly for the writer's share of the song in a lump sum. Killer Tracks was started a little later in 1989 by Sam Trust and was later purchased by BMG. Anyone driving in L.A. could not have missed their massive, audacious sign in front of their office building on Hollywood Blvd., in the '90s, next to the bar-restaurant Pig N' Whistle.

INTERVIEW WITH JONATHAN FIRSTENBERG—MUSIC PRODUCER

Another old friend of mine is Jonathan Firstenberg, who has a very broad background in the music industry. In fact, Jonathan was very instrumental in Universal's acquisition of MasterSource. Jonathan has served as an acquisition consultant, with his experience in strategic, creative, and business development for production music. Jonathan served as senior VP of

FirstCom

Royalty Statement (Income details: by Song and income type. Participant details: By song)
10/1/2010 through 12/31/2010

Client:
Address:

Song Title	Song ID	Income Band	Composers	Income Type	Royalty Amount
Autumn Road	FC-U98_3.00			Blanket	$8.29
		Domestic		Performance - Direct	$0.77
		Domestic		Blanket	$19.59
		Foreign			
				Song total: FC-U98_3.00 - Autumn Road	$28.65
Boardwalk	FC-U98_7.00			Blanket	$8.29
		Domestic		Performance - Direct	$0.77
		Domestic		Blanket	$8.81
		Foreign			
				Song total: FC-U98_7.00 - Boardwalk	$17.86
Down And Dirty	HM-011_3.00			Blanket	$4.32
		Domestic		Performance - Direct	$0.80
		Domestic		Blanket	$1.82
		Foreign			
				Song total: HM-011_3.00 - Down And Dirty	$6.95
El Paso	HM-011_5.00			Blanket	$4.32
		Domestic		Performance - Direct	$0.80
		Domestic		Blanket	$0.39
		Foreign			
				Song total: HM-011_5.00 - El Paso	$5.51
Emerald Isle	FC-U98_1.00			Blanket	$20.61
		Domestic		Performance - Direct	$1.90
		Domestic		Blanket	$17.52
		Foreign			
				Song total: FC-U98_1.00 - Emerald Isle	$40.03
Green Velvet	FC-U98_9.00			Blanket	$8.29
		Domestic		Performance - Direct	$0.77
		Domestic		Blanket	$21.85
		Foreign			
				Song total: FC-U98_9.00 - Green Velvet	$30.91

Strategic Development, VP of Business Development, and creative director and executive producer for Universal Music Publishing Group, BMG, and Zomba. He is a three-time Emmy Award winner for Outstanding Music Supervision and Composition for daytime dramas.

♫

From your experience both working for music production libraries and licensing from them, can you describe (to people who are not familiar with them) the importance of such libraries and how they fulfill the need in the industry?

Music libraries—sometimes referred to as stock music, source music, mood music, elevator music, canned music, production music, production music catalog, and most recently production music library (PML)—have been around since the 1950s. The motivation to both find and create this music was based on economics, as it was costly to score music for every TV, film, and radio production. The first uses of music libraries were heard during the era of radio. As radio got its foothold and new shows were produced, so did the need for inexpensive music.

The music that was heard, either as a feature or in the background, was more commonly used or accepted during the advent of the "radio soap opera." The drama of the stories needed accompanying music. A live organist was hired to add music to the scenes. When radio soaps transitioned to television, the organists kept their gigs . . . until the soap productions started working with composers who had compiled endless hours of background music, most frequently for exclusive use on a particular soap production.

In those days, as today, there was a never-ending thirst to create more music for all the varied forms of media that exist today . . . and what they will expand into in years to come. Music library cues, or instrumental tracks, are the music that is written to the invisible scene. Composers flocked to this new arena and wrote cues based on everything but the picture. They focused on styles, genres, moods, instrumentation, and tempo. This was the beginning of the "background" music industry, which has now become more in need and fully accepted than ever before. The proliferation of music libraries is staggering. There are composers everywhere, working on their rigs and creating their own styles and moods of music.

As film and television production increased, so did the appetite for keeping music budgets low. While the standard was to hire a composer for a TV show or film, it was customary for productions to depend on a music library, for music that would be too expensive to produce. For example, a scene takes place on a Hawaiian beach; cue the ukulele and slide guitar. How about the scene in the Parisian restaurant? Of course, the scene in a nightclub with a dance band playing in the background (BG) . . . Most PML's have a wide variety of source music . . . music that plays in the BG.

How did you get involved in music supervision on shows like Guiding Light and General Hospital, back in the day?

In the early '80s I was promoting my composition reel to music production companies in New York. One company called me back after hearing my music and said, "We like it, but we don't need any composers at this time. However, we are looking for a music supervisor." To which I replied, "What is a music supervisor?" They told me to go out to NBC in Brooklyn the next morning to learn more. That next morning I found myself on the set of soap opera, *Another World*. *Another World*, like most soaps at that time, was taped daily. My job, should I choose to grasp it, was to find music from an endless wall of fourteen-inch, acetate records, listen, match the music to the scene, mark with grease pencil, hand to audio engineer, who placed acetate onto turntable. Following the script and the camera cuts, I would turn to the engineer and utter, "Stand By," then a few seconds later, when dialog, mood, action, or subtlety takes place, I direct, "Play." Based on the interior elements of a scene I would give direction to the engineer by saying either, "Fade out," or "Let play and carry over." Scoring to script basically, treating the music and placement as though it had been scored by a composer who had watched the scene and written a custom cue. Prior to the advent of acetates, live organ music was widely used for soaps. In those days, the composer/musician would score the music for scenes, often improv.

Unlike other music supervision jobs in the industry where it is predominantly an administrative job, soaps uniquely put supervisors into the music editor seat; did you find this beneficial in placing the music yourself into the scene? If so, how?

I had to read every script . . . five or more scripts per week and score each one. Scoring means spotting the right place for the cue and then finding the cue that works . . . as though it was scored . . . so it matches the emotion closely . . . It's always a decisive moment . . . selecting the right music to start and end in the right place. Being directly involved in selecting the music, it helped enormously that I was charged with creating the sounds that worked best and understanding and following the creative directives of the producer.

Soap operas are unique, as the music you hear in soaps comes primarily from a repertoire that is recorded specifically with that soap in mind by either one or two hired composers or freelance composers. It's the job of the music supervisor to make sure the composers know the upcoming storylines so they can compose music that supports the characters and story involved. This is usually referred to as a "brief."

The advent of ProTools opened up an entirely new world to me while supping [supervising] *General Hospital*. For the first time I didn't have to lay the music in live. I could sit in front of a computer, select, and edit music at my own pace, fine tuning to make the sound like a scored show . . . like primetime.

Were libraries your major music resource? Were you limited to your choice of music licensing outside of the composers?

All soaps, or what are commonly referred to today as daytime dramas, depend heavily on music written specifically for each show. A daytime drama library has a ravenous appetite and needs to be constantly fed new cues. Every show has its own requirements for music. Some shows use recurring themes for characters, while others favor a looser format and style.

Outside music use was a constant on the soaps. If there were scenes that took place in France, I would search through outside music libraries for a French album (later on I would search for CDs) featuring typically and authentically French music . . . most probably written, arranged, and recorded by a French composer. For all these uses came licensing costs. They could vary from $100 to $500 and are still referred to today as "needle drops." In some instances a "blanket" license was negotiated with an outside music library so the show could use a pre-determined or unlimited amount of cues from that library. However, exclusively the soap opera production company owns 95 percent of the music one hears on soaps, as they invested in hiring composers and studio time for recording sessions. As many networks were signatories of local musicians' unions, a cue written for a soap had a life span of about one year. At the end of that year, the music had to be pulled from the library or a portion repaid to the union musicians who played on the cue. These days, daytime dramas have more flexible relationships with the unions and are not tied to a one-year music usage restriction.

One of the most important things I think budding musicians want to know is how to get placement? What is the best way for composers/songwriters to get their music into productions?

While on the soaps, I received calls every day from composers who wanted to submit music and write for the soap. As primarily a composer advocate, and following the networks and production companies' guidelines, I would always suggest that the composer send me their reel, cassette, CD, DAT, or link to me based on the music delivery [method] of the time. I made a point to listen to all submissions because of the theory, "grow the music library, and find new and great music." During the early '90s, more vocals were being used on soaps. Many of the music supervisors on the soaps were both composer and songwriter and would grow the library via their own material. In most cases, outside songs would be considered primarily by producers/director for the use of a pop or a well-known song.

What were the critical things you looked for in compositions/songs to emphasize a particular scene?

There are many elements that go into deciding on the proper cue/song to place in a scene. It starts with reading the script prior to selecting cues for that day's taping of the show. Some scenes require a short cue perhaps at the opening of a scene or at end. Some scenes "call for music" based on what is happening in the scene.

Is the character imparting good news? Bad news?

This moment in the script requires a music treatment . . . put in a cue. What kind of cue? Do you match the characters mood? Playing the reaction of the other person, waiting for either a physical or verbal response? Is the music simple, complex, emotional, or dangerous, romantic or playful?

This is where instinct comes in. You can use obvious formulas up to a certain point, but the final choice of music has to give you the same feeling that the writer, director, and producer are intent on conveying. The most important aspect of placing music into a scene is the ability to emotionally mirror the producers' or director's vision of the scene.

Finally, what advice can you give people who want to become involved in composing for music libraries? How can they get the edge over all of the other composers out there?

I have told countless composers, songwriters, and artists the way to make their music stand out. The first step is their desire to do so. As there are hundreds of music libraries, some niche, boutique, some midsized, some giant; your chances of at least having a shot at writing for a library is good. That is, if you compose at the level that music libraries demand. As the competition has grown, so has the quality of music that is signed and released by the libraries. It is often best to think of your submission as a complete album/CD featuring at least fifteen original cues with alternate mixes, and/or thirty- and sixty-second edits; libraries vary in their cue delivery and edit format, so you can be flexible on this. If your album fills the need of the library, you have a good chance to enter into an agreement. That agreement compensates the composer for anywhere from $300 to $1,000 per cue, depending on size and budget designated for new music, and based on size of production company.

There's also the ambition factor . . . or perseverance factor. Do you have the drive to make calls to the libraries, day after day? Do you *network* within the industry and attend events such as Billboard film and TV conferences, BMI and ASCAP workshops? Make sure you immerse yourself in the industry you are most interested in. There's always room for great composers and songwriters in the library system. Contracts are offered every day . . . the next one could be yours.

♪

Chapter 3

Mechanicals, Sync, and Masters

Now what's all this business with mechanicals, synchronization fees, and master fees, you ask? Do you really have to know about these technical terms? You're *damn right* you need to know. You're doomed from making money in this business if you don't! The only people that may not have to know are real, bona fide rock stars, and I don't mean guys who think they are rock stars because they once played with a famous singer on the road. I'm talking about the 100 million record sales club like the Eagles, Guns N' Roses, and Metallica, even now with the perpetual slow down of physical record sales, they have become more aware of sync/master fees and their true value. But I'm sure all these bands that have a writer's interest in their hit songs are well aware of their mechanicals.

MECHANICAL ROYALTIES

I don't want to get too technical in my descriptions of these terms, just enough for you to understand what they are and how you should be paid. First off, there are the Compulsory Mechanical License provisions of the Copyright Act. Once a song is recorded, commercially distributed, and sold throughout a territory, the composer/songwriters are entitled to Mechanical Royalties.

Furthermore, these same royalties are paid when there is a remake of the song as well. The copyright office sets the rate periodically and currently, from the 1997 Mechanical Rate Adjustment, it is set at "9.1 cents, or 1.75 cents per minute of playing time, or a fraction thereof per copy, for songs over five minutes."

Now the record company who manufactures the album and distributes it has to pay the mechanicals to the songwriter or, more commonly, to their publisher or representatives. This is where the Harry Fox agency comes into play. They act as a clearinghouse and monitoring service for licensing musical copyrights and act as a one-stop shop for licensing copyrighted material. They have a very detailed database of songs and will direct you to the copyright holder, if they do not represent a particular song. God knows I've used their services a lot when I was releasing the *Guitar Masters Series* through BHP Music, Ltd.

Also, if you are stuck and cannot find the copyright holder of a song, you can go to www.copyright.gov and take a compulsory mechanical license, which will keep you immune from a possible copyright infringement lawsuit if the copyright holder suddenly appears. Believe me, copyright lawsuits are a serious business and can be very risky.

FEDERAL CASE MISHAP

A few years back, I was producing the *Guitar Masters, Volume 2* and had licensed some tracks featuring famous guitarists—Santana, Jimmy Page, BB King, and Yngwie Malmsteen—from a certain major record label. Well guess which one of these artists literally made a federal case? Can you say Swedish meatball? Enough said. We released the record with a full color painting of these artists, plus a few others added in; keep in mind I had commissioned a painter to do the artwork for the cover so I owned it lock, stock, and barrel.

About three months after the release I started to receive threatening emails from a New York City attorney, asking where I had gotten this particular track and the right to use this artist's image. Well I know I had full clearance for licensing the track and went back to the agreement to double check its provisions. There it was in black and white, I had the right to use the artist's name and image and exploit the masters. I also had an indemnity clause in the agreement with the record label, which protected me from such lawsuits. So I called the label and they assured me there was no problem and that they would take care of the situation.

Well a few months passed and we were all served with a huge copyright infringement lawsuit filed in federal court, for the sum of several million dollars. I was dragged into the case, even though I had legally licensed the track from track. The reason being, if the label didn't have the legal right to release the track, then anyone who they sub-licensed it to, didn't either. On top of that, even though I had the right to use likeness and image of the artist in the agreement, they were suing for copyright infringement of likeness and name. Plus the song was a cover and I had properly taken out the mechanical license with Harry Fox beforehand. Thank God for the indemnity clause in my agreement with the record label because they covered all legal costs and had their own attorney.

Well, this dragged on for two years until we had to go to court to resolve this matter. I was dragged into this stuffy New York City attorney's midtown office and had to give a deposition—another life altering experience I could have done without. By this point I had already instructed my distributor to pull the release from the stores. It wasn't worth the headache and certainly was not selling enough physical copies to bother with.

The next morning we had to show up at the federal courthouse in downtown Manhattan on a muggy August morning at 8:00 a.m.—another experience I could have lived without. Anyway, I was the first victim there on that sunny morning, and then I saw the artist stumble out of the elevator with his team of lawyers, followed by the representatives from the record label. I knew then that we were in for loads of laughs! As I sat there at the table for this pre-court negotiation, the one last chance for both sides to come to some amicable conclusion before we had to go to actual court, I found myself staring out of the window, much like the times I spent in school, wishing for some sort of interruption of any kind to break up the boredom, like those infamous fire drills. No such luck though!

So there we all are, huddled around the conference table. I was in jeans, leather vest, and sunglasses; the president of the record label was dressed much the same; the lawyers dressed in tidy grey suits; and the artist in a suit that didn't fit, wrinkled as if he had slept on a park bench the night before. A magistrate justice, who was a very patient older gentleman, conducted this whole menagerie.

First the artist's side was asking for one million dollars from the record label, halfheartedly moving to $500,000, then softening to $250,000, quickly moving to $100,000, and desperately taking $50,000. So the big rock star had quickly reached out with grubby little hands for that $50,000, only to have to hand it over to pay his lawyer fees. Luckily, I was only a semi-involved spectator with all of this nonsense and nothing had to come

The Harry Fox Agency, Inc.
A SUBSIDIARY OF NATIONAL MUSIC PUBLISHERS' ASSOCIATION, INC.
601 West 26th Street, 5th floor
New York, NY 10001
Phone: 212-834-0100
Email: publisherservices@harryfox.com

Limited Quantity License for Physical Configurations

TO: Brian Tarquin   LICENSE NO.: 1073480417
     Old Chelsea Station   LICENSE DATE: Nov 28, 2007
     PO Box 47
     New York, NY 10113

    Refer to the provisions hereof reproduced in (E) varying terms of compulsory license provision of Copyright Act. The following is supplementary thereto:

A: SONG CODE: D14710
     TITLE: DAZED AND CONFUSED
     WRITERS: JIMMY PAGE

B: INCOME PARTICIPANTS: (R-HFArep N-Not rep D-Direct B-Blocked *-Contingent share)
     WB MUSIC CORP. OBO FLAMES OF ALBION MUSIC: R % 100

C: RECORD NO.: [(CD)BHP30011-1]
     ARTIST: INSTRUMENTAL REMAKE BY ARTIST BRIAN TARQUIN
     ROYALTY FEE (BASED ON STATUTORY RATE): $122.50
     PLAYING TIME: 6 MINUTE(S) 5 SECOND(S)
     QUANTITY OF PHONORECORDS LICENSED: 1,000

D.   ADDITIONAL PROVISIONS:
     THE AUTHORITY HEREUNDER IS LIMITED TO THE MANUFACTURE AND DISTRIBUTION OF NO MORE THAN THE QUANTITY OF PHONORECORDS STATED IN (C) SUPRA SOLELY IN THE UNITED STATES AND ITS TERRITORIES AND POSSESSIONS, AND NOT ELSEWHERE.

     CREDIT: IN REGARD TO ALL PHONORECORDS MANUFACTURED, DISTRIBUTED AND/OR SOLD HEREUNDER, YOU SHALL USE YOUR BEST EFFORTS TO INCLUDE IN THE LABEL COPY OF ALL SUCH PHONORECORDS, OR ON THE PERMANENT CONTAINERS OF ALL SUCH PHONORECORDS, PRINTED WRITER/PUBLISHER CREDIT IN THE FORM OF THE NAMES OF THE WRITER(S) AND THE PUBLISHER(S) OF THE COPYRIGHTED WORK.

     LICENSEE IS NOT REQUIRED TO COUNTERSIGN THIS LIMITED QUANTITY LICENSE.

     ALBUM: LED ZEPPELIN "GET THE LED OUT"
     DATE OF RELEASE: Feb 2008
     LABEL: BHP Music, Ltd.
     CONFIGURATION: CD Compact Disc
     VERSION: Guitar Instrumental Tribute to Led Zeppelin

E.   GENERAL VARIATIONS OF COMPULSORY LICENSE PROVISION:
     You have advised us, in our capacity as agent for the publisher(s) referred to in (B) supra that you wish to obtain a compulsory license to make and to distribute phonorecords of the copyrighted work referred to in (A) supra under the compulsory license provisions of Section 115 of the Copyright Act.

     Upon issuance of this license, you shall have all the rights which are granted to, and all the obligations which are imposed upon, users of said copyrighted work under the compulsory license provision of the Copyright Act, after phonorecords of the copyrighted works have been distributed to the public in the United States under the authority of the copyright owner by another person, except that with respect to phonorecords thereof made and distributed hereunder:

1. In consideration of the limited quantity of phonorecords authorized hereunder and, upon your requesting this license, your nonrefundable payment to agent for and on behalf of said publisher(s) of the full royalty fee set forth in (C) supra you need not otherwise pay royalties or account to us as agent. This license shall automatically be deemed null and void and of no effect if agent fails to receive timely, valid payment of all fees due with respect to this license.

2. This compulsory license covers and is limited to one particular recording of said copyrighted work as performed by the artist and on the phonorecord identified in (C) and (D) supra and this compulsory license does not supersede nor in any way affect any prior agreements now in effect respecting phonorecords of said copyrighted work.

3. You need not serve or file the notice of intention to obtain a compulsory license required by the Copyright Act.

4. Additional provisions are reproduced under (D) supra.

THE HARRY FOX AGENCY, INC.

---

out of my pocket except for giving up three hours of my life, which I won't get back. From where I stood no one won and everyone left that negotiating table feeling violated. Well, as they say, a fair deal is where both parties leave feeling unsatisfied.

SYNCHRONIZATION LICENSE

More commonly known as a sync license, this is when a show licenses the right to synchronize and perform your song throughout a particular territory (usually the Universe), which is defined in the agreement. It usually includes the right to subtitle the lyrics (including foreign translations) in "hearing impaired" and foreign language versions of the production, for exploitation, exhibition, and/or distribution of the production in all media.

Yes, they have to cover all of their bases today. They are also allowed to use the song, in any kind of promotions as trailers, advertisements, or any other form of media exploitation. (See Work-for-Hire contract in Appendix E.) It is absolutely essential that film and television productions get a signed sync license, or they will have committed copyright infringement. Even though this is just plain common sense, you would be surprised at how the largest companies in the world do not bother to abide by these rules.

I know firsthand, with all of the music I've supplied to productions. I have wound up in a few class action suits because of misuse. ABC-TV and its foreign affiliates ran into a huge copyright infringement case called the *Steiner* settlement. Basically ABC-TV was using commercially released music domestically and not taking it out when they shipped it to their affiliates in foreign territories like South America. ABC had a deal with certain record companies, which enabled them to use tracks from their commercially released catalogs, which in many cases waived sync/master license fees. However this deal only pertained to domestic broadcasting and was required to be stripped out of the shows and replaced with ABC controlled music before airing in foreign territories. I'm sure you can see where this is heading!

Long story short, ABC did not strip out the music on many of their shows before they aired in such territories as South America. Who knows, maybe someone later thought that South America was considered to be a part of the United States of America?

Well, it did not take too long for the class action suit to ensue and ABC had to settle on a multi-million-dollar payout for the suit. I remember first receiving paperwork to fill out, confirming that these were my songs. As the years went by, I thought to myself, will this case ever come to fruition or just die out? And just when I was about to give up hope, I received a very nice check in the mail from the settlement.

It took years. In fact I was single when the case started, but when I finally got paid I was married with two kids, but hey it still happened! The same exact thing happened with the class action suit against MTV/Viacom known as the *Music Force Class* settlement, except it was a lot more accelerated. Again, MTV did not strip out music for foreign airing and in some cases ignored licensing altogether. This should be a lesson for all shows, how extremely important sync licenses are. Even if you have music gratis for a production to use, you still need an agreement stating these terms.

MASTER LICENSE

Similar to the sync license, a master license grants the use of the master recording, which is owned and/or controlled in whole or in part by the licensor for use in connection with the audiovisual production, produced and/or distributed by the licensee and in promotions. Bear in mind that this is different from the sync ownership and pertains to the physical recording of the song, regardless of format: tape, vinyl, mp3, etc.

Think of the song as a pie, in which 50 percent equals the sync and the other 50 percent equals the master. Many times the sync and master ownership can be split across several entities, much like the writer and the publisher interests in a song. For a production, the more approvals from owner interests licensors have to get, the more complicated it can become to obtain a free and clear license. This is why music production libraries came into existence, to serve as one-stop shops for industries, especially for television productions that don't have the luxury of time to chase after multiple approvals, which may be spread across several continents.

It can also be problematic when a record company owns the master, but the sync is spread across a few writers and no one can agree on the fee they should charge. Ultimately, if one party wants to do the license and the other does not, the deal is dead in the water because you can't license half a song.

SONY
PICTURES

Diana Randell
Executive Director, Music Affairs Group

10202 West Washington Boulevard
Culver City, California 90232
Tel: 310 244-2788 Fax: 310 244-0080
diana_randell@spe.sony.com

11/29/2011

Mr. Brian Tarquin Browne

RE: THE STEVE HARVEY SHOW #318 / "Last Kiss Goodbye"

Dear Brian:

1   **REQUEST**
LICENSING INFORMATION
This is a **request** for a synchronization, performance and master use fee quotation in connection with your control and interest in and to the following musical composition(s) and master recording(s) which is/are being considered for use in the production, all as defined below.

Composition/Master:	
Composer/Artist:	Brian Tarquin Browne ,
Publisher/Master Owner:	Strat Kat (Ascap) / Brian Tarquin Browne
Production:	The Steve Harvey Show #318
Production Type:	TV Series
Producer:	Sony Pictures Television Inc., successor-in-interest to Columbia Pictures Television
Air/Release Date:	4/13/1999
Use & Timing:	Visual instrumental :50

2   **CONFIRMATION**
LICENSING TERMS AND RIGHTS **("Terms" and "Rights")** (All Rights shall be as defined in the Agreement [defined below]):
Terms:

	Fee:	$__4000.00_____, payable to Brian Tarquin Browne	Approved:
	Territory:	Universe	
	Term:	Perpetuity as of Air/Release Date	
	Credit:	N/A	_____
			o/b/o Publisher and Master Owner
Rights:			
	Media:	All media excluding only theatrical	
	Promotions:	In-context	Date:_____
	Option(s):	N/A	

We are proceeding in reliance on the above Terms and Rights, the Fee for which shall become payable **only** if the Composition and Master are used in the Production as commercially released.

If any of the foregoing is inaccurate, please contact me immediately by Tel: (310) 244-2788, Fax: (310) 244-0080 or via e-mail diana_randell@spe.sony.com.

3   **SHORT FORM LICENSE**
When executed by both parties below and subject to payment of the Fee, this document constitutes the Short Form License ("SFL"), effective as of the Air/Release Date, for the Terms and Rights set forth above, as modified below, if applicable, incorporating the terms of the Blanket Synchronization, Performance and Master Use License Agreement dated November 29, 2011 between Brian Tarquin Browne and Columbia Pictures Industries, Inc., Columbia TriStar Marketing Group, Inc., Sony Pictures Television Inc. and Sony Pictures Home Entertainment ("Agreement"). In the event of any inconsistency(ies) between the provisions of the Agreement and the provisions of this SFL, the latter will control.

Modification(s): ☐ None   Please initial changes (if any)
Revised Use:_____   _____   _____
Revised Timing:_____   _____   _____
Other:_____   _____   _____

By:_____   By:_____
An Authorized Signer   An Authorized Signer
o/b/o Producer   o/b/o Publisher and Master Owner

BLANKET SYNCHRONIZATION, PERFORMANCE AND MASTER USE LICENSE AGREEMENT
(Brian Tarquin Browne)

This Blanket Synchronization, Performance and Master Use License Agreement ("Agreement"), effective as of November 29, 2011, is between COLUMBIA PICTURES INDUSTRIES, INC., COLUMBIA TRISTAR MARKETING GROUP, INC., SONY PICTURES TELEVISION INC., SONY PICTURES HOME ENTERTAINMENT INC. o/b/o themselves and the Producer set forth in the short form license ("SFL") incorporating this Agreement by reference (individually and collectively, "Licensee"), and Brian Tarquin Browne o/b/o itself, the Publisher and the Master Owner set forth in the SFL (individually and collectively, "Licensor") and is subject to the following:

1. Short Form License. This Agreement, together with the SFL, shall constitute a license for the musical composition set forth in the SFL which is owned and/or controlled in whole or in part by Licensor ("Composition") and the master recording thereof which is owned and/or controlled in whole or in part by Licensor ("Master") (the Composition and Master are collectively referred to herein as the "Song") for use in connection with the audiovisual production set forth in the SFL produced and/or distributed by Licensee and in promotions therefor (collectively, "Production"). Each SFL is effective upon its execution, together with payment of the Fee, pursuant to the terms set forth herein. Except as expressly modified in the SFL, all terms and conditions set forth herein will govern each SFL, and are deemed incorporated in each SFL as if directly set forth therein. In the event of any inconsistency(ies) between the provisions herein and the provisions of the SFL, the latter will control.

2. Grant of Rights. Licensor hereby grants to Licensee the non-exclusive, irrevocable rights (but not the obligation) ("Rights"), throughout the Territory set forth in the SFL, for the Term set forth in the SFL, to use, synchronize and perform the Song for the use set forth in the SFL in the Production, including the right to subtitle the lyrics (including foreign translations) in "hearing impaired" and foreign language versions of the Production, for exploitation, exhibition and/or distribution of the Production in the media set forth in the SFL ("Media") and in promotions as set forth on the SFL ("Promotions"), subject to the following definitions:

(a) Media:

    i. "All Media" means any and all media now known or hereafter devised (including, without limitation, theatrical exhibition ["Theatrical"], non-theatrical, including, but not limited to, hospitals, oil rigs, all forms of transportation and common carriers - e.g., in-flight, coach, train and shipboard exhibition ["Non-Theatrical"], all forms of television, including, without limitation, streaming media ["All TV"] and a worldwide buyout for all forms of audiovisual devices now known or hereafter devised, including, but not limited to, videocassettes, videodiscs, internet, wireless, podcast, mobile and downloading ["AV Devices"], all for no additional fee including, without limitation, download fees and mechanical reproduction fees). Each of the aforementioned media rights may be licensed individually.

    ii. "All Media Excluding Only Theatrical" means All Media excluding only Theatrical.

(b) Promotions:

    i. "In-Context Promotions" means all forms of in-context trailers, clips, advertisements, promotions, featurettes, making-of's, specials, radio promotions, music videos and all other forms of publicity and other promotions, all in connection with the Production, and for any and all media now known or hereafter devised.

    ii. "Out-Of-Context Promotions" means all forms of out-of-context trailers, clips, advertisements, promotions, featurettes, making-of's, specials, radio promotions, music videos and all other forms of publicity and other promotions, all in connection with the Production, and for any and all media now known or hereafter devised.

3. Blanket License Term. The term of this Agreement is for two (2) years, commencing on the Effective Date. This Agreement shall automatically renew for a additional, successive one (1) year periods unless either party notifies the other in writing of its decision to terminate the Agreement not less than thirty (30) days prior to the expiration of the then-effective term. Notwithstanding anything to the contrary contained in this Agreement, should the Blanket License Term expire prior to the expiration of the Term set forth in the SFL, then the provisions of this Agreement will remain in full force and effect with respect to the particular Compositions and/or Masters licensed for use in the Production prior to the expiration of the Blanket License Term for the duration of the Term.

4. Trailers: The term "Trailers", as a Production Type set forth in the SFL, means all forms of in-context or out-of-context trailers, clips, advertisements, promotions, featurettes, making-of's, specials, radio promotions, music videos and all other forms of publicity and other promotions produced in connection with the exploitation of the Production.

5. Fee. In full consideration of the Rights granted herein, Licensee will pay to Licensor a license fee ("Fee") in the amount set forth in the SFL promptly following the later of execution and delivery of the SFL or the use of the Song in the Production as commercially released.

6. Credit: Subject to agreement by the parties and provided the Composition and/or Master is licensed for use in the Production, Licensee will accord the composer of such Composition and/or the Artist, whose performance is embodied in the Master, a screen credit substantially in the form as set forth on the SFL ("Credit"). All other characteristics of such Credit are at Licensee's sole discretion. No failure by Licensee or any third parties to comply with the provisions of this paragraph will constitute a breach of this Agreement.

7. Performing Rights. The right to publicly perform the Composition in the exhibition of the Production by means of all forms of television now known or hereafter devised (other than theatrically in the United States) including, without limitation, by means of network, local stations, DSL, broadband, high definition, "free television", "pay television", "pay-per-view television", "subscription television", "CATV", "basic cable", "closed circuit into homes television", internet, wireless, podcast and/or streaming (individually and collectively "TV Systems") in the United States, is granted subject to the following:

(a) Public performance of the Composition in the exhibition of the Production may be made by means of TV Systems having valid performance licenses therefor from the American Society of Composers Authors and Publishers ("ASCAP"), Broadcast Music, Inc. ("BMI") or other applicable performing rights society, as the case may be; and

(b) Public performance of the Composition in the exhibition of the Production by means of TV Systems not licensed for television by ASCAP, BMI or other applicable performing rights society, is subject to clearance of the performing rights either from Licensor, ASCAP, BMI or other applicable performing rights society, or from any other licensor acting for or on behalf of Licensor and in accordance with their customary practices and the payment of their customary fees. Licensor agrees that to the extent it controls said performing rights, Licensor shall negotiate a license with Licensee in good faith.

Rev.11282011

BLANKET SYNCHRONIZATION, PERFORMANCE AND MASTER USE LICENSE AGREEMENT
(Brian Tarquin Browne)

(c) It is agreed that clearance by performance rights societies in such portion of the Territory as is outside of the U.S. will be in accordance with customary practices and payment of customary fees for such Territory.

(d) For purposes hereof, a download of the Production does not constitute a performance of the Composition or the Master.

8. <u>Cue Sheets</u>. With respect to theatrical motion pictures and television programs, Licensee shall furnish Licensor and the applicable performance rights societies with a cue sheet of the Production promptly following the later of: (i) the execution of the SFL; or (ii) the first public performance of the Production or public exhibition of the Production at which admission is charged (except so-called "sneak" previews).

9. <u>Warranties</u>. Licensor warrants that:

(a) Licensor has the right to enter into this Agreement and to grant to Licensee each and every right granted to Licensee herein; that it owns and/or controls the percentage set forth in the SFL of the right, title, and interest in and to the Master and Composition; that the use of the Master and Composition hereunder will not violate the rights of any third party, including any third parties whose musical material may be embodied in the Master and/or Composition; and that no additional payments shall be due for the rights granted herein (including, without limitation, download fees and mechanical reproduction fees), other than those specified herein.

(b) The Master and Composition are free from any unlicensed "sampled" or other pre-existing musical materials; that any and all "sampled" or other pre-existing musical materials contained in the Master and/or Composition have been cleared by Licensor with the owner(s) thereof for use in the Master and/or Composition; and that Licensee shall not be required to obtain any additional consents or pay any additional fees for the use of such "sampled" or other pre-existing musical materials contained in the Master and/or Composition.

(c) Licensor shall be responsible for all payments to third parties, including, without limitation, the writer(s) of Licensor's share of the Composition and the Artist and producer of the Master, in connection with the rights and uses granted hereunder.

10. <u>Indemnity</u>. Licensor shall indemnify and hold Licensee free and harmless from any and all claims, liabilities, costs, losses, damages or expenses, including attorney's fees, arising out of any breach or failure of any covenants and warranties made by Licensor herein (including, without limitation, claims from mechanical collection societies). In the event of a material breach of Licensor's representations and warranties hereunder, Licensee may terminate its obligations hereunder. In the event of an anticipatory breach by Licensor, Licensee shall have the right, at its election and upon notice to Licensor, to remit payment of any monies otherwise payable to Licensor pursuant to this Agreement to a third party non-interest bearing escrow account until such time as (i) Licensee receives adequate assurances from Licensor that the anticipatory breach has been cured, in which case the monies shall be paid to Licensor, or (ii) such breach is confirmed, in which case all or part of such monies shall be paid to Licensee in satisfaction of Licensor's indemnity hereunder.

11. <u>Waiver of Additional Fees</u>. In the event that use of the Composition and/or Master renders the Production subject to the collection of mechanical reproduction fees in any portion of the Territory, Licensor hereby agrees to submit waivers of such fees to the applicable collection societies, promptly following receipt of notice that such fees are applicable. The foregoing requirement shall not apply in any situation where such fees are not waivable under applicable law.

12. <u>Remedies</u>. Licensor's rights and remedies in the event of a breach or an alleged breach of this Agreement by Licensee shall be limited to Licensor's right, if any, to recover damages in an action at law and in no event shall Licensor be entitled by reason of any breach or alleged breach to enjoin, restrain, or seek to enjoin or restrain the distribution or other exploitation of the Production and any promotions therefor.

13. <u>Notice</u>. All notices hereunder shall be in writing and shall be given by personal delivery to an officer of Licensee or Licensor, or by mail in the United States mail, postage pre-paid, at the address set forth below or any address as either Licensee or Licensor may designate by notice to the other, and the date of such personal delivery or mailing shall be the time of the giving of such notice.

To Licensee: Sony Pictures Entertainment Inc.   To Licensor:
                10202 W. Washington Blvd.
                Culver City, CA 90232
                Attention: Music Affairs Group

14. <u>Cure</u>. No failure by Licensee to perform any of its obligations hereunder shall be deemed a breach hereof, unless Licensor has given written notice of such failure to Licensee and Licensee does not cure such non-performance within thirty (30) days after receipt of such notice.

15. <u>Whole Agreement</u>. This Agreement constitutes the entire agreement between Licensor and Licensee with respect to the subject matter hereof and cannot be altered, modified, amended or waived except by a written instrument signed by the parties hereto. Should any provision of this Agreement be held to be void, invalid or inoperative, such decision shall not affect any other provision hereof and the remainder of this Agreement shall be effective as though such void, invalid or inoperative provision had not been contained herein.

16. <u>Assignees</u>. Licensee shall have the right to assign this Agreement or any of its rights hereunder at any time to any person, firm or entity. This Agreement is binding upon and shall inure to the benefit of the successors and assigns of the parties hereto.

17. <u>Law</u>. This Agreement shall be governed by and interpreted in accordance with the laws of the United States and the State of California.

AGREED TO AND ACCEPTED:

COLUMBIA PICTURES INDUSTRIES, INC., COLUMBIA TRISTAR   BRIAN TARQUIN BROWNE
MARKETING GROUP, INC., SONY PICTURES TELEVISION INC. and   o/b/o itself, the Publisher and the Master Owner
SONY PICTURES HOME ENTERTAINMENT INC.   (individually and collectively, "Licensor")
o/b/o themselves and the Producer
(individually and collectively, "Licensee")

By:_____   By:_____

An Authorized Signer   An Authorized Signer

Rev.11282011

Another point that is worth mentioning is that the fee for both master and sync are equal, meaning that if the sync fee is $2,000, then the master fee will be the same. Sometimes a production wants to use a known song and they don't have the money to do so. So they either hire a composer to do a sound-alike, where they would own the song outright and just pay the artist a work-for-hire fee, or they might license a cover song, in which the masters would be cheaper and all they would have to really negotiate would be the sync fee for the actual musical composition of the song. This is probably one of the rare times where the sync fee would be different from the master fee.

For example, if they wanted to use "Black Dog," by Led Zeppelin, knowing full well the master license would be out of their budget, they could license what is referred to as a "new master" (a new recording of a known song) and then request a sync license from WB/Superhype.

INTERVIEW WITH TANVI PATEL—CRUCIAL MUSIC
www.crucialmusic.com

Tanvi Patel is a 50 percent partner in Crucial Music Corporation and also serves as the company's president and CEO. Tanvi's career spans two decades in the broadcasting, record label, and production library industries. She launched her career in Cincinnati, working in promotions and music programming at WLW-FM (News/Talk), WUBE-FM (Country), and WVXU (Jazz). She then moved to Nashville where she landed her first label gig in the media department at BNA Records (a division of RCA Label Group), working with gold-record country recording artists like Lorrie Morgan and John Anderson. Tanvi left BNA to manage publicity, radio promotion, and sales for Jim Long at Honest Entertainment/The Gold Label, a multi-genre independent label distributed by Valley Entertainment.

Her achievements there included securing the #1 and #2 positions on the Gavin Jazz chart for Linn Records' jazz guitarist, Martin Taylor, and jazz vocalist, Claire Martin. She also scored media coverage in Billboard, NPR's "All Things Considered," and QVC placements for the label's artists, as well as helped to secure a Grammy nomination for Jack Jones's "Jack Jones Paints a Tribute to Tony Bennett."

Upon the sale of Honest Entertainment/The Gold Label, Tanvi moved into the library business, managing production and securing placements in film and TV for Jim Long's production library, OneMusic Library (distributed by FirstCom). Her placement credits included *20/20*, *Six Feet Under*, *America's Most Wanted*, *Boston Public*, *Dark Angel*, *White Chicks*, *American Pie 3: American Wedding*, *Exorcist: The Beginning*, and others.

In 2005, Tanvi moved to Los Angeles to manage the Point Classics catalog of over 2,500 classical compositions, securing ringtone deals, CD licenses, digital distribution, and film and TV placements that included Oscar-winner *Brokeback Mountain*, *Ocean's 12*, *Land of the Dead*, HBO's *Classical Baby*, *Wildfire*, *Judging Amy*, *Malcolm In the Middle*, *The Simpsons*, and more.

♫

From your experience starting the company Crucial Music, can you describe (to people who are not familiar) the importance of such services and how they fulfill the need in the industry? How does it differ from the days you were working at OneMusic?

> The film and television industry today, as opposed to the early 2000s (my OneMusic Library days), has an insatiable thirst for independent songs. Productions have demanded real songs for background uses in addition to feature uses. It used to be that production library instrumental tracks would work for deep background uses, but that has changed. Even if the song is buried in a restaurant scene, they want the lyrics of the song to reflect the moment. As a result, film and TV placement services for independent artists have become a clearing house for supervisors. Rather than dealing directly with two thousand artists, they can call a company like Crucial Music who has two thousand artists in its roster, all of which are pre-cleared for use. Supervisors can work with a handful of companies they have come to trust and get all of their needs met without worry. Companies like ours have made the supervisors' and studios' jobs easier.

What types of shows and films tend to use your service and have you seen an increase in usage from the industry through the past years?

All types of productions use our service: shows from primetime net-work sitcoms *(The New Normal)* and dramas *(The Following)* to cable scripted dramas *(Californication)* and comedies *(Veep)*; independent films *(The Sessions)* to feature films *(The Incredible Burt Wonderstone)*. As production budgets and music budgets have decreased, the need for songs has increased, and so the volume of usage has increased in the seven years we have been in business. We are now seeing an increased demand from web programs (webisodes) and Internet, long-form, corporate branding videos; both of which have minimal budgets but want real songs.

One of the most important things I think budding musicians want to know is how to get placement? What is the best way for songwriters to get their music into productions?

I think the best thing an artist can do is sign his or her songs with a company who specializes in film/TV placement, so they can be left to focus on creating music. Maybe they don't want to give up a share of the revenue, but 100 percent of zero is zero. Artists bombard supervisors every day; and they are not going to be happy taking calls, and I bet most artists hate making calls. Companies like ours have the contacts and supervisors take our calls because they trust us to pitch the music that makes the most sense for the productions they are currently working on . . . we have a proven track record . . . we'd be out of business if we didn't.

What are the critical elements your clients look for in compositions/songs for their particular productions?

The most important element of any song, when it comes to film and TV is: Does it fit the scene? Does it enhance the message being delivered? . . . Whether it's a breakup singer-songwriter song for a montage usage or it's a traditional jazz track playing in the back-ground at a jazz club, before it can get to that point, the song has to be recorded in the highest production value possible for the genre. It also has to have great lyrics or a memorable melody. Basically what-ever makes a song a hit on the radio . . . all of those elements have to be in the song before it can be pitched for use in film and TV.

Finally, what advice can you give people who want to become involved in composing for productions? How can they get the edge over all of the other composers out there?

> Composing for film/TV is different than writing songs. If you want to be a composer, I think the best thing you can do for yourself is develop a unique sound. Something that sounds like no one else . . . Don't try to be like somebody, just be yourself. Trent Reznor took his industrial rock style and was able to apply it to cinematic scores very successfully with *The Social Network* and *The Girl with the Dragon Tattoo*. Thomas Newman's *American Beauty* score put him on the map . . . When you hear it you know it's him. Even John Williams has an identifiable sound. Be fresh and unique. I think that goes for songwriting too. Look at Willy Moon, Jack White, Amy Winehouse (in her time), Adele, Florence + The Machine; all artists that don't sound like anyone else, and all are breakout hits.

♫

INTERVIEW WITH BRIAN PERERA—CLEOPATRA RECORDS
http://cleorecs.com

Cleopatra Records is a Los Angeles-based independent record label founded in 1992 by entrepreneur and music fan Brian Perera. It has since grown into a family of labels, including Hypnotic Records, Goldenlane, Stardust, Purple Pyramid, Deadline, and X-Ray Records, encompassing a variety of genres with emphasis on unique and experimental artists. Cleopatra Records specializes in gothic rock, hard rock, heavy metal, electronic, dubstep, and reissues of out-of-print music.

In the mid-1990s, Cleopatra released tribute albums of Goth, techno, and industrial bands covering artists such as The Cure, Siouxsie and the Banshees, The Sisters of Mercy, and New Order. Other Goth and industrial acts were compiled to cover songs by AC/DC, Pink Floyd, The Smashing Pumpkins (see: A Gothic-Industrial Tribute to The Smashing Pumpkins), Guns N' Roses, and the arguably uncoverable Dead Can Dance and Skinny Puppy.

Cleopatra Records has been primarily known for ushering in the second wave of Gothic and Industrial music with an eclectic roster of artists including Christian Death, Switchblade Symphony, Leæther Strip, The Electric Hellfire Club, Razed in Black, X Marks the Pedwalk, Kill Switch . . . Klick, Genitorturers, Download (featuring members of Skinny Puppy), as well as New Wave artists Gary Numan, Missing Persons, Information Society, and others. When the revival of '80s Hollywood Metal exploded around the turn of the century, the company started a subsidiary label, Deadline Music, to handle releases by Quiet Riot, White Lion, Warrant, Cinderella, and Poison's Bret Michaels.

♫

How did you start Cleopatra Records? Can you give us a little history of the label?

I started Cleopatra Records by licensing well known acts from Europe including Motorhead, Kraftwerk, Syd Barrett, and Hawkwind. I then put that investment to start recording bands that I signed such as Christian Death and Electric Hellfire Club. Within a short time we became a leader in the Goth and industrial movement of the mid '90s.

What kind of changes have you seen in the industry since the digital revolution has occurred? Is it a positive change for the way records are sold?

I basically saw firsthand the big decline in retail, and people were getting laid off in the hundreds. It was a terrible thing to see but I think a change was needed. With the digital revolution I've seen more opportunities than ever to get your music out there and have a fair chance for getting it heard.

How did you amass such a large catalog with such icons as Santana, BB King, etc.?

Some of these iconic bands are artists we have either bought masters or we have long licensing deals with. A lot of iconic bands we put back in the studio to re-cut their big masters. This tends to be very popular with music supervisors since we don't charge as much as what a major label would charge. We are very flexible in working out fair deals.

Have you seen an increase in film and television music licensing as opposed to hard sales?

> Yes, I have seen a large increase. I think now with the Internet people can find us and the music we have is more accessible. Although, I have also seen a small growth in hard sales based on the new interest in people collecting vinyl.

Finally, what advice can you give budding musicians on how to get a record deal? What is the best way for bands/songwriters to get noticed today?

> I recommend to the artist, don't chase the labels, and let the labels chase you. You can attain great attention by playing live shows and putting out your own material through outlets such as CD Baby. A label will then check your Soundscan numbers. If they look good, I guarantee you will hear from someone. Once a label sees your hard efforts you can then get their attention. Labels are looking for acts that have built up their own following through social media such as Facebook, YouTube, and playing live shows. Labels love to see bands with lots of activity.

♫

INTERVIEW WITH AARON FREEMAN—REDEYE DISTRIBUTION

Aaron Freeman is the Chief Operating Officer of Redeye Distribution. He oversees company functions for over fifty-five employees, which includes Redeye Distribution, Yep Roc Music Group and 11spot Direct-to-Fan. The responsibilities of the position include oversight of overall company structure, all company systems, company processes, and budgets. He is responsible for ensuring overall profitability and for hitting company profit goals. Also under his purview is oversight of the accounting department, IT department, and operations department, the latter of which includes all warehouse, inventory, manufacturing, and digital metadata functions.

♫

*From your experience working at Redeye can you explain (to people who
are not familiar) how record distribution has changed through the years?*

> I think the biggest change is that the value of distribution is now
> seen in sales and marketing efforts, rather than simply getting prod-
> ucts to the stores and digital providers. Delivery of products and
> assets remains important, but the sales and marketing value is what
> makes one distributor stand out from another. This ability to seize
> on opportunities is especially evident in the digital marketplace
> where delivery of assets is done by lots of companies, while very few
> can successfully market these releases in a way that increases sales.

*Is physical retail still a large part of your business or have digital downloads
become more of a priority?*

> My answer is yes to both questions. Physical retail is absolutely
> a large part of our business and we feel this will remain the case.
> Digital sales are also a huge priority as that segment of business
> continues to grow year after year. There is a huge advantage in work-
> ing with both physical and digital products since both formats can
> be incorporated into a comprehensive marketing plan. For every
> release there are different types of fans, and a marketing plan that
> focuses on both physical retail and digital allows a label to vary their
> offering to this range of fans. Specifically for Redeye, we continue to
> open up smaller, more curated (often vinyl-only), indie stores, and
> see that as a growing part of our business. This is a direct response
> to the demand for vinyl we're seeing from our customers and some-
> thing that continues to set us apart from our competitors.

*One of the most important things I think budding musicians want to know
is how to get their music distributed. What is the best way for bands/song-
writers to get their music sold without going through labels?*

> It really depends on the musician and the type of distribution they
> need. For developing artists who simply want their music on iTunes
> or for sale online, there are companies that can help with that and
> for an affordable price. Once an artist establishes more of a fan base
> and requires a more robust sales and marketing plan to help sell
> more to a wider range of stores (physical and digital), a more full-
> service distributor is needed and an artist should make that contact.

Regarding selling music without a label, artists do this every day using popular web services to sell directly through their websites. Once an artist reaches a certain point, though, a label (even if it's their own label) can play a critical role in their success. Labels provide the infrastructure and experience that helps maximize the potential of a release, which includes publicity, promotion, social media, access to distribution, and manufacturing.

What kind of resurgence has vinyl made and is it really the end of physical CDs?

Vinyl has indeed seen a resurgence in the past few years. That said, CD sales still make up the majority of physical sales industry-wide. There are lots of different kinds of music fans out there and each has their own preference—whether it be CD, vinyl, digital downloads, streaming, a limited edition deluxe package, or all of the above. The job of an artist or a label should be to accommodate their fans by providing their music in a format that their fans enjoy purchasing and listening to it, whether it be CD, LP, or digital.

Finally, how do you see the future of distribution?

The current distribution model is strong, though I do see a continued trend towards a more fan-centered approach. This translates into a continued focus on sales and marketing efforts at physical retail and digital providers ("How do we get this music in front of the right audience?") as well as the actual products offered. Ten years ago, most releases involved only a CD format. Today, many releases involve a CD, an LP, a deluxe package, a digital download (album and track), digital streaming as well as videos, each involving a marketing plan designed to sell a release in different ways. Specifically at physical retail stores, distribution has changed in recent years with more focus going towards connecting fans to the artists through all possible retail outlets and by providing the appropriate messaging to help drive traffic. There are more ways than ever for artists to get their music to fans, and a distributor's job is to facilitate that.

♪

CONCLUSION

We've gone over the specific differences between Master, Sync, and Mechanical licenses and how they pertain to different parts of the composition. We've also peeked into the process a production goes through when they license specific tracks for their shows. Again, like everything that has such great rewards, a lot of muscle and sweat goes into achieving the end goal.

Chapter 4

PROs: What They Do

Performance Rights Organizations (PROs) are a very important part of the puzzle in the music world. Simply, each country or territory has a PRO and here in America we are blessed to have three to choose from: SESAC, ASCAP, and BMI. These companies represent hundreds of thousands of copyrights and issue licenses to users like broadcast stations, radio, cable, etc. They then collect the monies from the users and pay their affiliates. What I've found in twenty years is that everyone has his or her own experiences with each society, which can be drastically different from case to case.

I preface this chapter with this—I am writing about my actual life experiences with these societies through the last twenty years. Now you can speak to other people with completely different perspectives. You can also call each one of these companies and speak with a writer-relationship person that will BS you all day on how great they are, but the truth is: How do they behave under fire? The following is my reality and what I have found.

ASCAP

When I first started composing for music production libraries many moons ago, no one told me there was a choice. The guy I was working with just said, "Call ASCAP." I couldn't pronounce the name let alone know what they did. So like many young composers, I requested a membership application, opened up a publishing company and joined as a composer, having absolutely no idea what the hell to expect. Well, the next years were certainly eye opening to say the least. I noticed that as my catalog grew and I received more airplay, the ASCAP statements seemed to be written in some sort of secret code, especially when it came to foreign royalties.

Every quarter when I received the statement, I would sit down and try to make sense of the statements. This is why I always requested cue sheets from shows whenever possible, so I could at least cross reference the cue sheets with the statements. Inevitably, there was always a show payment missing or an underpayment. I found myself on the phone with a representative that knew far less than I did about how it worked. I remember finally one representative saying to me, "You can't expect to get paid for every airing!" Well, hells yeah!

The running joke with members of ASCAP was, "It wasn't caught in our survey," because they would all say that when they couldn't explain how the monitoring system worked. I felt like saying to this lady, "How about your boss comes down to your little cubicle in the corner of your stuffy midtown office and tells you casually, 'I can't pay you this week, because your hours weren't caught in our survey.' I bet that would make you think twice!"

This is why I always had problems with music administrative people in the industry. They break your balls when you try to find out the simplest things about your artist catalog, while giving you attitude on the other end of the phone. They barely know their own job, and what they don't realize is that some of us actually make a living composing music. What we deserve is respect, not contempt. If it were not for all of *our* music fueling the company, you wouldn't have a job! This is not just ASCAP, mind you. It can be a host of other industry, paper-pushing workers in various companies, such as; publishing, recording labels, marketing, radio, etc. Anyway, this is when I realized that I had to take charge of my music and educate myself on how royalties worked.

Unfortunately, a lot of musicians prefer not to take a proactive stance when it comes to the business side of music. I don't blame them; it is the other side of the brain that we don't like venturing into if we can help it. It can be very uncomfortable dealing with all of these administrative people and challenging them at their own game.

To be honest that's why I'm writing this book, to help fellow musicians overcome this challenge and become more knowledgeable in this subject. So the next time you speak to your PRO or to a production company, ask more questions and don't be afraid to say "No," if you do not accept their terms.

Unfortunately, ASCAP is way behind in monitoring technology and always has been. I remember in the late '90s befriending a guy who worked in the radio department as a musicologist. In fact he knew of me because the radio hits I had at the time; that's a nice ego boost. ASCAP would place him alongside a host of other people in a large room with cubicles containing headphones and cassette players at each desk. They would listen and record radio broadcasts from around the country and then decipher the tapes.

Typically, these music guys and gals would sit in vans at various US marketplaces and record hours of different radio formats and then physically mail them back to the ASCAP headquarters in Lincoln Center. Excuse me, what century are we in? *Are you kidding me?* This is the technology you used thirty years ago and you still can't find a modern way to monitor radio—ever heard of BDS, Broadcast Data Systems?

I would not have believed it if he hadn't take me up to his office and showed me the setup. Holy smokes! I was convinced then that ASCAP had no plans of moving forward any time soon. What a waste of manpower and money to pay for crews to go out on location and decipher music. How accurate do you think that was? And the mistakes that must have been made—I hate to think of it. They since were forced to abandon the system and go with BDS. Talk about wasting affiliates' monies; this was the poster child for it.

BMI

I do have publishing companies with all three societies, which is a great way to compare payments, especially if you have a song that is split between two or more societies. Which leads me to my next story, this time about BMI.

I had a number of radio hits back in the '90s in the NAC format, which later became Smooth Jazz. One of my songs, "One Arabian Knight," released by *Instinct Records*, charted #4 on R&R/Gavin radio charts when there was such a thing. There were two other writers with me on the song and the song was split between BMI and ASCAP. I controlled 100 percent of the publishing and collected performances through both societies on the publisher side. After comparing the statements between ASCAP and BMI, it was clear that BMI barely even acknowledged the format, least in royalty payments. For every $500 that ASCAP paid, BMI only paid $50 for the exact same song and the same publisher splits. Meaning that the two other writers had 15 percent each on the song and I had 70 percent. Now between those two writers, one being BMI-assosciated and the other ASCAP, BMI only paid 10 percent of what ASCAP paid for the same airplay and percentage.

No trick mirrors or brain surgery, BMI was screwing the other writer and my publishing company. So, as I have always done in my life, I picked up the phone and called BMI. I proceeded to be transferred to every office from L.A. to Nashville, then to New York. In addition, I mailed (this was before the email generation) them the ASCAP statement and the BMI statement as proof.

Finally, after weeks of trying, I got through to some clueless secretary to the VP of writers' affairs. I explained the whole story to her and her response was, "I's never heard of that song before!" Houston we've got a problem . . . beam me up, Scotty! I don't believe I asked you if you were familiar with the song; in fact, I only asked to speak to your boss! This is the kind of unprofessional behavior we're all up against!

Bottom line, I did in fact speak to her boss later, who was dumbfounded that I would ask such a question. But why wouldn't I? I had the numbers right in front of me and there was a big discrepancy. His conclusion was simple: BMI did not care about the format (NAC), had put very little resources into monitoring these radio stations, and yes, the old cliché, "it wasn't caught in our survey." (What a surprise!)

Ironically, around this time BMI had a policy in place that advertised to members that they would match payments in these situations to that of ASCAP. I bet you know what happened next? BMI weaseled out of it and said they no longer honored that policy. I have no use for people like this, so it was time to move forward and learn from these experiences so that I wouldn't make the same mistakes. Live and learn.

SESAC

When I moved over to SESAC, I knew things were going to be much different and they were. First off, SESAC is a privately owned, for-profit organization, whereas ASCAP and BMI are not-for-profit organizations and are legally bound to a consent decree. Basically, ASCAP and BMI have certain restrictions they have to abide by on court settlements concerning antitrust problems. So clearly SESAC has much more flexibility as a company in court negotiations. In fact, SESAC was just sold in 2013 to a private equity firm for $600 million. Hey, there is absolutely nothing wrong with being a for-profit organization; truthfully this is what drives American businesses. I believe that with the sale, SESAC's affiliates will benefit greatly.

I have spoken to several board members of ASCAP and they think it's sacrilegious to be a for-profit PRO company. I say, piss off! Let me tell you that ASCAP is trying to keep the masses ignorant! Look who sits on the board of ASCAP and in the presidency: all Tin Pan Alley writers from the Brill building days of music publishing.

The fact of the matter is that those songs do not constitute the majority of music licenses any longer and haven't for a long time. It's already been proven, years ago, that 80–85 percent of the music broadcasted over all media is background source music and themes. But if you have the older generation that benefits from the status quo, which have special interests in the current royalty system, well they aren't about to change it and take money out of their royalty-lined pockets. It's like expecting Congress to voluntarily ask for a pay cut; it just not going to happen.

Now back to SESAC, there are a few important things that make them stand out. They have quite a large catalog now because of the catalog acquisitions of Bob Dylan, Neil Diamond, Rush, and television composers like Bruce Miller and Jonathan Wolf. For one, their reps are very easy to talk to and open to discussion.

For instance, like the BMI issue I mentioned earlier, I had a similar situation occur when I was writing for daytime television. SESAC's daytime rate was lower than ASCAP's, I brought it to their attention, showed them the ASCAP statement and the SESAC statement as proof and you know what? They matched the royalty fee for that airplay and any future royalties! Now that is what I'm talking about, R-E-S-P-E-C-T! Finally a PRO that gets it! There was no chasing or arguing; I simply showed them the situation and they made good.

VERANCE AND THE VALUE OF WATERMARKING

What I like about SESAC is that they are proactive with technology. They are always trying out new ways to get the affiliates paid faster and more accurately. One of the large reasons I went to SESAC back in the late '90s was because they had partnered with a new technology that involved watermarking music. This to me was such a fantastic idea that I couldn't believe no one had come up with it sooner. The idea was to digitally place an inaudible watermark on a piece of music so it could be detected if used in broadcasting, as well as under a voiceover or buried in the mix of a television show.

Once Verance—the company who was monitoring and issuing the watermark—got up and running, I have to tell you, it worked damn well! Verance in turn would supply the monitoring details to SESAC to pay their affiliates accordingly. My SESAC statements literally went from being fifteen pages to being over a thousand pages. I kid you not! It contained all kinds of detections from every small local station to major networks and cable channels.

The first thing I did was to watermark the commercial releases and library CDs I had composed and produced for Megatrax, FirstCom and Sonoton. The only drawback was that since music had to have a physical watermark placed in it, you couldn't redo music that was already released, unless you were doing a second pressing. Also, it is worth noting that as an "everyday composer," I couldn't send the music to get watermarked at Verance while I was doing daily and weekly shows. However, since I was writing for major networks I wasn't worried about the watermark for them. It was the local markets that were troublesome.

I am convinced that the local markets do not bother to create cue sheets or hassle with submitting paperwork to the PROs. They think music is free and anyone can use it as they see fit. Some, at least, abuse the rules of engagement to an extent. It's mostly with library music, where the water-mark becomes so useful.

Case in point, I heard a number of songs that I composed for FirstCom on a Fox Sports channel, so I recorded it. I contacted FirstCom who in turn contacted the channel to look into this claim. I even sent them the actual video with the music. First, Fox didn't even have the cue sheets for the shows; then, when put on the spot by FirstCom, they made one up out of the blue, just grabbing any library CDs on the shelf, except for the ones they really played of course, just to appease FirstCom. If we had had the watermarking system working at the time it would have been there in black and white on the detection report. The major networks like ABC, CBS, and NBC are very diligent in submitting cue sheets to the PROs, so there's never a really big issue with them.

By the way, for those of you who don't know, a cue sheet is a document created by the user, network, cable station, etc., which lists all music used within a particular television program, movie, or miniseries. It contains all of the pertinent information about the music: song title, writer/publisher information, song duration, and how the music is used, as in theme or background.

Unfortunately, because of costly lawsuits and monitoring systems, Verance abandoned the project after only a couple of years. SESAC went on to try another failed watermarking system and is currently using a finger-print technology like BDS. However, they have not found one that has the same far-reaching success into the local markets as Verance had, but here's hoping the future brings success.

It is worth noting that both ASCAP and BMI refused to pay affiliates from monitoring data supplied by Verance and that the SESAC was the only PRO that paid on this system. In fact, ASCAP and BMI bought their own watermark technology and never did anything with it. I believed they only bought these technologies to sit on them so no one else would use them, and never had plans to actually put them to use. Again, the board members who run ASCAP and BMI, who are old singer/songwriters, certainly don't want to use a technology that will certify what everyone has known for years and decrease their own royalties. Ultimately, it is your decision in the end what PRO you choose to represent your works.

KNOW YOUR AFFILIATES

I always loved the story a former president of SESAC told me when Bob Dylan resigned from ASCAP and took his whole catalog over to SESAC. No one contacted Dylan when he decided to leave, not even a farewell phone call from ASCAP asking him to reconsider his decision.

On the other hand, I got a call from ASCAP before I left; that's crazy! I figured the kids at ASCAP at the time had no idea that Dylan's legal name was Robert Zimmerman, so it slipped right by them at a costly price! It was a good thing for SESAC affiliates that Bob Dylan and Neil Diamond came over, because it really put SESAC on the map and more importantly it gave them negotiating leverage for radio and television licenses, especially with the Television Music Licensing Committee (TMLC). Now TMLC couldn't say they don't play any SESAC artists, so they had to pony up to the table with decent license fees; a real turning point for SESAC.

The other thing you have to understand is that, by decree, ASCAP and BMI have to accept every applicant, whereas SESAC being a private company can pick and choose their affiliates. ASCAP has 450,000 members and BMI has 550,000, while SESAC is small in comparison with only a few thousand members. But being a very selective society, it gets the cream of the crop!

RESIGNING FROM A SOCIETY

One thing to keep in mind if you are a current writer-member of ASCAP or BMI, is that it can be tricky to resign because of their rules and regulations. Both societies have a very small window of opportunity in which you can actually resign. The resignation period for ASCAP is in September on specific dates, otherwise you will have to wait another year before you can leave. Also, it is better to leave your catalog there because if you take it they will refuse to pay you for the last six months of royalties, putting the money into the slush fund.

Upon my resignation I instructed ASCAP to continue to represent my catalog, starting fresh with new material at SESAC. BMI plays a similar game whereby, if you miss the resignation date you are renewed automatically for another two to five years, depending on their current licenses with broadcasters. So be very punctual if you want to move to another PRO.

INTERVIEW WITH HUNTER WILLIAMS—SESAC

www.sesac.com

Hunter Williams is senior vice president of Strategic Development/ Distribution & Research Operations at SESAC. Hunter is responsible for developing new business opportunities, utilizing SESAC's licensing, distribution, and copyright management capabilities. He also oversees all royalty distribution operations, including the development of the company's distribution policies and performance tracking systems. He's in charge of the company's research division, which helps drive the strategic development of the company through business and industry analysis. Williams began his career with SESAC over sixteen years ago.

Under his leadership, SESAC has pioneered the use of digital fingerprint and watermarking technologies to track and pay royalties for performances on radio, television, and new media. Williams has a bachelor of science degree in mass communications/music business administration from Middle Tennessee State University. He currently serves on the board of advisors for the Music and Entertainment Industry Educators Association (MEIEA).

♫

From your experience working at SESAC can you describe (to people who are not familiar with PROs) the importance of such companies and how they fulfill the need in the industry?

A PRO [performing rights organization] allows businesses like broadcasters, digital music services, live music venues, etc. [music users] to efficiently and quickly get the rights to play, transmit, or perform the music of multiple songwriters and publishers. Likewise, it allows songwriters and publishers to authorize multiple users to perform their music without having to issue licenses to each one individually.

Can you briefly describe how PROs collect license fees from various broadcasters and how SESAC in particular pays its writer and publisher affiliates?

Most licenses with broadcasters are negotiated as "blanket" licenses, meaning the broadcaster has access and authority to play any or all of the music in the PROs repertoire for one flat fee. The fees vary from broadcaster to broadcaster, but are typically paid once a year.

SESAC collects this money then determines which songs in its repertoire were actually performed by analyzing usage reports from each broadcaster. Royalty payments are then determined for these performances using a payment formula that weighs performances on things like frequency, duration, time of day, how the music was used, and more. This weighting formula results in credits for each song performed and song credits are multiplied by a credit value to determine royalty payments. These payments are then disbursed monthly for radio performances and quarterly for all other media.

What kind of changes have you seen in the industry since the digital revolution has occurred? Is it a positive change for PROs and its affiliates?

The biggest change, in my opinion, has been the access to, and the affordability of, technology and data. The digital revolution has been the great equalizer for artists and musicians, making it possible for anyone with a computer and midi controller to create great sounding music, distribute that music to hundreds of online music sites, and track that music using audio-recognition technology like Tunesat or YouTube's content ID system.

Is this a positive change for PROs and their affiliates? Change presents opportunity. There's more music being produced and consumed than ever. The economic models of the music business may change, but songwriters, artists, and musicians will always need service providers to help them navigate the vast, often turbulent seas of music distribution, licensing, and administration. I believe there's great opportunity for companies like SESAC to help music rights holders manage and monetize their musical assets in the digital space.

How are foreign performance royalties paid? Do they measure up to domestic royalties at all?

SESAC, ASCAP, and BMI all have reciprocal agreements with performing rights organizations in other countries all over the world. These agreements stipulate the licensing, tracking, and payment of each other's repertory in our respective territories. So, in Australia for instance, the local society, APRA, licenses the SESAC repertory, collects the money, and remits payments to us on a periodic basis.

Each foreign PRO has its own licensing and payment rules, so the resulting payments can vary quite a bit. However, royalties from performances on a global basis can be quite substantial. It's not uncommon for foreign royalties on catalogs with substantial global activity to generate two to three times what they might receive domestically.

Can you explain how SESAC differs from ASCAP and BMI and why writers and publishers can benefit so much more from your services?

All three PROs have their benefits. At SESAC, our affiliates benefit from our personalized service, faster payment, and clear and efficient tracking and reporting.

Where do you see the future of PROs and will there be a drastic change in royalties with the constant devaluing of music?

Traditional revenue streams may change in value and therefore the royalty payments that are derived from them. The stakeholders and gatekeepers in the revenue streams may change as well. However, there are more revenue streams from music today than there were ten years ago. Plus the costs of making and distributing music are less expensive. I believe a thriving marketplace will exist for artists, rights holders, and service providers that are forward-thinking, educated, technologically sophisticated, and that employ good asset management practices.

♫

"THE INSIDER'S GUIDE TO SONGWRITING CONFERENCES"
by Dan Kimpel (Courtesy of *Music Connection* magazine)

http://musicconnection.com

If You Write Verses and Choruses, Songwriting Conferences are the Bridges to Career-Making Connections

Songwriters can often be solitary creatures: ensconced in claustrophobic rooms, hunched behind keyboards, poring over laptops. But consider this irrefutable fact of songwriting in the present tense: collectives of songwriters whose names read like law firms write the majority of hit songs. What this signifies for songwriters is that alliances within the music business—with artists, producers, and potential collaborators—are essential building blocks for any songwriter's career.

Sure, you can network on the Web, read message boards, and collaborate with others long distance, but there is no better opportunity to make an impact on other songwriters than face-to-face at a conference. The trick is to zero in on the conferences that are geared toward what you want to accomplish.

A Bit of an Overview . . .

The very first Songwriters Expo—envisioned by John Braheny and Len Chandler, co-founders/directors of the Los Angeles Songwriters Showcase

(LASS)—was held in 1977 and continued for over two decades. Since then, many replications and variations on the theme of educating and connecting songwriters via multi-day events have sprung up, based on the original LASS concept.

Bigger is not necessarily better: some of the smaller conferences afford intimate personal contact with the industry guests and with the other visiting songwriters.

For readers who reside in the music capitals of Los Angeles, Nashville, New York, and Atlanta, conferences also present a welcome opportunity to bond with other attendees when you meet them in the airport, on the plane and the hotel shuttles.

Conferences are an investment. Funds are required for transportation, admission, hotel rooms and incidentals. These can add up quickly, so researching events, talking to people who have attended in order to find the event that best matches your music, and planning a trip in advance to take advantage of early-bird admission specials are recommended steps. If you can attend more than one event, this is advantageous.

If you have to choose a conference, choose it wisely. You will also need to manage your expectations. Conferences are about opening doors to the future. And while you might not leave with a publishing or sync deal, you might be one step closer. In this exclusive feature, *MC* will spotlight, define and describe, in alphabetical order, some key career-making confabs that can educate, connect and inspire songwriters.

ASCAP "I Create Music" EXPO

Carly Simon, the Smeezingtons (Bruno Mars, Philip Lawrence, Ari Levine), Lindsey Buckingham, Quincy Jones, a conversation between Justin Timberlake and Bill Withers, John Mayer, Ann & Nancy Wilson (Heart), Jeff Lynne, Jon Bon Jovi & Richie Sambora, Jackson Browne, Steve Miller, Randy Newman and Tom Petty: The ASCAP "I Create Music" Expo is the most expansive and comprehensive of the songwriter conferences.

If you aim to attend, be aware that by planning you will save substantially on the admission fee. If you are arriving from out of town, staying at the Loews Hotel at Hollywood and Highland, where the event is held, will afford you maximum participation. Teaming up in rooms with visiting friends and new acquaintances can make for some fun networking opportunities.

With the riches of panels, listening sessions, one-on-ones and work-shops, pre-conference research is essential in order to maximize a visit and tailor-make it to specific needs. Without a plan, this experience could be overwhelming.

You will be in the heart of Hollywood, and as such, there is much to experience. The EXPO is also excellent for connecting with music supervisors and finding out about the latest trends in the business for those creating music for film, television and games.

The EXPO is held the same week of the ASCAP Pop Awards, so the odds are excellent that the most distinguished names in the Society's roster will be on hand for the conference.

There are five hundred One-on-One Sessions made available, with an additional $30 processing fee. They are available on a first-come, first-served basis and every year they have sold out. The next EXPO is April 18–20, 2013 [April 24–26 in 2014] in Los Angeles, CA. Registration begins Nov. 1st. http://ascap.com/eventsawards/events/expo

Durango Songwriters Expo

With two events held annually—one in the mountains of Colorado in the fall, most recently just outside of Boulder, and a February event in Santa Barbara, CA, Wine Country—The Durango Songwriter Expos certainly qualify as two of the most scenic songwriter celebrations. The picture is even better inside the events, as a gracious community welcomes longtime participants and newcomers alike.

There is a distinct advantage to the more intimate scale. Both of the Durango events limit the number of participants, and if you've got the goods you will be noticed. This is a very social event (especially as wine corks pop in the fabled Santa Ynez Wine Country) and enduring alliances have been formed as a result.

The hotel halls breathe with music as co-writers conspire in suites, rooms and stairwells. There is no shortage of artists such as Mindy Smith; Shawn Mullins; and Michelle Shocked on hand, and serious songwriters: Dan Wilson (Adele); Jeffrey Steele (Rascal Flatts, Faith Hill, Tim McGraw); Big Al Anderson (George Strait, LeAnn Rimes); J. D. Souther (the Eagles);

Chuck Cannon (Toby Keith); and many others who create the hits for major artists.

The listening sessions are intimate and real as publishers, music supervisors, label reps and many others spend quality time with the songwriters, giving feedback and suggestions. As befits the Expo's congeniality, it is a supportive and nurturing environment.

There is also a looseness to the event that can seem laid back and spontaneous. The evening concerts featuring the hit songwriters are revelatory—especially for fans of solid nuts and bolts song craft. The partying opportunities are plentiful.

DSE also sponsors a Write With A Hit-Maker Songwriting Contest, where the winner collaborates on a song with a prominent hit songwriter.

The Kauai Music Festival

Blessed by breezes from the Pacific Ocean at a Hawaiian beachfront luxury resort, The Kauai Music Festival (KMF) songwriter conference is a four-day celebration of the art and craft of songwriting. Industry guests convene with attendees for one-on-one meetings, configure small group sessions, conduct workshops and participate in panel discussions. Each night features performances and open mic activities. Industry guests include Grammy, Emmy and Na Hoku-winning songwriters, a contingent of producers, TV & film music supervisors from Hollywood and top A&R executives from Nashville, New York and Los Angeles including Music Supervisor Liza Richardson (*Hawaii Five-0, Parenthood, Friday Night Lights*).

The attendee range from Music City hit writers to musical creators from the other islands—hobbyists and beginners will not be out of place.

For fans of Hawaiian music, the Saturday night Pua Hana concert is a singular opportunity to absorb the breadth of modern island music: from ukulele sensation Jake Shimabukoro to HAPA and Charles Michael Brotman. The preceding night, Friday, Mainland hit writers and performers share the stage at the Poalima Concert. (Concert tickets are an additional $25 fee per show or $40 for both concerts.)

In addition to the Festival's Gold Sponsor County of Kauai and the Hawaii Tourism Authority, this confab is generously supported by BMI, and past participants have included hit songwriters from that Performing Right Organization's ranks including Kris Kristofferson, Kara DioGuardi

(Christina Aguilera, Carrie Underwood, Cobra Starship), Bonnie McKee (Katy Perry, Taio Cruz, Leona Lewis); and Evan Bogart (Beyonce, Jason Derulo, Jennifer Lopez). Hit songwriter, author and songwriting sage Jason Blume is also a regular guest.

Flip-flops, cut-off shorts and sunscreen—you won't feel underdressed on casual Kauii. The schedule of the event allows for plentiful networking and sightseeing opportunities on the Garden Island. Evenings are filled with well-orchestrated open mics that flow deep into the night.

At past events, the Kaui Music Festival has been opened with a blessing chant from a Hawaiian holy woman. KMF is paradise for songwriters and a breathtaking destination of unparalleled beauty. http://kauaimusicfestival. weebly.com

NSAI Tin Pan South/Spring Training

NSAI's annual Tin Pan South Songwriters Festival, taking place in the incomparable song town that is Nashville, TN, presents the greatest song-writers in modern music in intimate performances at a variety of venues. Last year's event kicked off with John Oates of Hall & Oates performing an acoustic version of "She's Gone." The educational element to the week is the two-day "Spring Training."

Spring Training has an appealingly casual vibe: "Lunch with the Pros" features a roster of Nashville hit makers sans panels or formal lectures: just folks sitting down and eating together. Ole Music Publishing presented hit writer Chris Wallin and Marty Dodson in a session titled "Hitsville" where an attendee left the session with a single song contract offered by the company.

Indie artists are a focus of the information, and Publisher Break-out Sessions afford a one-on-one meeting with a publisher of choice and a guaranteed opportunity to play one song with the possibility of multiples should time afford.

The event is held at the Maxwell Millennium House hotel, situated on the banks of the picturesque Cumberland River. It's a short drive to Music Row, downtown, and other areas (including the hipster hotbed of East Nashville,) so you might need to rent a car, although the hotel does have a shuttle service.

NSAI is Nashville Songwriters Association International, and it's not just for country writers exclusively, but the nightly shows are primarily Americana, roots and country of any and all varieties with artists like Josh

Turner, Radney Foster, Dierks Bentley and Jim Lauderdale performing with the intimate song circles featuring luminaries like Greg Barnhill, Jimmy Webb and Jack Tempchin.

NSAI also presents Song Camp, in late July, with close to 100 participants gathering in Nashville for educational lectures, intense song critiques and performances. http://tinpansouth.com

SESAC Bootcamp

At a price point of "Free" for SESAC affiliates and a mere $40 for non-affiliates (and this includes breakfast and lunch!) the one-day SESAC Bootcamp, held at the Skirball Cultural Center in Los Angeles, CA, is certainly the least expensive of the conferences. But its value is tremendous. It happens in the summer, when participants can enjoy a full day symposium devoted to offering information on all aspects of the music industry to artists, songwriters and producers.

Guru and music industry tastemaker Ted Cohen was one of the forward thinking guests at this past year's event. Managers, publicists and indie artists offered insights on what it takes to build a career in the new business model, using time-tested strategies and new technology.

SESAC's roster of songwriters and artists includes Mumford & Sons, Bob Dylan, and Neil Diamond. The Society also reps many of Hollywood's most eminent composers and songwriters for film and television, so there is emphasis in this direction plus music for advertising and games.

With writer-producers like Bryan Michael Cox (Mariah Carey, Chris Brown, and Mary J. Blige) and Angela Hunte ("Empire State of Mind" by Jay-Z and Alicia Keyes) on the roster, SESAC is the organization of choice for eminent R&B songwriters. The Bootcamp is host to creators of urban music, so writers and artists working in hip-hop and R&B will be in excellent company.

The Skirball Cutural Center is a gorgeous setting, and that free lunch (while tasty) is also a prime opportunity to connect with other writers and industry members at this friendly, low-key event. http://sesac.com

TAXI Road Rally

A prime benefit of the independent A&R organization, TAXI, is free admission for the member plus a guest to attend the company's annual Road Rally in Los Angeles, CA. This year [2012] the Rally will be held Nov. 8–11 with hit songwriter Diane Warren receiving the TAXI Lifetime Achievement Award with a corresponding keynote interview.

The Road Rally is immense, and is an event that requires tactical pre-planning as TAXI takes over the Westin Los Angeles Airport Hotel. Songwriters and music industry professionals of all stripes throng the ballrooms, classrooms and exhibition hall for a serious selection of heavy hitting guests and invaluable music industry information.

Numerous listening sessions are a key draw. Last year a group of execs from Disney, Universal, RCA Records and Sony Music were on hand for a Listening Panel.

New media, fan management and public relations for independent artists are key Road Rally panel and class topics. Befitting a conference held in the entertainment capital of the world, great attention is paid to film and television music, and how to write and create for games.

TAXI is heavy on the one-on-one mentoring sessions and the always-boisterous Mentor Lunches (where participants are joined at 10-minute intervals by a roving band of music industry professionals), plus open mics and other performance opportunities.

A large contingent of TAXI's international songwriters is also on hand, so you can create cross-cultural collaborations. Hobby and beginning songwriters are welcome. The airport is not near the center of Los Angeles, so plan on staying at the host hotel (or check out cheaper options nearby) and rent a car and stay extra days to take advantage of the trip. http://taxi.com

West Coast Songwriters Conference

Held in early September on the campus of Los Altos College near Palo Alto, in Northern California, the West Coast Songwriters Conference is the longest running event—32 years—specifically for songwriters. WCS is a powerhouse organization with a dedicated community and grassroots organizers. They currently hold over 20 monthly events to enhance aspiring writers and performers with creative and career development by music industry professional.

The Conference is the organization's highlight of the year. It kicks off with a Friday night party, and then takes place over two days with classes, panels, one-on-ones, performance evaluations, song screenings, a noontime concert series, a Saturday evening show with hit songwriters, and much more.

Given its proximity to Los Angeles, the Conference attracts music supervisors, publishers and songwriters from Southern California. Also present are songwriters and industry from Northern California—for example, attorney Elliot Cahn, who has managed both Green Day and Papa Roach. Steven Memel's performance workshops are consistently rewarding, and new media is well represented with panels and workshops on social and new media.

Hobby, older and beginning songwriters will feel very welcome in this warm community. Also, writers whose songs vary from the mainstream won't be marginalized here in ever-so-tolerant NorCal. There are panels on children's music (courtesy of WCS co-founders and hit songwriters Michael and Patty Silversher) and songs with social significance. There is a strong Nashville contingent, and regular guests include publisher Dan Hodges, who has a long history of discovering hit songwriters, such as Josh Kear and Chris Tomkins. http://westcoastsongwriters.org

CONCLUSION

One of the most important topics in the book is royalty payment! We have a better conception of what Performance Rights Organizations (PROs) are supposed to do and how they pay. Hopefully, it's clear what to watch out for with PROs and most importantly to stay on top of them for your royalties. You should have a better understanding of how the money is generated from the broadcasters, as well as how it is collected by the PROs, which then pay out to the composers and publishers.

Chapter 5

Music Supervisors and Editors

Music supervisors and editors are valuable people to know for getting your music placed. Supervisors usually do the administrative work, clearing the tracks with publishers and record companies or whomever holds the rights to the masters. A supervisor's job is to make sure the correct licenses are acquired from all of the parties, so there is no possible copyright infringement.

Editors do the actual job of syncing the music to the show in postproduction, much like so many people today who use programs like Final Cut at home to make their own music videos. Now on some occasions, as in daytime television, the music supervisor also edits the show. I know this was always the case on the soap operas.

I wrote for *All My Children* for ten years and when I delivered the music, the supervisor would then load it into Pro Tools and sync it up with a scene. I found it much easier to work with people like this because they could explain exactly how the song worked or didn't work for the show. They knew how to explain it and understood the mechanics of the whole process, making it easier for me to understand and to know what to give them next time.

The problem I've run into many times, both in film and in television, is that the music supervisor is really a liaison between the composer and editor/producer/director. By the time the message is relayed through the channels something is always missing or misinterpreted. It's bad enough dealing with people who aren't musicians, but when they make up words that are thrown around to describe a song, I know I'm in trouble.

COMMUNICATION IS KEY

For example, early in my career, I worked in a jingle house and I heard some of the most ridiculous descriptions from the advertising people. Like can you make it more "green sounding" or can you make it sound more "potential." *What the heck are you talking about?* That's it. I was done with advertising after my experience in Vancouver, B.C. with Ogilvy & Mather, in which we produced a Barbie commercial that had little to no music, yet the copywriter kept spewing nonsense terms during production. I know. I grew up in NYC with parents in advertising and between that and the Son of Sam I had enough of the whole thing! So off I went to Hollywood!

I remember in L.A. I was composing a session for ABC-TV and the head of music was on the phone with me about some promos I was doing and she kept saying, "Lower the *Boom Boom* sound," repeatedly, until finally I figured out that *Boom Boom* meant the kick drum. She had me on speakerphone when she announced to her assistant, "You know, we really should get someone in here who knows about music." *Oh my God! You're only the head of the department.* How did you get the job? . . . No, I don't want to know.

I had this same experience with an Artist & Repertoire (A&R) guy when I was a recording artist finishing my album in the UK. I remember vividly going over the songs on speakerphone, and he asked the producer, "What's that sound that rotates from side to side?" Lo and behold, this idiot was talking about the real suitcase Rhodes (an electro-mechanical piano) we recorded. What's even scarier was that he was a so-called keyboardist himself.

Soon after that, I was at the Gavin Radio Convention when an A&R guy announced that all of the current singles are now using drum programming and we should too. Huh? Are you kidding us? We just spent two weeks recording the songs with live musicians, onto two-inch tape; so his comment was just replace the drums with a drum machine. This guy had no clue, everyone played together off of each other with a feel, a vibe that added to the song. You can't just take the drummer out and insert fake drum loops. You lose the magic of that moment.

So here we are again heading down the same old road. This is the same guy who at the mastering session kept yelling "QUIET" in the studio, so he could determine the space in-between each song. Should it be two or three seconds; he was in deep thought. This was his great contribution to music? Please, use communication accurately to get things done right or it is just a waste of time.

FILM AND TELEVISION MUSIC GUIDES

One of the best ways to find out about music supervisors and editors is to buy a copy of the Music Registry's *Film & Television Music Guide*. It has detailed information on everyone, plus you'll be able to cross-reference it with other guides like the *Hollywood Reporter* so you can see exactly who's working on what production. Remember, this is not as easy as it may seem. It takes lots of patience to do cold calls, and most of all you have to be thick skinned and able to take rejection. There's no doubt that rejection just plain sucks, but you have to understand that this is not personal; it's just timing. You can make twenty calls in a row, but all it takes is just that one contact that can make your day and license your track.

In the beginning of my career, I represented a jingle house in New York City for one year and hated it. I couldn't sell anything. But it taught me how to take rejection, plus I repped for my parents' company growing up, which gave me a good introduction to the business. This is how I learned how to shamelessly self-promote, because if you're not a famous artist, managers and agents won't do anything for you, straight up.

Don't be afraid of approaching as many supervisors and editors as you can, because even if they don't need your music now, they may in the future. These guys move from show to show very quickly and do a lot of work during the off-season, as well for pilots and movies. I've had this happen often where a supervisor couldn't use my music on his current show, but winds up using the same song in a film a few months later. Bottom line, relationships are important and keeping them through the years is even more important. Offer to take them out to lunch when it slows down for them. It's a great way to make a lasting impression. I hate to use the word, but for lack of a better one, "schmooze."

I think self-promoting is even harder than repping someone else because it's so personal. When rejection is given from the outside world, it is hard hitting because it is directed to you. But the way it goes is you can play something for someone who hates it and then go down the hall and play it for another person who might love it. It's very subjective, but at the end of the day all you are trying to do is get your music licensed. Also, you need to research what styles of music the supervisors and editors are looking for in their upcoming shows. If you are a songwriter with country music, then of course you're not going to contact a show that primarily uses hip-hop.

7 TIPS TO MAKE YOU SUCCESSFUL
previously published in *Music Connection* magazine

1. Use Resource Guides

I've always found that resource guides are a good place to start making connections. Having more than one guide or directory is even better—you can cross-reference them. *The Music Registry* publishes a host of reference guides for the music industry, like the *Film & Television Music Guide* and the *Music Publisher Registry*. They were one of the first companies to tackle this type of directory for TV and film music contacts back in the early '90s. What is most impressive about this guide is that it carries pertinent information about music supervisors, music editors, and music departments, among other things. There are other resources, too, like the *Hollywood Creative directory, 411 directories,* and the *Blu-Book directory* that are available, but *The Music Business Registry* is still the most thorough of its kind. And do not overlook *Music Connection*, well known for its guides and directories.

2. Do Your Homework

Once you have a list of contacts to approach, make sure your music is appropriate to submit to these particular contacts. Meaning, if you are a pop vocalist, be sure that these people you are contacting actually license vocal music and not just sixty-second promo instrumental music or blues. The best way to research this is to first watch the shows in question and make note of their likes and styles, so when you contact them you sound well informed. Also before making cold calls, try to get a referral from someone they know. How do you do that? If the contact person is not able to use your music, *always* ask them whom they can recommend! If they are able to give you a name, then you know you can use that person's name for a referral to make the new contact. Keep a detailed log as well. Write down the date you spoke to a contact and any other pertinent information, such as, "Told me to call back in June to follow up on new show."

3. Build A Catalog

Product, that's what you need! When you start shopping your music for licensing possibilities, have at least a CD's worth of material. It seems fruitless when people shop only one song to a music supervisor, unless it's a huge hit from an artist that everyone knows, like Lady Gaga. Sure there is always a possibility that one song could be perfect for a scene and they could license it, but if you are going to all this trouble of contacting people, it just makes better sense to have a number of tracks to shop to get a fighting chance. Especially in today's digital revolution, you can put tons of music on thumb drives and mail it off.

4. Pick The Right Contacts

It will save a lot of time if you make preliminary calls to the music departments to see if they, in fact, license music from outside contributors. Certain companies have exclusive licenses with music libraries and are restricted from using outside sources. Also, there are certain shows that don't license outside music and only use one music composer for the show. Please keep in mind that a lot of your success is determined by timing and whether a show needs your type of music.

When speaking with the music supervisor always try to see what kind of music they may need in upcoming episodes and attempt to get a gauge on what their future licensing needs are. Inquire if they are developing other projects—if they can't use one of your songs now, they may be able to use it in the future.

5. Understand Music Libraries

A common question I get is, "What is a Music Production Library?" Simply, they are music companies, like FirstCom, Megatrax, Sonoton, etc., who hire composers to produce music that's affordable for all sorts of broadcast and film productions. So if a show wants a pop vocal song and can't afford licensing a track by Rihanna from Def Jam, they go to a place like Killer Tracks and license a sound-alike. It's pretty straightforward and simple for productions because these libraries own both the masters and the sync (publishing), so it's a one-stop shop.

In the new millennium there has become a new business model for these libraries, places like Crucial Music, Pump Audio and Rumble Fish, where these companies aren't hiring composers to build their catalog, but instead licensing tracks from a plethora of musicians out there and offering the songs up for licensing.

6. Check Out *The Hollywood Reporter*

This has been the classic guide for TV and Film people through the decades. Thing is, it is also a great resource for music placement contacts. They offer an online Industry Tools feature that lists both TV and film productions, with the specific production data, like phone numbers and addresses. This resource doesn't offer music supervisor information, so you have to call the main production number for each listing and ask them for the appropriate music contact. This is where cross referencing with your other directories comes into play; sometimes people are reluctant to give emails or numbers over the phone; as long you have a full name you can look it up. More than likely you'll find the detailed information you need.

7. Target Music Editors

While a music supervisor is more of an administrator, licensing the music from the various sources, a music editor physically places the music in the shows. A lot times music editors might *temp* in a piece of music and it will end up staying in the show as a final. It is good then for editors to have your music at hand, so it's immediately available to be placed. In the past, I've had a lot of success like this and it has sometimes turned into a productive business relationship. Some will even call on you personally to compose original score for them down the line.

As with music supervisors, the best way to connect with music editors is to reach out by phone and see if they are open to using outside source music and are able to license directly from artists. They can also refer you to the music supervisor they are working with on current shows. This goes for post-production facilities as well. You can contact post supervisors at the various houses and see if they are in a position to license music directly. Like editors, they drop in music at the last minute if a scene is not working. Access to your music is key for these people to place it in their productions.

INTERVIEW WITH BARRY COFFING—MUSICSUPERVISOR.COM

http://www.musicsupervisor.com

I sat down with Barry Coffing of MusicSupervisor.com and Ritch Esra from the Music Registry to find out their take on being successful in music placement. They have some very good insight for artists in the twenty-first century.

Barry Coffing is a music business entrepreneur who grew up in Houston and graduated from the High School for the Performing and Visual Arts. After a short stint at the University of Houston, he began his professional music career in Houston. For six years he was not only performing in bands locally, but also a top jingle singer, music producer, and composer. It was then that Steve Tyrell and Barry Mann discovered his talents and invited him to Los Angeles. After several trips resulting in two of his songs being placed in movies, he decided to move to L.A.

Over the next seventeen years he amassed a great deal of credits and awards with over 200 tracks placed in movies and on TV, BMI songwriting awards, multiple #1 hits and an Emmy nomination. He continued to be the voice behind the scenes in movies like *Moulin Rouge, The Brady Bunch Movie,* and the Winnie the Pooh movie, *Pooh's Grand Adventure.* He wrote TV themes for *California Dreams, The Pyramid* (starring Donny Osmond), and *The Heights.* His song, "How Do You Talk to an Angel" went on to become a number one hit and sell over five hundred thousand copies worldwide. Currently, he is a music business entrepreneur who represents over ten thousand record labels and publishers for film and TV licensing. His company, Music Supervisor, Inc. places hundreds of songs each year in films, TV, and advertisements. Every major film company and TV network uses the software and services of Music Supervisor, Inc.

♫

From your experience of starting the company MusicSupervisor.com, can you describe (to people who are not familiar with them) the importance of such services and how they serve the industry?

Making music is a full-time job. Not every artist gets to work that way, but they should. There are over five thousand movies made every year. How could any one person, let alone a composer or artist working part time, hope to keep up? The answer is they can't. I believe art is a team sport. No one, not even the Beatles, made it based solely on their talent. With no manager to pitch them and no producer to mentor them, then we never hear of them. Currently we are pitching music for over seventy projects a month. That's more than two a day, but we are only scratching the surface of the licensing market.

MusicSupervisor.com was designed as a program for music supervisors to help them do their jobs. We built a state-of-the-art search engine designed for the real granular searches that music supervisors are faced with every day. So they could search by sad cue that is mid tempo and features an accordion, and in seconds be listening to cues. Our goal was to streamline the process so that composers could just compose and music supervisors could just search and listen without researching who owns what all day.

For composers and songwriters, our deal is non-exclusive. We do not retitle any of the composers' works and you can leave at anytime. We get a percentage of what we license, so we are basically a commission-only sales force. If you don't make money, we don't make money.

Working in sales, what types of shows and films tend to use libraries, and have you seen an increase in usage from the industry through the past years?

I have seen every type of production from student films to multi-million-dollar, Spielberg, WWII epics use music from a library. From a cost and time perspective, great library music is a real lifesaver. I had a great indie film I was working on and I licensed a classical piece for the opening of the film because they had a big crane shot of a college with its brick buildings and perfect spacious lawns, so Mozart worked perfectly in two ways. One, it screamed of being taught about and by old white men, and two, it had an eighty-piece live orchestra, which made the movie look expensive. I scored the rest of the film with solo piano and moody guitar cues. I would say I have seen an increase in the number of projects and that has raised the number of library cues used, but the library use is about 20 to 30 percent of total music licensed. It hasn't changed much as a total percentage over the last few years.

One of the most important things I think budding musicians want to know is how to get placement. What is the best way for composers/songwriters to get their music into productions?

> If you want to really clean up as a composer, get a series, or pretend you have one, don't just write one cue in one style; write a whole series of cues that could be used to score an entire episode. Make sure you have a sad cue, a chase cue, a heroic cue, a long background cue; a traveling cue that has movement; a flashback, otherworld type cue; plenty of tension cues with some ending in action and some just tapering out; a warm family cue and plenty of alternative versions and cut downs with and without lead instruments.

> Make sure to use the same instrument palette and keep them in the same keys or a relative minor so a good editor can cut between them to create even more cues.

What were the critical things your clients look for in compositions/songs for their particular productions?

> Here is the checklist that I go through myself and when picking out what to pitch to a client:

> Does it work for the picture and does it make my scene come alive?

> Does it enhance the emotion without competing with the dialogue?

> Does it sound real? In 90 percent of the cues, if it's samples we don't want to know that it's samples, so learn how to write within their capabilities. Don't just write it on a score pad and expect it to work and sound like the real thing. Use samples while composing not after the fact.

> Does it work within the budget? Usually with library music that is not a problem, but if the cue has a full orchestra on it, we charge much more because it's worth it and we can get it.

Finally what advice can you give people who want to become involved in composing for music libraries? How can they get the edge over all of the other composers out there?

First I think you need to have scored a film before you start cranking out cues without really knowing what a real cue needs to do. Do student films or documentaries. Scoring commercials will not help you because they usually have one feel and they stay there. You need to face every composer's nightmare—the five-minute dramatic scene full of people doing nothing but talking: no gunshots or car crashes on screen, but with actors are trying to create the same excitement with simple words. It is all about the timing and the tone.

As far as getting the edge on other composers, it is not a sport where one guy must lose for the other to win. You need to find a niche that you do as well as anyone and create as much great music as you can. Your enemy, if you must have one, is the numbers. The more cues the more lottery tickets and the better chance you will win.

♫

INTERVIEW WITH RITCH ESRA—THE MUSIC BUSINESS REGISTRY http://www.musicregistry.com

Since 1992, Ritch Esra and Stephen Trumbull have been running the *Music Business Registry*, which includes the *A&R Registry*, the *Publisher Registry*, the *Music Business Attorney Registry*, the *Record Producer Directory*, and the *Film and Television Music Guide*.

"The directories give everyone vital, accurate, and the most up-to-date information they need to contact the entire A&R [Artist & Repertoire], music, publishing, legal, and film/TV music communities," says Ritch. "Each directory tells you how to reach these industry veterans by regular mail, email (including websites), direct dial telephone, and fax. Additionally, we provide the exact title, street address, the name of their assistant, and the style of music that each executive deals with. Due to the volatile nature of A&R, the *A&R Registry* is completely updated and reprinted every eight weeks and often has over 100 changes in a single issue. There's no directory of this kind anywhere in the world."

Ritch says that among the subscribers are record company executives, music publishers, managers, agents, attorneys, studios and various other music business professionals in Los Angeles, New York, Nashville, Chicago, Atlanta, Toronto, London, Dublin, Copenhagen, Tokyo, Stockholm, Sydney, and Munich.

Ritch started out as a promotion coordinator for A&M Records in Los Angeles in 1980–81. He coordinated releases with radio stations as well as the national field staff, providing promotional prerelease information on what competitive stations are playing, informing stations on status, on how a record was selling, and on overcoming objections and resistance to broadcasting new releases. He also ensured that all field staff had product and took care of any product needs for radio stations.

From 1981–1987, Ritch was director of West Coast A&R for Arista Records. He signed the Thompson Twins to their US deal, as well as Mara Getz. He worked extensively with the publishing and songwriting communities for material for Whitney Houston, Aretha Franklin, Dionne Warwick, Melissa Manchester, Tanya Tucker, Jennifer Warnes, and Jermaine Jackson. He also coordinated music for the *Ghostbusters* and *Perfect* soundtracks.

From 1988–1991, Ritch worked on various independent projects. He produced the award-winning educational video for artists and musicians, *How to Get a Record Deal*. "At the time, it was the only video of its kind examining the frequently misunderstood process from five different perspectives: record company executives, A&R VPs, artist managers, record producers, and sixteen major artists including Los Lobos, Mark Knopfler, Phil Collins, Jody Watley, Karla Bonoff, Michael Bolton, Fleetwood Mac, Chick Corea, and Kenny Loggins," says Ritch. Producers Phil Ramone and Jeff Baxter are also interviewed in the video.

Ritch has organized and coordinated the events and activities of the Independent Music Conference in Los Angeles, sponsored by BMI. The three-day symposium addressed problems facing recording artists, including publishing, management, touring, obtaining record deals, and exploring alternative ways to bring music to the public.

♫

Why did you start the Music Registry? I remember it back in the day as a small, self-printed, thin reference guide, which I thought was a great idea.

We started it in 1992 because I felt that the era of only having annual directories was something of the past. It was apparent that the information in A&R was changing far too rapidly to only have it once a year.

You offered this service at a time when printed editions were a very integral part of the business model. How did you deal with the distribution part of it?

> We shipped books all over the world. It was a pain because often they were lost and had to be replaced, which was costly. As we grew, so did the amount of pages in our registries, as well as the cost of shipping them.

In the beginning, was it a challenge to get all of the contact information?

> It was a challenge in that I wanted not only the data of the company, but I also wanted to include all of the assistants' names and direct dial lines as well. I felt that assistants were the real unsung heroes in the business in that they were the ones that got so much of the work done. Whether you wanted your song heard, your act checked out live, or your invoice paid, you needed to get to know who the assistants were and make friends with them, because they were the ones who got the work done.

How did you go about obtaining all of the names, when industry people can be very secretive at times?

> They can be, but I had been in the business for twelve years already and so many people at the labels knew me. But it was, and still can be, very difficult at times, though most people know us now and we've become the industry standard over the last twenty years.

From your experience, what are the critical things companies look for in compositions/songs for their particular productions?

> The one thing they look for above all is "Could this song be a hit for one of our acts?" They also look for writers/producers who have great production chops, as we live in an age where there really is no such thing as a "demo recording" for the most part in the pro songwriter/music-publisher world. When you hear the productions that the top, hit songwriters submit to recording artists, they're nearly finished records.

Finally, what advice can you give prospective licensees to be successful in getting music placed in TV and films?

> The most important advice that I can give *anyone* looking to place music into film or television is:

a) Remember, it's not about someone listening to your music and finding a place for it—it's about you serving the needs of the film or TV show. If you can truly get that, you'll do very well.

b) The other piece of advice that is very important is never submit music for a TV show that you don't watch or know the musical sensibility of. That's career suicide. Again, your job as a music creator is to serve the needs of the TV show or film, not have someone find a use for your music.

Have you found that phone calls are more effective than email blasts?

There's no one answer to that question for everyone, but I would say you'll have better luck building a relationship initially with email than calling on the phone, unless you know them personally.

♩

INDUSTRY PROFILE: P. J. BLOOM NEOPHONIC, INC.

By Larry LeBlanc (Courtesy of CelebrityAccess MediaWire)

http://celebrityaccess.com

Slash loathes *Glee.*

In fact, Guns N' Roses, along with the Red Hot Chili Peppers and Kings of Leon, have refused to allow their songs to be covered by the cast of *Glee.*

Glee, nevertheless, is a pop cultural phenomenon.

As well, *Glee* has become the must-go-to platform for any music publisher intent on finding a sizzling promotional vehicle for their copyrights.

Each week after the musical comedy-drama television series airs, digital sales of the music featured on the show skyrocket.

The series—if you don't know—follows the fictitious lives of the members of William McKinley High School's glee club, called the New Directions, as they deal with life, sex, and being supercharged teenagers in Lima, Ohio.

The show's track record for snaring attention is downright impressive.

Nineteen Emmy nominations (and four wins); a Peabody Award; a Golden Globe for best TV series, and two Grammy Award nominations.

The show's first soundtrack, *Glee*: The Music, Volume 1, received a Grammy nomination for best compilation soundtrack album for a motion picture, TV, or other visual media. *Glee* also received a nomination for best pop performance by a duo or group with vocals for the cast's version of Journey's "Don't Stop Believin'" (regionals version) on the *Glee*: The Music-Journey to Regionals album.

Traditionally, television has motivated fans to purchase music—often preexisting third party songs—that they hear on a show. *Glee* is absolutely unique in that its fans buy both the new version performed by the program's cast as well the original by the pop superstar act.

How the show came about was that in early 2008, after the success of his cutting-edge, FX show, *Nip/Tuck*, the show's co-creator and director, Ryan Murphy, read an edgy independent film screenplay by Ian Brennan titled *Glee*.

Murphy became so fixated on the title that he asked Brennan to redo *Glee* as an acerbic television comedy. Then, with co-writer Brad Falchuk, they successfully pitched the show to Fox Television executives in the spring of 2008.

The potential for the show's music to be a digital sales powerhouse was demonstrated when the *Glee* pilot aired on Fox on May 19, 2009, greatly benefiting from a sizable lead-in of *American Idol* viewers during finale week.

The pilot episode achieved 9.6 million viewers on it first broadcast, and 4.2 million viewers when a director's cut version was later aired.

The pilot featured one song placement after another—more than twenty in an hour's time—including Amy Winehouse's "Rehab," energetically performed by the glee club members, decked out in frilly, blue, polka-dotted skirts.

After Murphy had committed to making Journey's "Don't Stop . . ." the signature song for the pilot, the production team began the process of turning one of the best known pop/rock songs of all time into one of the greatest *Glee* triumphs.

Murphy, however, hadn't cast his actors for the series yet. This resulted in no less than twenty different demo versions being created by two different producers, sung by everyone from the top session singer in Los Angeles to a Journey cover band front man.

In the end, *Glee* producer Adam Anders created what we needed, which, in turn, was sung by the cast. The rest is showbiz history. The *Glee* cast's version of "Don't Stop Believin'" has racked up one million sales, according to Nielsen SoundScan.

In season 2's opener, besides performing Lady Gaga and Beyoncé's "Telephone," Filipino singer, Charice, sang a powerful rendition of the latter's "Listen."

The choices of such recent contemporary hit fare signaled that *Glee* had shifted from being reliant on catalog to really entering the pop superstar sweepstakes.

Now that *Glee* is *GLEE*, it has the latitude to explore newer songs on their way to becoming mega-hits.

The program has the clout, in fact, to add to the hit-making machinery.

This was evidenced by Blaine and his Dalton Academy classmates singing Katy Perry's "Teenage Dream" that landed first-week sales of 214,000 digital downloads; as well as cast covers of Travis McCoy's "Billionaire" and Cee Lo Green's "Forget You" being mega-hits as well as reigniting sales of the original recordings.

In October 2010, recordings by the *Glee* cast overtook the Beatles in terms of the number of songs placed on the Billboard Hot 100. To date, *Glee* has placed 102 songs on the chart.

For the show's success, give credit where credit is due: to Murphy and the team of producers, writers, directors, and editors who are encouraged to contribute their creative input to the show.

Also, overseeing the music in *Glee* for the show's production company, Ryan Murphy Television, is the very versatile P. J. Bloom, a partner at the music supervision firm Neophonic, Inc.

Once Murphy picks a song for inclusion in *Glee*, Bloom tries to clear the rights with its publishers. Songs are then rehearsed, choreographed, and recorded. The process begins six to eight weeks before an episode tapes, and can finish up the day before.

For over a decade, Bloom has been one of Hollywood's most prominent music supervisors.

He has supervised, coordinated and consulted on everything, from small independent films (such as the 1999 documentary *Better Living Through Circuitry* on electronic music and rave culture) to major studio projects by such filmmakers as Steven Spielberg, Jerry Bruckheimer, Ridley Scott, Michael Mann, John Frankenheimer, Norman Jewison, Mike Nichols, and others.

His impressively long list of credits include *Terra Nova,* the sci-fi drama television series that aired on Fox in 2011; as well as such TV series as: *CSI:*

Miami, *United States of Tara*, *Nip/Tuck*, *The Shield*, *Angels Over America*, *Lincoln Heights*, *Trust Me*, *State of Mind*, *Night Stalker*, and *Baywatch*.

Bloom has also been a music consultant at HBO Films since 1998, overseeing such projects as *Angels in America*, *The Life & Death of Peter Sellers*, *Maria Full of Grace*, *The Gathering Storm*, *American Splendor*, *Generation Kill*, and *The Ballad of Bettie Page*.

Born and raised in Los Angeles, Bloom first worked at honing his craft in the soundtrack divisions of Columbia Records, and Arista Records. As well, he worked at the Grammy Foundation, operated by the National Academy of Recording Arts & Sciences (now known as the Recording Academy).

Along the way, Bloom has been a prominent club DJ, a music journalist, an Internet radio host, and part of the creative team behind Disneyland's "Rockin' Both Parks" event which updated the soundtracks for both the Space Mountain and California Screamin' roller coasters in 2007.

As well, he was music supervisor for such feature films as *Eat, Pray, Love,* and *Running with Scissors*.

With your job, is it hard to listen to music for pure enjoyment?

I just don't have time. I am juggling so many projects here, and I need to stay so far ahead. That is what, in a lot of ways, producers and directors who hire me expect. I don't have so much personal time to spend with any one [music] thing. If I did, I would just lose too many hours of the day. I have to be constantly rifling through new stuff.

You also have a two-and-a-half year old son.

Yeah, so I don't have any friggin' time to sit down, and listen to music [at home]. I am chasing him all over the place, and trying to be a husband and a father while I do this music business thing in the day.

Do you find yourself listening to music thinking, "Maybe I can use that"?

I don't think there's any moment I spend with music these days that I'm not thinking about how I can apply it to my work. That is just a double-edge sword of what I do, and how long that I have been doing it. It all seems to factor into the visual media for me in some way, shape, or form.

Was that true when you started doing music supervision?

I guess when I discovered soundtracks, I was lucky enough to find a creative area that really coincided with who I am as an artistic person. I was excited to be able to apply my love of music to music supervision, and that I actually had an outlet to do it. I think I was proactively trying to figure out how I could take everything I was listening to, and apply it to the projects that I was working on. Now it is completely unconscious.

The main thing about my career, and my relationship with music, is that I've essentially sacrificed my fandom for the work. I don't have time to spend with back catalog or to listen to albums I love from back in the day. I'm constantly looking forward, and living this ephemeral existence with music. And, I do love that part of it. But, it's unusual that I listen to albums more than once or twice.

That's kinda sad being a music junkie.

I couldn't imagine doing anything else with my life and yet, as blessed as I am, there is this downside to crossing commerce and art that no one who's not in [the music business] can understand. As overjoyed as I am with what I've managed to accomplish, I can't just sit and listen to music anymore without overanalyzing if/how it relates to my work, which zaps a lot of the pure enjoyment. Makes me long for the old days when I was an impoverished, jobless stoner surrounded by a sea of vinyl that I spun all day long.

I hosted an Internet radio show [Hunnypot Radio] for four years, up until recently. The best part about it was just getting to play my favorite tunes for three hours a week. No business, just music. It was so great.

The music business is a business few people understand.

Well, it's definitely not the real world. It is not the world that we really live in. Everybody else lives in the real world. I really hope that this music business thing continues to work out for me because if it doesn't, I'm screwed because I do not have any real world skill sets. If I'm forced to go and push a pencil in a cube somewhere, it will be a rough road for me. I think that I'd sooner put on a backpack and go and wash dishes across Europe.

What makes you and Ryan Murphy work so well together? *Glee* **isn't the first series you have worked on together. You worked together for six seasons on the FX series** *Nip/Tuck* **and the 2006 film** *Running With Scissors.*

Honestly, I think that the thing that makes my relationship with Ryan work so well is that I just get him what he wants. Ryan is very sure about his wants, his desires, and his needs. We have a very good shorthand, and he tells me what he wants to do, and I make it happen for him. If he wants my creative input I am happy to share it with him. But, in terms of facilitation, I get him what he wants, and I get the job done, and I get it done on time and on budget. I think that he is appreciative of that.

You and Ryan must be on the same wavelength for many things.

I think so. I think that Ryan appreciates my intensity about [music] and my conviction. He is a very intense guy himself. He knows exactly what he wants. He has a vision, and I think that he appreciates that from me as well. And I think that he appreciates the progress that I have made as well.

When we first started working together, I was not nearly the music supervisor that I am now. He gave me an opportunity to show him that I could do what I said that I could do, and it worked. And I think for one of the first times in his career his projects have been recognized for the music, and he's been recognized as a music person—someone who pays very close attention to soundtracks. I think I can take a little bit of credit for that.

Does your company Neophonic handle all of the musical clearances for the show?

We do. I prefer it that way. We are very hands-on here. Clearance, in a lot of ways, is the backbone of music supervision. We pride ourselves on doing an incredible administrative job, and having a very tight business affairs ship. I personally believe that while it's positive and a good thing to know music in a creative way and have some artistic ability, I do not think that is a primary component of music supervision. I think that music supervision is a very specific skills set that includes creative, but it also includes technical and business affairs, money management, and politics. All of these things that so many of the younger "music supervisors" don't necessarily appreciate or know how to do.

Obviously relationships are important in your work.

Yep. That's our entire business. In the music business and the entertainment business in general, relationships are a lot of it. And, you are only as good as your last job.

Now that *Glee* is so popular, have you gone from where music was hard to clear to suddenly the floodgates are open?

It's definitely [now] more the latter. It was a huge uphill battle at first. We had this incredibly ambitious endeavor in an episodic musical. The episodic musical had failed miserably over the years with shows like *Cop Rock* or *Viva Laughlin*, which went a whopping two episodes [on CBS] before it got canceled. So we were behind the eight ball for sure. A lot of my time was spent convincing all of these A-list songwriters and major publishers that "This is going to be different," and "We're going to be great," and "It's going to mean so much," and "It's going to be so wonderful."

No doubt, these publishers and songwriters were all saying, "Show me the money."

There was a lot of that stuff. People are still saying, "Show me the money." Now with the show, obviously everything has changed. We're incredibly popular. We sell a lot of records. So there's a huge ancillary income stream [for creators]. There's a huge marketing component. When our songs go into the charts, the original versions reenter the charts as well. It brings recognition back to the original artists. There is just a lot of great stuff that happens for everybody who is associated with the show.

***Glee* has spent an unprecedented amount of money on music for a scripted network drama. Do you still battle for music rights on your other film and TV projects?**

Every show is a battle. *Glee* is no different. It's not like I just sit back in my chair and pick the things that I want. There are still a lot of money conversations. Any songwriter or any publisher is still concerned about content; especially using huge songs by certain acts, like the Beatles, Billy Joel or any of these huge catalog acts; or even these new acts, like Lady Gaga. They want to make sure that they are being really represented [in the show]. Just because we say that it's *Glee*, it's not a given that it is all going to be good and positive for everybody. There's still a lot of work to be done.

How did it feel having the show's cast overtaking the Beatles on Billboard's Hot 100 singles chart?

It is difficult to process when you see it there in print. It's amazing, and at the same time it feels a little bit blasphemous to a music person like me. There are just certain things that you are not supposed to mess with. Obviously, it feels incredible. I am thrilled for the success of the show, and Ryan's success, and my own success because of it. At the same time, we are doing covers. We didn't overtake the Beatles' singles record by writing songs, so it needs to be kept in perspective. But, you know, it's awesome.

Sir Paul McCartney didn't send a telegram?

Paul has been an incredible friend of the show. We've used several of his songs and we will continue to use several of his songs. We have also used a couple of Beatles songs. We've have been talking to Paul and his camp about doing a Paul McCartney tribute episode which will definitely happen at some point.

So many people are excited about being involved with *Glee* because they all have kids and grandkids.

If there is an accolade that Paul hasn't won over the years I would be surprised. So I would assume that he wasn't too broken up by *Glee*'s success.

> The episode that will feature Paul McCartney's songs has yet to be announced. According to Reuters, Ryan Murphy was a sent a set of mix CDs by McCartney "It came out of the blue in a package, handwritten, and it had two CDs and it said, "Hi Ryan, I hope you will consider some of these songs for *Glee*," Murphy said. "So, of course, we are going to do something with him."

Ryan has been teasing a Justin Bieber episode.

Justin Bieber will be represented shortly. His episode is coming around in February [2011]. Everybody has Bieber fever right now. *Glee* is no different. We're not immune.

One of the most fun things of *Glee* for me is that we get to participate in all of these cultural things that are happening right now. The first season, in a lot of ways, was built on catalog. We needed to have these huge hit songs that everybody knew in order to establish the series. Now, in season 2, now that we are so much more popular, we get to really attack the charts as they are happening. Whether it is Katy Perry or Justin Bieber, we have our versions of these songs coming out within weeks of these songs becoming charts hits.

Are there concerns from the original artist's labels that by using a song with the *Glee* cast, you are taking away from what they do?

No, no one is really concerned. There are certainly questions that are talked about because the record companies are running campaigns with their artists, and we're doing our things. What has happened is that (covering original songs) only spikes sales for the original acts. We do our Paramore song ("The Only Exception") and Paramore comes back onto the charts. We do a Katy Perry song ("California Gurls"), Katy Perry sells more records.

Everybody buys them both, especially the younger demographic, the teenagers and the young 20s. These folks are out there buying music and they are spending time on iTunes. They are buying, and they are re-buying. They are buying digital and then they will go ahead and buy at retail.

Was the show's 15th episode "The Power of Madonna" on April 20, 2010 a watershed for the program? Covering Madonna was risky, but the show went so well. It was so popular.

Certainly from a business standpoint [the spotlight one performer] hadn't been done. It took us weeks and weeks to set this deal up. Madonna and her team were integral and Warner-Chappell, her publisher, was integral in helping us with that. So was Geoff Bywater over at 20th Century Fox, who is the head of music television there. This show could not run without him. It took the best of all our efforts to make the Madonna thing happen. Once we were able to get the deal on its feet, Ryan and his team just took the creative part to another level. I think that we were all excited about the way it turned out. We were all pleased. At the same, you have to give birth to it. You hope to put it out there and the world responds. If you do justice arguably to the biggest female act in the world, people will respond.

> The Madonna episode was the first time the music on *Glee* was turned over in its entirety to one performer. According to Nielsen, the episode was watched by 13.5 million viewers in the U.S. Michele's lead performance of Madonna's "Like a Prayer" sold 87,000 digital downloads, according to Nielsen SoundScan. The stand-alone "Power of Madonna" soundtrack from the episode debuted at #1 on the Billboard 200.
>
> Sony Music Label Group chairman Rob Stringer explained to Ann Donahue in Billboard (May 8, 2010

issue) that "The Power of Madonna" was a risky album release being that it was based on the songs from a single episode. "It's kind of weird," he said. "It's a different marketing angle, but the episode is so bloody good."

Getting Madonna's approval for the "Power of Madonna" episode and the album that followed was, by no means, easy. Her camp originally passed on the concept. Further pitching was done, and the deal was only greenlighted after Ryan Murphy sent an appeal letter directly to Madonna.

Glee covers aren't identical covers of the original recordings.

Glee doesn't try to be something that it is not. We pay homage and honor to all of the songs, and all of the acts that we cover. We're certainly unique out there in the world, but we are not trying to completely reinvent the wheel.

We have some of the best singers in the business. We have incredible actors. Ryan is a master story-teller, and there's all the creative team. Everyone on this team is incredible at what they do. Kudos to Geoff Bywater and to the production executives and creative executives at 20th Century Fox. Everybody has been so gracious with their talent and has worked so hard to make this thing [show] so great.

The addition of Darren Criss—who sang the show's cover of "Teenage Dream"—as a cast regular and recurring guest stars like Charice must give Ryan and you a greater range to pick songs.

Absolutely. Every cast member brings something different to the table. A lot of new people coming in, and people who are going to visit in the future, just add a new dynamic and broadens our ability to do different kinds of creative things. It allows us to keep fresh.

According to Laraine Santiago of the Santa Ana Celebrity Examiner, Ryan Murphy has confirmed that Charice is returning to the show. "She is coming back to *Glee* in a big way; we're finishing the year with her. She's coming back for five episodes at the end of the year. She's gonna be great! Lots of big, big ballads for Charice."

So when do we get a Nirvana/Led Zeppelin/Sex Pistols episode?

[Laughing] I would enjoy that one. I'm told that the Nirvana camp is up for it. I've been told Led Zeppelin would potentially consider it. Sex Pistols? I really haven't gone there. I haven't had the pleasure to talk with Johnny [Lydon] about it. I would hope if that day comes, it would come to pass.

Didn't you license Nirvana's music for *CSI: Miami* in 2006?

That deal disintegrated just before the finish line. I spent quite a long time working on that, and quite a lot of effort. Unfortunately, that was not meant to be. I certainly believe that my efforts laid the groundwork to what came after it, because prior to that Nirvana had never been on a scripted television show in that way. That has since happened, it probably would have happened, but I certainly teed it up.

> The 2007 season premiere of *Cold Case* featured eight Nirvana songs: "All Apologies," "Stay Away," "If You Must," "Lithium," "Drain You," "Something in the Way," "Come As You Are" and "Heart Shaped Box."
>
> In Oct. 2006, *Forbes* magazine had reported that four Nirvana songs, including "Come As You Are," would be used on *CSI: Miami* in November 2006. However, no Nirvana tracks were on the soundtrack when the episode aired.
>
> In the third season's finale of ABC-TV's *Lost* in 2006, Jack Shephard is driving down the street listening to Nirvana's "Scentless Apprentice," right before he arrives to the Hoffs/ Drawlar Funeral Parlor. This was the first usage of the band's music on a network television program's soundtrack.

Vanity Fair magazine outed you as a Rush fan.

Rush are truly one of my all-time favorite bands. My wife loves them too, actually which is fun for us. I've never met them. I know Neil [Peart] has made mention of *Glee*, so I feel I'm like one degree of separation from the band.

You're a David Bowie fan too.

David Bowie is probably my singular, all-time favorite artist. He is the ultimate pop/rock artist, and songwriter. I would kill to be involved with him in some way. He is an artistic chameleon—changes every time he comes out with a new album. Just as a representative of music and rock and roll, he is my all-time, all-time favorite. I've never had the opportunity meet him. He's one of very few people I would be star struck by.

Music supervision for film and TV has changed considerably over the past decade. Ten years ago music supervisors were often dropping in licensed tracks in postproduction.
Nowadays, music supervisors can front-load the creative, business ,and production elements of a soundtrack well in advance of shoot days. Often you are brought into script and concept meetings.

I would say that ten, fifteen, or twenty years ago, music supervisors were facilitators in a lot of ways. Now, we—at least some of the best ones—are known for our creative prowess, and what we bring to the table. We all do a very different thing, a very unique thing. We are brought on to not only handle the production, technical, and the business affairs needs of the show, but as a true creative component.

We are also in one of the few above-the-line roles that are in the trenches—working with the filmmakers and television producers from day one, really. We are there on the set. We are there during the editing process—start to finish.

There weren't many popular soundtracks in the '60s and '70s that successfully licensed eliciting third party songs. In the '80s, I remember the popularity of *Stand By Me* (1986) reigniting Atlantic Records' catalog.

There was also *The Big Chill* (1983). The concept of licensing existing third party songs en masse for film soundtracks is something that is relatively recent, as in the last thirty years. In the '40s, '50s, and '60s, it was all about original music. If it wasn't a musical where the songs were created specifically to support the story, [studios] were commissioning [original] works. It was never about licensing twelve, fifteen, or twenty tracks for a film. It was about commissioning that one big song to anchor the project.

> The soundtrack of *Stand By Me* reached #31 on the Billboard 200 in 1986, staying on the chart 45 weeks. *The Big Chill* reached #17, and stayed on the chart for 161 weeks.

Studios either had an orchestrator, music composers, and lyricists in house, or had orchestrators like Alex North, Leonard Bernstein, or Henry Mancini do the music.

Exactly. It was just an entirely different medium back then.

Warner Bros. Records was originally established in 1958 as the recorded music division of the American movie studio Warner Bros. Pictures. Among the label's early releases were albums by Warner contract players such as Tab Hunter, Edd Byrnes, Connie Stevens, Jack Webb, and William Holden. That was a rare planned marketing matchup of TV and music.

Absolutely. I would also say that back then that these film companies never really looked at soundtracks as a marketing tool. [The soundtrack] existed solely to support the body of the film, and the creative aspect of the film. Later, when you get into the '80s, the Michael Mann era of television with *Miami Vice* or the early '90s with *Beverly Hills, 90210* you have these soundtracks that were not only driving the episodes but they were also being used as marketing tools by the studios and the [TV] networks.

Michael Mann was one of the first to bring a sound and a look to a TV series.

Absolutely. I did a series with Michael Mann [as executive producer], the short-lived *Robbery Homicide Division* [in the 2002-03 season for CBS]. At the time we were going up against *CSI, Crime Scene Investigation*, the original Las Vegas one. We absolutely got killed by that show. *Robbery Homicide Division* went off the air after a short ten episodes. But Michael did tell me a couple of great stories about licensing music for *Miami Vice* back in the day. Nobody really cared back then. It wasn't a money-making operation. The music industry didn't really care about the licensing because everybody was still selling records and making money at retail. So, for him to license a song like Phil Collins "In The Air Tonight," he said that he paid in the neighborhood of a few hundred bucks, and the deal was done in a day.

Some directors and producers are more attuned to music than others.

Yeah, there are a lot of directors I've worked with who have incredible taste in music and an incredible sense of it. Ryan Murphy is definitely one. Unfortunately, I think, more directors and producers really just have a sense of story, and a sense of picture, and not so much a sense of music. I find that, more often than not, most people are looking to [license] their favorite songs, which may or not apply to the film or the television show. Usually what makes a favorite song is that you have your own incredible memories when you first heard it, like getting laid in the back of a car during prom [night] or on your wedding night, whenever it was. That's what they look to. Your memories are never the same as the world's.

And those are usually the tracks that are impossible to clear because they are such big hits.

Right, exactly. In some cases, they are such a small hit that they have no significance whatsoever.

You worked in the soundtracks department of Columbia Records in the early '90s?

I started my whole [music supervision] journey at Columbia back in the '90s. I was doing soundtracks. That's where I discovered the trade. I ended up getting a job with Maureen Crowe, [then VP of Soundtracks at Columbia Records] who had just come off *The Bodyguard* soundtrack, which was one of the big-selling soundtracks of all time. She was offered a department at Columbia Records. She started up the soundtrack department there, and I got a job working with her.

You left Columbia after a year.

After leaving Columbia in 1995, I went to NARAS [the National Academy of Recording Arts & Sciences—now known as the Recording Academy] and worked for the Grammy Foundation for a while during the Mike Greene era. Jim Berk was running the foundation at the time. I was glad I was exposed to what NARAS was doing, but it was not my bag. Then, I opened up a nightclub in Los Angeles.

A nightclub in Hollywood?

It was called The Night Watch. Do you remember the club Simply Blues on top of the Sunset and Vine Tower? It was there for about twenty years on the top floor of the Sunset and Vine high-rise on the south-east corner of Sunset and Vine. That's where our club was.

You lost your ass.

Oh, absolutely. We spent about eighteen months building the club, and we were open for about nine months before we had to close, but it was fun. We booked live talent and had a dance club. It was another thing to add to my music repertoire. In some shape and form, my journey.

After that, you had to look for a job.

I had been exposed to soundtracks by that point, and I wanted to stay in [that field]. I ended up finding a job with Evyen Klean, who is now my partner in music supervision. His partner, at the time [in Klean/Broucek Music], was Paul Broucek [now president, Music, Warner Bros. Pictures]. I was their assistant for a little while.

Six months into that, Evyen and Paul got asked to, essentially, become the music department at New Line Cinema. Evyen had pretty much lived his entire existence as an independent music supervisor, and he didn't have any kids. Paul Broucek, on the other hand, had two kids who were imminently going to college. So the idea of steady income was more enticing to him. So they ended up splitting up. Paul went on to run the music department at New Line Cinema [as President, Music, 2004-2008 until New Line Cinema was folded into Warner Bros. Pictures].

So, that left just me and Evyen doing the music supervision thing when Evyen had [*Baywatch*]. All of a sudden I was thrust into this greater role. I got to spend my early days finding music for Pam Anderson running down the beach with her boobs flapping around.

Welcome back to the music supervision business.

Yes, exactly. That's when I really thought, "You know what? This is for me."

Didn't you also launch Hunnypot Unlimited with John Anderson?

John and I founded Hunnypot together. It started about ten years ago.

You started out by throwing free parties.

We did. The soundtrack world was starting to have a real voice within the music industry as digital started to come around, and physical retail was meaning less, and soundtracks were meaning more. There was a much greater spotlight cast on this industry.

As a way to bring people together in a social way, John and I started throwing these parties around town [Los Angeles]. We would do them, probably, quarterly. They were great. It was everybody in the then-burgeoning film and television music business. We were all having fun. We were all doing really cool creative stuff. We were making money for the business. We were all having a good time. There wasn't a whole lot of pressure. We weren't supporting the rest of the record industry like we are now. We were flying just below the radar. We had enough prominence where we had the respect, but didn't have so much of the responsibility and accountability that we have now. It was a lot of fun throwing parties for this group.

> A decade ago, Bloom and "Hot Tub" John Anderson (senior VP of film, TV and creative for Windswept Music Publishing), started throwing film and television music mixers to coincide with the then-burgeoning soundtrack field. About thirty to forty people showed up at the early parties. As the world of film and television music grew, so did their events.
>
> Hunnypot parties have had as many as a many as 1,000 people, and have included live bands and tastemaker DJ's. Hunnypot has also had a presence at several music conferences, including CMJ and South by Southwest. In addition, Hunnypot broadcasts a weekly online radio program.

Flash-forward about eight years, John and I decided to try and monetize this thing, and get into the [music] publishing world. We found some money, started signing bands, and began working with different acts.

In 2008, Hunnypot Unlimited joined with EverGreen Copyrights for a music publishing, placement and marketing venture.

EverGreen were the first people to come in and fund us. That was a difficult experience for us. It was fun trying to get funded, to go out, and look for money. We had a couple of suitors at the time, but we decided to work with EverGreen. They were funded in an around-about way by Lehman Brothers Merchant Banking Group [now known as Trilantic Capital Partners].

It was difficult to work within the music business medium, especially publishing, when developing new acts. There is probably a three or four year arc before you see any money, or any movement, on the acts that you are working with. But we were involved with bankers who were getting quarterly reports. So every three months, we would have these huge conference calls, and board meeting type of affairs, where they would keep asking us, "Where are we? What's our progress? How much money have we made?" The answer, generally, was, "Well, we're nowhere. We haven't made any money. We are still spending money. We are still developing."

We would talk in all of this esoteric street jargon with a bunch of suits-and-ties that were using a bunch of economic acronyms that I didn't really know about, or care about.

Is Hunnypot Unlimited still active?

John and I are still partners, although I no longer participate in the day-to-day (business). We have a publishing deal with [the electro-dance group] Far East Movement, among others. They currently have an international super hit with "Like a G6" (which reached #1 on the Billboard Hot 100). Their second single "Rocketeer" is in the Top 30 and rising.

You are from L. A.

I am from L. A. I grew up in the Benedict Canyon area. It is technically Beverly Hills, but I am just embarrassed to even say that.

Don't tell me you went to Beverly Hills High School.

I did. There are two other successful music supervisors from my high school class—Lisa Brown, who has done a lot of Disney stuff over the years, and Ann Kline.

Your parents are in entertainment.

My father, George Bloom, is an Emmy Award winning screenwriter. My mom, Sue Bloom, is in fashion. She has dressed a lot of very famous people over the years.

Your dad has been nominated for three Emmys, and won as head writer for *Cyberchase* in 2007.

He worked on Lou Wasserman's team at MCA from '62 to '68, and was involved in shows like *The Alfred Hitchcock Hour*, *Wagon Train*, *Ironside*, and *It Takes a Thief*. Then he became a freelance writer in the later '60s to now. He wrote for *Starsky & Hutch*, *The Incredible Hulk*, and *Maude* in the '70s, and wrote the film *Last Flight of Noah's Ark* starring Ricky Schroeder and Elliot Gould. He switched to children's programming in the '80s to now, writing for *Transformers, My Little Pony, Magic Schoolbus, Cyberchase,* and other shows.

You got a taste of Hollywood while very young.

Growing up, I would go with my dad to all of the studio lots. I grew up going to 20th Century Fox when they still had the old *Hello Dolly* set there or going to the old Paramount Studio. I'd go with him to take meetings or I would go with him when he was on set to shoot. So the whole concept of being in Los Angeles, being in the entertainment business, and being surrounded by Hollywood for all of this music stuff, is very natural to me.

Did you hang out at Tower Records on Sunset Boulevard?

I worked at Tower Records in the summer of '87. I'm the real deal in that way. It's amazing to me that it doesn't exist anymore. I still live in Los Angeles and I drive down the Sunset Strip all of the time. I look over to where this iconic record store used to be, and it just seems odd that it's not there.

Where did you go to college?

I went to the University of Colorado [in Denver]. I got a degree in music and a degree in interpersonal communications there. I went there as a piano performance major. I ended up getting in a bit of a row with the head of the piano department. She was a strict classicist and insisted that we did the theoretical lessons by performing music by dead people, music by dead composers. I wanted to exploit the theoretical lessons by writing my own stuff, which is what I thought was kind of the idea of going to music school and learning how to play and how to perform. Apparently, she disagreed.

So at that point, I lost interest and wanted to drop out of the [music] program, but one of my professors there was Dick Weissman [then a tenured professor in the Music & Entertainment Industry program]. I think that he's also one of the top claw-hammer banjo players in the country. He's written books on the music business. I credit him for putting me on the path. I took classes from him. He suggested that, if I was going to drop out of the music program that I should stay and get into the very young music business program at that time. I loved taking classes with him.

A member of the legendary folk trio the Journeymen with John Phillips and Scott McKenzie, Philadelphia-born Dick

Weissman is also a renowned teacher and writer of over 20 books, including:

The Music Business: Career Opportunities and Self-Defense, The Folk Music Sourcebook, and *Which Side Are You On? An Inside History of the Folk Music Revival in America.*

You collected records for years.

[Record stores] were a big deal for me. (I can remember) all the Rhino Records backlot sales, all of the penny sales that they used to have. Record Surplus down on West Pico Boulevard—all of these places. For me, my father is a screen writer, but I developed this sort of music passion on my own.

I DJ'ed for a long time at clubs and I would lug my vinyl around everywhere. It just meant everything to me, it still does. I love to see these statistics where CD sales go down 30% every year, but vinyl goes up 200%. That is just amazing.

Do you miss the warmer sound of vinyl?

I have really expensive gear in my office. I've got tube amplifiers. I try to pull as much warmth out of (music) as possible. When I still DJ, I work with the digital vinyl medium Serato (Scratch Live). I basically take my turntables, and play actual physical vinyl that it is encoded so it reads the MP3s that I have on my computer. I still have my hands on the vinyl in that way.

Do you still own vinyl?

I don't. I don't really have that much at all. The bulk of my major collection was stolen about a decade ago. I had it in storage and the storage facility was broken into. So the bulk of my collection was stolen. The rest of it I either gave away or . . . I'm not so much a believer in the physical manifestation of music anymore. I was in that for a long time. I don't know what it means to me anymore. I'm in this incredibly unique position of having everything at my fingertips at any time. I've taken that to, "So why do I need to own it?"

One flick of the wrist on the Internet, you can listen to what you want.

It's true. And you can stream these bootleg concerts. Go to a show, and the next day you can hear the show that you went to. I love all of that as someone who grew up in the world of record stores, and rifling through the bins.

I was always nervous for the next generation of the record-buying public, just knowing how voracious my appetite was back then, and how excited I was to leave my house and to go to the record store, be there at midnight when the album of the big band that I wanted went on sale or taking the bus to the record store and spending every last nickel that I had rifling through the used record bins.

I didn't think that the world of digital retail would have the same kind of meaning. I thought that there would be some apathy from the record buying public. But what has ended up happening is the world has now been unified and people can now go on the Internet, and find anything that they want at any time. It has given people a new kind of curiosity to try to find as much as they can. They have developed a hunger and an appetite for (music) in a different way.

Then there's a medium like Pandora where you input one type of music that you like, or one band that you like, and Pandora spits out, "Well, if you like this, maybe you will like this music." It gives you a playlist of everything that is kind of like this one band or this one act or this one genre that you like, which is also kind of a neat thing.

Anyone in a rural area 30 years ago couldn't get access to diverse music. Now, they have access through the Internet.

Access is everything. Back 20 or 30 years ago, we had to leave the house and go to the record store or go to the concert if we wanted to hear music. There was no access. The challenge was finding (records) and getting (records). If you were one of the few people who caught onto one of these things, you were revered for it. Now access is everywhere. So the acquisition of it doesn't mean the same.

The Internet has also exiled the traditional gatekeepers to music such as radio programmers. There's no format on the Internet. A kid can be listening to Journey followed by the Sex Pistols, and Charlie Parker.

I would say that is true of terrestrial radio. For me, terrestrial radio has been a big waste of time for a lot of years. I don't (really) listen, and when I do listen, I find myself just completely frustrated searching around the dial for something that I want to hear. The world of satellite radio or Internet radio is rife with creativity, and much more reflective of what free-form radio used to be back in the day.

Terrestrial radio is still out there, and has an audience, but a 17-year-old today can make up their own playlists on the Internet.
Absolutely, and that is a beautiful thing.

> Larry LeBlanc is widely recognized as one of the leading music industry journalists in the world. Before joining CelebrityAccess in 2008 as senior editor, he was the Canadian bureau chief of Billboard from 1991-2007 and Canadian editor of Record World from 1970-89. He was also a co-founder of the late Canadian music trade, The Record. He has been quoted on music industry issues in hundreds of publications including Time, Forbes, and the London Times. He is co-author of the book "Music From Far And Wide: Celebrating 40 Years Of The Juno Awards."

INTERVIEW WITH MARK NARDONE
Editor-in-Chief of *Music Connection* magazine
http://musicconnection.com

Since 1999 Mark Nardone has been the senior editor of *Music Connection* magazine, the world's best resource for the indie musician. Previously, he was a segment producer for MTV, Disney, and *TV Guide Online*. *Music Connection* magazine is a monthly music trade publication catering to musicians, industry pros, and support services. *Music Connection* exists to serve artists and music people, to offer connections to the unconnected, and to provide exclusive information that can help our readers take their music to the next level. From its unique vantage point, *Music Connection* magazine sets its sights on every aspect of the business, from decision-making in corporate towers to performing in small clubs. Whether offering expert tips on raw survival or the factors contributing to breakthrough success, *Music Connection* examines and defines the realities of music making. Founded in 1977 on the principle of bridging the gap between "the street and the elite,"

Music Connection has garnered a solid foundation of active readers with a broad appeal that encompasses the songwriter, publisher, producer, studio manager, agent, attorney, publicist, label executive, and, of course, the professional and semi-pro musician.

♪

As editor and chief of Music Connection magazine can you explain (to people who are not familiar) the importance the magazine has in connecting musicians to various opportunities for placing music in film and television productions?

> Since its inception in 1977, Music Connection's mission has been to connect music-makers who are unconnected, give them the tools they need—professional advice as well as contact info for influential people in the industry. For the past ten years we have been at the forefront of providing pro advice and specific information related to licensing opportunities. Our magazine's film/TV section and our website's homepage regularly feature opportunities for artists to get their music into shows.

Working in editorial, what types of challenges do you see musicians come up against in our endless changing world of technology?

> All of this technology is fantastic, but there is the danger—and I see it pretty frequently—of artists getting so involved in the hi-tech marketing aspects of their career that they lose their edge as artists. I advise artists to place a firm limit on how much marketing/promoting they do—first make great music. The rest will follow.

One of the most important things I think budding musicians want to know is how to get placement. What can songwriters do to get their music into productions?

> The bottom line in much of the business is that producers still like to do business with people that they know. Which means that artists need to make friends and associates in the music business, particularly in the area of licensing and placements. If, say, the call goes out for a specific type of tune for a movie, chances are that a composer the production folks know, and can depend on will quickly fill the opening. They don't want to take a chance that some artist

whose tune is great does not have full ownership of his song's rights, or some other glitch [poor mastering] that might prevent the song from being used.

Since Music Connection has always been a leading industry source, have you seen a shift in concentration by publishers/record companies towards music licensing as opposed to retail sales?

Yes. Because of the upheaval in how consumers get, use, or buy music, record labels are going crazy trying to not only hang onto their copyrights, but also figure out how to maximize every new revenue stream that pops up. Licensing has been one of the juicier streams. There are new labels we've profiled, in fact, whose sole reason for existence is to do film/TV licensing; they don't even bother to release a physical product. Due to the recent shift toward the free streaming from sources like Spotify, publishers/record companies see film/TV licensing as a prime source of revenue.

Finally, what advice can you give people who want to become involved in composing for music productions? How can they get the edge over all of the other composers out there?

We interview lots of people who have broken through to careers in composing for film and TV and they all have a unique way they got there. There is no set career or breakthrough path. The one thing they have in common is that all of them were determined, and they found a way to get their music to someone who could do them some good. Often, they impressed a person who was connected to the director or producer, like a film editor. In many cases, it comes down to hanging out—actually socializing with people who are in the film and TV industry. Even in the age of Facebook and LinkedIn, personal face-to-face introductions are still the gold standard when it comes to getting opportunities. That said, it is just as important to have what it takes to deliver the goods once you get the chance. That includes being a team player that can take criticism and can meet the demands of those who are paying you for your time and talent.

♪

CONCLUSION

Now we know what music supervisors do and how they interact with publishers and editors. We've seen how so many things can determine the use of a song for a scene and how it can affect the characters. Appendix A contains a list of music supervisors and post houses, so it's time for you to go to work and sell your music! Are you ready?

Chapter 6

Liberation of Digital Distribution

All I can say is thank God there is no more physical distribution with hefty reserves, breakage charges, and of course those nasty returns. It is a good-bye to brick-and-mortar record sales and a hello to a new age of selling music. Of course, this does come with a price to the artist and the record company, but it is still early in the developmental stage and it is a better system for all parties involved. Don't get me wrong—I miss Tower Records, both as an artist and as a consumer, but I believe this is a more efficient way to sell music. The record industry has been selling physical music the same way through distribution chains since Edison's invention of the phonograph in 1877.

BRICK-AND-MORTAR DISTRIBUTION

The whole process of physical distribution—whether it was for vinyls, 8-tracks, cassettes, or CDs—was very convoluted. A record company would basically pay for a distributor to get the release into a mom-and-pop store or a national chain like Tower or Barnes & Noble. These deals were long contracts that would specify term, warehousing inventory, bill and collect monies from retail stores, etc. (See Appendix F for a standard distribution agreement.)

Some deals were called P&D deals, which stood for pressing and distribution, whereby the distributor would front the money for the cost of manufacturing, as well as the cost of distributing the releases to retail. Everything was considered to be cross-collateral, meaning that every expense the distributor incurred for promoting, distributing, or manufacturing would be set against any profits the entire catalog would make, until all expenses were recouped. The costs for all of this varied, but the percentage could be in the mid-20s of gross receipts, taken off of the top by the distributor.

For example, a typical clause in a distribution deal would read

> Twenty (20%) percent of the amount invoiced by us during each Billing Period will be retained by us as a reserve against anticipated returns and credits. The reserve established with respect to each Billing Period, to the extent not reduced for actual returns and credits, will be liquidated and paid over to you within fifteen (15) months. If at any time during the Term, returns exceed initially established reserves for sales, then we, in our reasonable business judgment, may establish a longer liquidation period. If your returns exceed thirty-three (33%) percent of the previous six (6) months' gross sales or if you are "upside down" with us and a current (excluding returns reserves to be liquidated in the future) balance is due us, we are entitled to retain your inventory as collateral, refuse you access to the inventory, and liquidate your inventory.

Plus, all costs for co-op advertising, like listening-booth programs, end-cap displays, out-of-bin placement, you name it, the label pays for it either upfront or the distributor advances the money and it's another expense to be added on for recoupment. Ironically, as bad as this deal looks, it was the standard in selling records commercially. Basically, you pay retail to have your CD at their stores and they have a certain amount of time to return them if no sales occur. This is known as consignment sales and every label, large and small, had to do business this way. That's why the smaller label deals do cross-collateralization between artists' royalties and mechanical royalties, to try to recoup all of the expenses associated with releasing a record.

I try to explain to artists that even if they give me the record for free with no advances, it's going to cost a lot just to release it, especially for an unknown artist. This is not even taking into consideration all the costs of marketing and promoting to get the word out. This is a huge risk with the possibility of no CD sales. Believe me, this is a record label's and an artist's worst nightmare, and I've seen both. This is exactly why labels had large reserves in their contracts, to prevent any overpayment to the artists in royalties, if there were huge returns on their releases.

When you really think about this business, it sucks for everyone, except maybe the store. I never could understand how in the world a successful business like Towers Records went bankrupt and out of business. Think about this: everyone you hire on floor is paid minimum wage and all the merchandise in the store is paid for by the labels (flats, posters, listening stations, end caps, displays). Where did the money go? The actual retail space was probably the most expensive thing, so how the hell did they sink into a hole to the tune 100 million dollars? This company had nearly 100 stores in the US and 144 locations overseas that used the Tower brand. In 2006, when they were forced to liquidate, this really was the end of an era. There was no other chain in this country that could fill the gap and soon Virgin Mega stores pulled out of the American market and Borders dissolved.

DIGITAL AGE

Hence we have the birth of digital downloads. I must admit I started out fighting it as a consumer, because I just thought the sound quality of an MP3 at the time was awful. Since then, they have improved, but I am still a vinyl collector and nothing sounds better than a record spinning on a turntable. Holding a record like David Bowie's *Diamond Dog* with the bi-fold opening up and seeing such awesome images while reading the credits as "1984" plays—man, what great memories. Onward and upward, download the damn thing now and you'll get the booklet as a bonus if you purchase the whole album. Not the same, but close enough.

Well, I've grown fond of downloading music, and in fact I have a library consisting of thousands of downloads. As a consumer it's great, because I'd never be able to find eclectic favorites in modern retail like, Billy Cobham's *Spectrum*, The Crusaders' *Those Southern Knights*, or Al di Meola's *Electric Rendezvous*.

It was in 2009 that I realized that the physical retail market was on its last legs and if you wanted to sell music it was digital downloads. Of course, there are still a few indie retail stores out here, but for the most part they specialize in hip-hop or alternative and are not full service record stores. So I turned my attention to IODA, a digital distributor, which later merged with The Orchard in 2013.

Before that discovery, my label was with a physical distributor who cross-collateralized my whole catalog with digital and physical sales. From there I saw the shift to digital sales and I never looked back. Understand, that even though the tracks are cheap, they are one-way sales. This means no returns and the distribution fee is lower than physical sales, so you start earning money right away. To think of all the blunders that the record industry has made through the years is nothing compared to the blunder they made on downloads.

In the late '90s, major record companies were suing Napster and young teenagers for copyright infringement. Yes, they were infringing on copyrights, but it could have been handled differently. Listen, Napster, at the time, was one of the first music download sites that offered this one-of-a-kind service with over a million subscribers. You don't shut them down; you acquire them! You don't sue a thirteen-year old girl for downloading a U2 song. That's not great PR. Labels could have done something with this new technology. Remember, this was years before iTunes and the iPod.

Here's an idea: buy the site, acquire all of the subscribers and charge them per download, at that time they could have charged two dollars a song and it would have taken off. I guess it was too easy. A few years later, as Apple computer sales started to slump, Steve Jobs came up with a little device that played music files: the iPod. On top of that, Apple opens, acquires, and further develops a piece of software dedicated to downloading music to play on the iPod: iTunes. OMG, someone was paying attention to the marketplace and how the majors screwed up! The new standard of music retail was born, thank you very much.

THE ORCHARD

Today The Orchard/IODA sports a very cool Dashboard site that lists a breakdown of all the digital revenues coming in. As an artist, you can see statistically where downloads are being purchased—such as iTunes, Spotify, Deezer, Amazon, and Nokia—as opposed to streams. It has the ability to compare track popularity and my personal favorite, which countries are downloading your tracks. Big in Japan, anyone? They even have this program called iTunes Heatmap, whereby you choose a release that shows a graphic of the globe with highlighted colors representing the popular areas for your music downloads.

Hell, try to get detailed information from your distributor back in the day, when they couldn't even give you an accurate number of how many CDs they exported, let alone the countries to which they exported. Many more traditional distributors are getting into digital distribution these days, just based on the pure fact that physical retail sales have dropped and continue to do so. The name of the game is building up your catalog and start watching your digital royalties add up. Putting a couple of songs or titles up there won't produce much in the way of income, if it's not a blockbuster hit. But building a catalog is key to offering rewards in the near future. See Appendix G for a foreign distribution agreement.

IODA Royalty Statement

Funds Received During January 2013

Balance Forward: $0.00
Services Net Receipts: $475.39
Check to be issued 15 Mar 2013: $475.39
Outstanding Balance: $0.00

Service	Original Currency	Net Receipts
7digital		
(Europe) **1 Oct 2012 - 31 Oct 2012**	EUR 0.48	**$0.61**
Amazon MP3		
(France) **1 Dec 2012 - 31 Dec 2012**	EUR 0.52	**$0.66**
(Germany) **1 Dec 2012 - 31 Dec 2012**	EUR 1.04	**$1.33**
(Germany) **1 Nov 2012 - 30 Nov 2012**	EUR 5.19	**$6.61**
(Japan) **1 Nov 2012 - 30 Nov 2012**	JPY 794.75	**$8.33**
(United Kingdom) **1 Dec 2012 - 31 Dec 2012**	GBP 0.83	**$1.25**
(United Kingdom) **1 Nov 2012 - 30 Nov 2012**	GBP 5.83	**$8.78**
(United States) **1 Dec 2012 - 31 Dec 2012**		**$17.43**
Aspiro		
(Norway) **1 Nov 2012 - 30 Nov 2012**	NOK 19.13	**$3.29**
Deezer		
(Europe) **1 May 2012 - 31 May 2012**	EUR 2.13	**$2.71**
(Europe) **1 Sep 2012 - 30 Sep 2012**	EUR 3.91	**$4.98**

Service	Original Currency	Net Receipts
(Europe) **1 Aug 2012 - 31 Aug 2012**	EUR 2.97	**$3.79**
(Europe) **1 Jul 2012 - 31 Jul 2012**	EUR 2.11	**$2.69**
(Europe) **1 Oct 2012 - 31 Oct 2012**	EUR 3.91	**$4.98**
(Europe) **1 Jun 2012 - 30 Jun 2012**	EUR 2.25	**$2.87**
(Europe) **1 Mar 2012 - 31 Mar 2012**	EUR 2.72	**$3.47**
(Europe) **1 Apr 2012 - 30 Apr 2012**	EUR 2.07	**$2.64**
eMusic		
(Europe) **1 Oct 2012 - 31 Dec 2012**		**$6.00**
(United States) **1 Oct 2012 - 31 Dec 2012**		**$30.64**
Google Music		
(Germany) **1 Dec 2012 - 31 Dec 2012**	EUR 8.92	**$11.37**
(United States) **1 Nov 2012 - 30 Nov 2012**		**$1.19**
(United States) **1 Dec 2012 - 31 Dec 2012**		**$0.60**
iTunes Music Store		
1 Dec 2012 - 31 Dec 2012		**$0.01**
(Australia) **1 Dec 2012 - 31 Dec 2012**	AUD 14.39	**$14.30**
(Australia) **1 Dec 2012 - 31 Dec 2012**	AUD 0.04	**$0.04**
(Canada) **1 Nov 2012 - 30 Nov 2012**	CAD 7.74	**$7.39**
(Canada) **1 Dec 2012 - 31 Dec 2012**	CAD 0.04	**$0.04**
(Canada) **1 Dec 2012 - 31 Dec 2012**	CAD 2.98	**$2.85**
(Europe) **1 Dec 2012 - 31 Dec 2012**	EUR 0.08	**$0.10**
(Europe) **1 Dec 2012 - 31 Dec 2012**	EUR 41.11	**$52.39**
(Hong Kong) **1 Dec 2012 - 31 Dec 2012**	HKD 0.03	**$0.00**
(Japan) **1 Dec 2012 - 31 Dec 2012**	JPY 302.60	**$3.17**
(Mexico) **1 Dec 2012 - 31 Dec 2012**	MXN 0.27	**$0.02**
(Mexico) **1 Dec 2012 - 31 Dec 2012**	MXN 7.14	**$0.54**
(Switzerland) **1 Dec 2012 - 31 Dec 2012**	CHF 0.03	**$0.03**
(Taiwan) **1 Dec 2012 - 31 Dec 2012**	TWD 10.20	**$0.33**
(United Kingdom) **1 Dec 2012 - 31 Dec 2012**	GBP 0.07	**$0.11**
(United States) **1 Dec 2012 - 31 Dec 2012**		**$0.59**
(United States) **1 Dec 2012 - 31 Dec 2012**		**$118.98**
JB Hi-Fi		
(Australia) **1 Nov 2012 - 30 Nov 2012**	AUD 0.63	**$0.63**
Last.fm		
1 Oct 2012 - 31 Oct 2012	EUR 0.06	**$0.08**
1 Oct 2012 - 31 Oct 2012	EUR 0.27	**$0.34**

Service	Original Currency	Net Receipts
MediaNet Digital		
(United States) **1 Nov 2012 - 30 Nov 2012**		**$0.05**
(United States) **1 Dec 2012 - 31 Dec 2012**		**$0.00**
(United States) **1 Oct 2012 - 31 Oct 2012**		**$0.06**
Muve Music / Cricket		
(United States) **1 Dec 2012 - 31 Dec 2012**		**$3.30**
Rdio		
(Australia) **1 Dec 2012 - 31 Dec 2012**	AUD 0.06	**$0.06**
(Brazil) **1 Nov 2012 - 30 Nov 2012**	BRL 0.06	**$0.03**
(Brazil) **1 Dec 2012 - 31 Dec 2012**	BRL 0.10	**$0.05**
(Canada) **1 Dec 2012 - 31 Dec 2012**	CAD 0.03	**$0.03**
(Canada) **1 Nov 2012 - 30 Nov 2012**	CAD 0.17	**$0.16**
(Denmark) **1 Nov 2012 - 30 Nov 2012**	DKK 0.29	**$0.05**
(Germany) **1 Nov 2012 - 30 Nov 2012**	EUR 0.03	**$0.04**
(New Zealand) **1 Nov 2012 - 30 Nov 2012**	NZD 0.01	**$0.01**
(United Kingdom) **1 Nov 2012 - 30 Nov 2012**	GBP 0.03	**$0.05**
(United States) **1 Dec 2012 - 31 Dec 2012**		**$0.57**
(United States) **1 Nov 2012 - 30 Nov 2012**		**$0.52**
Rhapsody		

Exchange rates for this statement period

- AUD to USD, 0.99398500
- BRL to USD, 0.47053500
- CAD to USD, 0.95486970
- CHF to USD, 1.03122500
- DKK to USD, 0.17081000
- EUR to USD, 1.27442500
- GBP to USD, 1.50660500
- HKD to USD, 0.12255000
- JPY to USD, 0.01048135
- MXN to USD, 0.07495500
- NOK to USD, 0.17176000
- NZD to USD, 0.79695500
- TWD to USD, 0.03239500

INDUSTRY PROFILE: RICHARD GOTTEHRER, THE ORCHARD

By Larry LeBlanc (Courtesy of Celebrity Access)

http://celebrityaccess.com

Richard Gottehrer is the co-founder & chief creative officer of the digital distributor, The Orchard. Gottehrer is also a prominent Bronx songwriter, record producer and the co-founder of Sire Records. Gottehrer never planned on a music career. In 1962, after becoming the first in his family to receive a college degree (in history, from Adelphi University in Long Island), Gottehrer enrolled at the Brooklyn Law School.

However, a career in law didn't follow.

In 1961, while at Adelphi, Gottehrer had co-founded his first record production company, and had recorded as Troy & the T-Birds.

In 1963, an impromptu writing session with Bob Feldman and Jerry Goldstein led to the trio co-writing and co-producing the Angels' #1 Billboard hit "My Boyfriend's Back." It was followed two years later by their production of the McCoys' "Hang On Sloopy" which also reached #1 on Billboard.

As the Strangeloves, Gottehrer, Bob Feldman and Jerry Goldstein had their own string of hits, including the 1965 single "I Want Candy." The song has since charted with Bow Wow Wow in 1982, and Aaron Carter in 2000.

In 1966, Gottehrer and Seymour Stein co-founded Sire Records. Gottehrer left Sire in 1976, and produced Blondie, the Go-Go's, Joan Armatrading, the Fleshtones, Mental As Anything, Dr. Feelgood and many others. In 1997, Gottehrer and Scott Cohen co-founded The Orchard. In 2003, Dimensional Associates acquired The Orchard, and it merged with the Digital Music Group in 2007. Headquartered in New York and London, and with offices in 29 countries around the world, The Orchard licenses and globally distributes more than 1.3 million songs and 4,000 video titles through hundreds of digital stores and mobile carriers.

The Orchard has continued to outpace the digital industry substantially through key acquisitions (including TVT last year,) leading distribution alliances (including those with Vice, and Nokia) and its strategy as a value-added media services company. Under its buyout of TVT, The Orchard assumed control of the company's catalogue of recorded masters, artist contracts and physical record distribution infrastructure. The addition of physical distribution from TVT may be seen as making The Orchard a more competitive company, one that can better address the needs of select record label partners in the US marketplace.

In February, The Orchard negotiated a secured, revolving credit line with Palo Alto's Peninsula Bank Funding, which could provide both the opportunity to continue its acquisition of assets and as a hedge against tough economic times.

On March 26th, The Orchard reported financial results for the fourth quarter and year ending Dec. 31, 2008. Revenues were $16.2 million compared to $9.9 million for the same quarter in 2007, an increase of 64%. Net loss for the quarter was $0.3 million compared to a loss of $2.4 million in the same quarter of 2007.

For 2008 overall, revenues doubled to $57.4 million from $28.5 million in 2007. Net loss for 2008 was $2.3 million, compared with a loss of $7.6 million in 2007. In addition to managing the digital retail relationship on the labels' behalf, The Orchard has incorporated features like online sales reporting, synch licensing databases and other analytical tools to help their clients take advantage of opportunities traditionally left to bigger companies.

In addition, The Orchard drives sales of music through its marketing and promotional campaigns; brand entertainment programs; and film, advertising, gaming and television licensing. The Orchard also tries to place their clients on the widest possible selection of services. For example, last year, Merlin, A2IM, Koch and others in the independent music community lambasted the indie digital deal offered by MySpace Music, arguing that it didn't give them the same equity stake as the major labels. So they balked at the MySpace Music terms. However, The Orchard jumped in, and signed up.

You don't believe in the death of the music industry?

I don't believe in the death of the industry at all. The future is a lot brighter (than what others think). What has happened is that we have seen an absolute change in the industry.

The Orchard had a very strong fourth quarter in 2008.

I am very happy about the growth of The Orchard when you think it is something that Scott Cohen (VP Europe) and I started in a basement on Orchard Street (in New York) in1997. To see it growing like this and see it in the hands of great leadership now [is great]. The day-to-day is run by our Greg Scholl (president & CEO) with some great people. Greg is not only a great business person but he's a music lover.

The Orchard has no debt load. Is this a reflection of the tough economic times we are now in?

We have been fortunate in growing the way we have and to be able to have the continuity and cash flow to function and operate. We'll continue to grow.

You launched The Orchard during a time that American investors were throwing money at dotcoms. Most of them disappeared.

We never got the money. That was both good and bad. It was bad because we didn't enrich ourselves but if we had (outside investor financing) the company would have been gone. It wouldn't have been able to survive the dotcom crash. The demand by investors to repay the money would have probably been overwhelming. A lot of great ideas went awry in that period because of that.

The Orchard grew organically for a few years.

It grew organically until 2003 when it was taken on by *Dimensional Associates* (a private equity firm and a subsidiary of JDS Capital Management) and Greg was put in as CEO. From there, it continued to grow partially organically but also through sound management. Scott and I are great entrepreneurs. Having people who understand the business of true business and who can take a company that is a great idea and build and grow it as the (music) industry continues to contract, is absolutely the most positive thing.

The Orchard's merger with the Digital Music Group in 2007 gave the company further market clout.

It changed the impression of The Orchard because they were a public company and, as we merged into them and were the surviving party, the name changed to The Orchard. We are now publicly listed.

The merger with DMGI gave us over 4,000 hours of video and a starting point to expand further into video. It made us a full service company. Not only can we create great opportunities but we are capable of doing business at the level of any company, including the major labels.

Video isn't formed as a sales medium in the digital marketplace yet.

We are still in the early stages. People aren't buying a lot of videos digital or what we have, a lot of independent stuff. What the merger did was that it showed The Orchard to be serious on becoming an even bigger leader in an emerging industry. Then you add on TVT with another catalog and with a physical (distribution) component that allows us to get involved with a company like *Vice*.

The company seems to be searching for assets it can own.

Obviously, we look at other ways of growing. As we expand our marketing capabilities, and our ability to feed this expensive global system, we'll look for others way to grow. That includes finding catalogs that bring more value to the company.

The TVT acquisition brought us some great catalog music. We also moved down to the space that they occupied in Soho from uptown (New York). Now we are in an environment that is more conducive to the music that we release.

The TVT acquisition gives you the ability to now offer physical distribution. Was there a demand by labels to have both a digital and a physical distribution presence?

Labels we might be interested in might not look at us in the same way if we can't offer them physical as well. When we took on TVT, there was a physical team in place which we have expanded by bringing in some top people.

Some indie labels do more business with digital.

The physical business is not a growing business. It's a value add-on (component of our business). We are a digital company, and our future is in developing more and more outlets for digital distribution

We have our global reach and an ability to function in all of the different aspects of the music spectrum—marketing, sync/advertising placement and brand awareness. The word "360" is silly but music today is a total picture. In order to succeed today, the musician should succeed on multiple levels. Not necessarily an, "Is anyone going to buy their record?" type of thing.

Of all the businesses in the music industry affected by the evolution of digital distribution, no area has benefited more than the indie label community. The majors were slow in adapting to digital distribution but they've recently jumped in with both feet.

At this point, the writing is on the wall and things have changed for the industry. I think they missed the boat. They didn't move quickly enough. But in fairness, there is an obligation attached to being the owner or creator of a copyright of music. You just can't give it away, even if people want it or free.

What should the majors have done in the early days of music on the Internet?

I don't know what the answer is. They probably should have embraced the change. They should have worked as an industry instead of suing people for not doing what they wanted them to do. They should have tried to find ways of monetizing the music. Maybe they should have tried to license music to the ISPs or mobile (phone) operators.

I can't say anything negative about anyone running a big company. But, in the end, that spirit of originality and entrepreneurship and the ability to go beyond quarterly operations escaped them. There was nobody who stood up and said, "I am the head of this company. We are going to license Napster. This is what the future is." Nobody did that because it wasn't in their purview. There was nobody strong enough to stand up at a corporate meeting and say, "If we don't do this, our business will begin to deteriorate."

Do we need to own music today?

It depends on how peoples' concepts develop. We needed to own (albums and CDs) because they were rare things packaged and created for us. We associate the ownership of a record or a CD with personal use.

Today, there are people who just want to go to iTunes, buy music and own it. There are others who don't care about owning music as long as they know it is available on subscription or whatever. They might as well stream (their music). As society changes from having the desperate need to own things, and music becomes less rare, streaming will become a bigger part of the future.

The Orchard made a controversial deal with MySpace Music last year. Was the motivation to just get into that market?

Absolutely. If you are not in the game, you have no chance of winning. If Universal, Sony and EMI own a piece of (MySpace Music), so what? They have music that more people want. If they can enforce that kind of leverage, that's fine.

As The Orchard, we have an obligation to the people that have licensed us their music to not only monetize the music but to introduce them to new ways to (distribute music) while the music is paid for. We are not talking about giving it away for free. Other independent people that don't participate aren't going to be paid.

It is the same with telephone use coming with music. What's wrong with that? Buy a phone, you get the music. Part of the revenue stream then goes back to the rights owners.

> The Orchard is now offering its member labels and artists access to an iPhone application development program called Mobile Roadie, provided by partner Fluidesign. The company has added the Mobile Roadie program to its Artist/Label Workstation program, an online management tool that aggregates sales, assets and other information for Orchard users.

The entry point into the music industry today for an artist is similar to when you entered it in the '50s.

Right. You know what? It was never about anything but luck back then. You went out on the road, and you played. If you did well maybe you got a chance to make a record. If it was great, what were the chances of it being heard? If it was heard, what were the chances of someone buying it? How could you predict that? Back then, you could make a lot of music but you had to be lucky at the same time. It is the same today.

You entered an industry that, like today, only had a few major labels, Decca, EMI and Columbia. It was a world of independent labels back then.

That's true. There might have been major labels but they weren't corporate controlled. It was still the business of music. However, the majors were not necessarily interested in what we called the new music—which was R&B or black music. But there was a group of young people then discovering and experiencing music from a different perspective—be it socially or racially different, then turning that into something of their own (rock and roll).

Columbia Records didn't get into rock and roll until Mitch Miller [the powerful head of the company's popular division] left in 1961. He passed on both Elvis Presley and Buddy Holly.

Mitch Miller thought rock and roll was useless. At Columbia, he was still alive and vital into the '60s. But there was also (producer) John Hammond who supported Bob Dylan and a lot of other great things. He was able to recognize a true talent that deserved to be recorded.

For years, ASCAP wouldn't sign R&B or country songwriters because they weren't considered legitimate songwriters.

I am still a member of BMI. When I entered the business, it was during the early days or rock and roll. That's where all the new songwriters went. You were frowned upon at ASCAP.

You played in several bands in high school. Were they rock and roll bands?

We played YMCA and YMHA dances. We would play all of the pop standards from the "fake" book, four-chord ballads like (the Penguin's) "Earth Angel" or songs by (crooner) Rusty Draper. We'd also insert a boogie woogie or a rock and roll song into sets. We found a guitar player who had country roots and could play rockabilly.

You studied history at Adelphi University, and later law but you were too interested in songwriting to graduate.

Early on, I would write for my own sake. I was a piano player and I learned to write songs by experimenting. It seemed easy to me.

At Adelphi, I met a couple of guys and one of them introduced me to Allan Chesler. His father was Lou Chesler, the head of (the film company Seven Arts Productions which had a record label (Seven Arts). Allan wanted to do something in the (music) business as well. So we formed a production company. He introduced me to Morty Kraft who was running the label. [A producer and also owner of Melba Records] Morty is a legendary music industry figure. He was always telling me, "Kid you should go back to law school. What are you doing here?" Of course, I didn't. I made a couple of records. One of them Morty gave me recently. It's called "Twistle" and came out under the name Troy & the T-Birds on Seven Arts.

> Lou Chesler has been described as a front or associate of underworld crime bosses Vito Genovese and Meyer Lansky through the Florida real estate company General Development Corp. which he owned with another Lasky associate, Wallace Groves. In 1967 his company, now called Seven Arts, acquired Jack Warner's controlling

interest in Warner Bros. Pictures and other interests, including Warner Bros. Records and Reprise Records for $84 million. The company was renamed Warner Bros-Seven Arts.

You started hanging around The Brill Building?

I was walking around with my songs. I met a couple of publishers and I had a few songs recorded. On one occasion I was waiting outside a publisher's office with two other guys. We got stood up by the publisher so we left. One of them had a room somewhere and we sat down and started writing songs. That was with Bob Feldman and Jerry Goldstein.

That led to co-writing and co-producing "My Boyfriend's Back" by the Angels that reached #1 on Billboard in 1963.

Yes, that led to "My Boyfriend's Back." But we wrote other songs before that were recorded. We were beginning to get a bit of a reputation. We learned how to (produce) records by making the demos. We were making demos of our songs to show to artists. In those days, (pop) artists didn't write their own material. They look to publishers who had the new generation of young songwriters under contract to write songs that fit their style.

(For the Angel sessions), we used studio musicians and worked out the arrangement with the arranger, Leroy Glover. He wrote the arrangements out so we were able to record four songs in three hours.

In 1965, you, Bob Feldman and Jerry Goldstein produced a #1 hit with "Hang On Sloopy" by the McCoys. As well, "I Want Candy" which you three recorded under the name the Strangeloves, reached #11 on Billboard. Both were on Bang Records.

We became friends with (Bang Record owner, producer/songwriter) Bert Berns and we sat around and wrote "I Want Candy" with him. Then we recorded the song as the Strangeloves and put it out on Bang Records, the record label Bert started with Ahmet and Nesuhi Ertegun and Jerry Wexler from Atlantic Records.

Didn't the Strangeloves also record as the Beach-Nuts?

We were the Beach-Nuts and we continued working with the Angels. The Strangeloves had three hit singles very quickly. "I Want Candy," "Cara-Lin" and "Night Time," a great song I sang that has been recorded by the J. Geils Band and George Thorogood. Our songs have been recorded by many others over the years.

Do you have a favorite version of "I Want Candy?"

Bow Wow Wow's version became the definitive version.

> "I Want Candy" was also covered by Melanie C for the 2007 film of the same name and Good Charlotte covered the song in the film "Not Another Teen Movie."

Though you three were basically a production team, you also toured as the Strangeloves?

We weren't very good performers but we went out anyway. We could sing a few songs. We could do "I Want Candy," "Time is On My Side," and "Hang On Sloopy" (recorded by the Vibrations in 1964 as "My Girl Sloopy" on Atlantic Records). And a Chuck Berry song. That was our show.

You didn't really have to tour then. You could go on television. We did NBC's "Hulabaloo" that was hosted by Sammy Davis Jr. with guests the Supremes, the Lovin' Spoonful, and Sonny & Cher. And there we were . . . the Strangeloves. And because we were passing ourselves off as Australians, they put us in a thatched roof hut wearing skin vests to do our hit. It was a bit of spectacle.

How did the production team come to produce the McCoys' "Hang On Sloopy" on Bang Records?

When we would go out and perform, there would be a backup band. In a show near Columbus, Ohio, Rick and the Raiders were the backup band. They got as big a reaction from the fans as we did as national stars. Being producers, we took them right off the stage, met their parents the next day and suggested we could make records with them. The band, including their parents, followed us back to New York in a caravan of cars. We already had the track for "Hang On Sloopy." It is the same version as on the Strangelove's album ("I Want Candy" in 1965).

"Hang On Sloopy" is pure American pop recorded in a very organized, calculated way by people who were at the top of their game of making American pop records. It's pretty perfect for a pop record.

Sire Records started as Sire Productions in 1966, co-founded by you and Seymour Stein.

I met Seymour when he was hired by Bang to promote the Strangelove's version of "Hang On Sloopy." Seymour was a great promotion man. He learned his trade through working at Billboard in the chart department and from working with (King Records owner) Syd Nathan. Seymour and I became friends and the production company seemed like a good idea at the time.

Did you have a concept for the company?

Not at first. It was only a production company at first. We had no money but we got an advance from Epic Records, and we produced some good R&B records for them but nothing sold. Seymour had a relationship with a one-stop distributor (known as a rack jobber) in Fall River, Massachusetts named Danny Gittelman. He put up some financing and we got a distribution deal with London Records, the American arm of British Decca. We produced a couple of folk type records with David Santo and Allan Thomas.

Then you and Seymour started going to Europe and picking up acts?

We got the Climax Blues Band, Barclay James Harvest, Renaissance, the Social Deviants, and Focus by going to Europe. We would work with the export departments of record companies who had American affiliates. They were making great records but if they weren't hits in the UK, labels like Capitol or London, wouldn't want to put them out in the US. So we would license them.

We would go over there with cheesecakes from Turf Cheesecake Company (in Harrison, New York). We'd bring about 20 cheesecakes over and give them to people, and they would give us records.

By this time Danny wanted out of the partnership. I think we found some money and bought him out. We continued going to Europe.

Sire was developing with these European bands as radio was shifting in North America from AM Top 40 to free-form rock formats on FM.

We had the music when this shift happened. While we were smart enough to get the music, we didn't necessarily anticipate the shift. But the shift certainly happened, and it benefited us.

Sire itself never became a real stand alone record label. It was always under the auspices of a larger entity. First with London Records, then at Polydor where we didn't do that well, and then at Famous/ABC where we brought Focus. That is where we really became a record label. They provided (promotion and marketing services) for a small fee.

Did you leave Sire in 1976 to get back into producing?

I guess. I was dissatisfied with my role. It was probably time for a change.

Have you and Seymour remained close?

We're friends. We are probably better friends now than in ages. It's like having family. You have a brother and you may not talk to him for whatever reason but he's still your brother.

Any misgivings about leaving Sire given what a powerhouse label it grew into?

No. I did all right. I don't think I was cut out to run a record company. With Sire, it's fine that it went onto the successes of Madonna, Depeche Mode, the Pretenders and so on. That's brilliant. Seymour's ability to recognize that uniqueness in people is what makes him a great A&R person.

You have produced an astonishing number of contemporary acts—everything from Blondie to Beat Rodeo to Aerosmith, and including the Go-Go's, Joan Armatrading, Robert Gordon, and Richard Hell.

What do you look for in deciding to produce an act?

I always look for songs and some degree of personality. But the thing that separates artists, that makes one great as opposed to being good, are the songs. After awhile, you will burn out on the image of someone.

When I first went to see Blondie, for example, I obviously noticed that Debbie (Harry) has a very commercial voice and she had a great image and was beautiful. But what really made the difference for me were their songs. On their first two albums, which were the only two I did with them ["Blondie," and "Plastic Letters"], you can't forget those great songs. And that was before "Heart of Glass" (in 1979).

It was the same with the Go-Go's. It was the songs that made the difference. The fact that they were all girls playing their instruments, fine. But without the songs . . .

You still do some production work today.

I do go into the studio occasionally with the Ravonettes. They are real special and, if I can help, I will try to. Outside of that I don't spend much time recording.

Despite the wide range of your production work, you seem to have a pop music heart.

That's essentially true. I even look at music that way today. I see great bands and I think, "Wow, if they just had that one magic song."

> Larry LeBlanc is widely recognized as one of the leading music industry journalists in the world. Before joining CelebrityAccess in 2008, Larry was the Canadian bureau chief of Billboard from 1991-2007 and Canadian editor of Record World from 1970-89. He was also a co-founder of the late Canadian music trade, The Record. He has been quoted on music industry issues in hundreds of publications including Time, Forbes, the London Times and the New York Times.

CONCLUSION

As we have learned, music distribution has changed dramatically through the past ten years. Brick and mortar has succumbed to the digital revolution, giving the artist more freedom and control. This is actually a good thing because, every year, there are more music subscribers on the Internet. In fact, for the first time in years, since the turn of the 21st Century, 2012 saw an increase of 20 million digital music subscribers.

Chapter 7

Royalties, Copyrights, and What to Expect

First, let's take a realistic view of how much composers/artists can earn from their performance royalties, also referred to as backend royalties. As we discussed earlier, PROs pay writer and publisher affiliates from the licenses obtained from a number of sources like universities, clubs, restaurants, hotels, radio and television stations, as well as networks, web radio, and hundreds of other entities. However, the real moneymaker is royalties generated from the broadcast outlets, such as network and cable stations. Don't get me wrong, all of the others are welcomed, but they don't equal much in revenue. Since we covered the PROs earlier in chapters 1–4, let's take a look at other companies monitoring digital media performances.

SOUND EXCHANGE

Through new technology, companies have evolved, specializing in collecting digital revenue royalties. One of the most prominent companies is Sound Exchange, which is a non-profit performance rights organization. They collect statutory royalties from satellite radio (such as SIRIUS XM), Internet radio, cable TV music channels, and other outlets that stream music recordings. A special set of copyright judges had to be appointed by the US Library of Congress called the Copyright Royalty Board to determine rates and terms for the digital performance of sound recordings. They basically named Sound Exchange the sole company in the US to collect and distribute digital performance royalties on behalf of master right owners, like record companies and recording artists. They also represent all independent artists who control their own masters.

According to the Copyright Royalty Board's website, and I quote:

> On February 14, 2013, the Copyright Royalty Judges issued their Final Determination setting rates and terms for the digital performance of sound recordings and the making of ephemeral recordings by preexisting subscription services (PSS) and preexisting satellite digital audio radio services (SDARs) under the statutory licenses set forth in Sections 112 and 114 of the Copyright Act for January 1, 2013, through December 31, 2017.

In fact, Sound Exchange announced on their news page that in 2012 the total distribution was $462 million, which was an historical moment for them. These royalties continue to grow for everyone; I've seen my Sound Exchange royalties grow greatly through the past years. In order to get the most accurate royalties you need to provide them with what is known as a metadata sheet—painful, time consuming, yet very rewarding. This has become a standard in the digital world. Either you or someone you hire will have to list all of your releases and breakdown all administrative data, like artist, writers, publishers, song description, and album title, etc.

RECORD ROYALTIES

Now in the case of physical sales, artist royalties are determined by record sales based on a percentage of records actually sold and not returned. If it is a compilation of artists on a release, then it is calculated on the same percentage, but royalties are proportionally divided across the amount of artists that appear on the release, commonly known as pro rata.

Early in my career, I worked in the business affairs/finance department at Virgin Records in Beverly Hills, now defunct. What I got out of that job was seeing, firsthand, the nuts and bolts of the music industry, which later helped me in my career; most importantly, how record deals were structured, the details of royalties, and how royalties were calculated.

Number one rule, *every expense* the label incurs pertaining to an artist's release is recoupable! Not just the obvious ones like recording expenses and advances, but marketing phone calls, FedEx shipments, lunches, dinners, airfare, faxes, Xeroxing, and any and all expenses connected with the release.

<u>Compilation Record Sales Formula</u>

1. Distribution Fee = 15%
    Multiply unit price by 15% & minus amount from
    Store price

2. Artist Royalty 15% Pro Rata
    Multiply unit price minus Redeye fee by 15% = royalty amount

3. Divide royalty amount by number of tracks on unit = individual Artist royalty

4. Multiply individual Artist royalty by the number of physical units sold = Final Artist royalty amount

Example:
(Important-when calculating put infinity decimal point on)

Guitar Masters Vol 1
$12.99 x 15% = $1.94
$12.99 - $1.94 = $11.04
$11.04 x 15% = $1.65
$1.65 divided by 18 = .09 cents per artist
.09 cents x 1554 (units sold) = $142.98

You name it; they recoup it. In fact, all of an artist's releases are cross-collateralized. Meaning that if an artist had not recouped their expenses on album number one and two, royalties from his third album with the label would have to recoup the previous titles before he or she saw any royalty checks, even if number three was selling well.

If the artist did not sell enough CDs, then of course the label would drop the artist. You'd be surprised how many artists did not understand recoupment and were completely in the dark with how the industry worked. I always thought it should be mandatory for every artist to work in some part of the record industry before they are signed to a label. This way they would have some kind of inkling as to how they could make it as an artist.

PERSONAL WORKING EXPERIENCE

I remember having to go through Diners Club and FedEx statements, placing artist codes next to every charge; there were codes for Lenny Kravitz, Janet Jackson, David Bowie, and The Rolling Stones. This code would associate the artists with his or her respective charge and be added into their recoupment accounts. I've seen the most trivial expenses from postage stamp charge-backs to $50,000 for travel expenses. So when artists say the record company pays for everything, I have to laugh because they do, but it's coming out of your royalty pocket. The only difference with them and a bank is that they won't come after you and your assets if you don't recoup.

It was unreal on how much Virgin would owe the Diners Club credit card each month. I mean $200,000-plus and they would wait until absolutely the last freaking moment to pay them. I used to help handle this account and I would go line by line, coding the artist's recoupment expenses and my boss would always ask for an extension from Diners Club. Then when the extension was up, the staff would all be frantically trying to get the VPs' signatures on the checks to make FedEx pick up by 6 p.m. Absolute madness! But even with all of those recoupments, some artists still did very well with royalties.

Lenny Kravitz was making around 1.5 million every royalty period from his release "Are You Gonna Go My Way," which was a few years old by then. Funny, I remember meeting some of the artists when they dropped by the label for a meet and greet, (Lenny Kravitz, David Bowie), and thinking, "Man, if you guys only knew what the hell happens behind the scenes."

Later, when I became an artist, all of these experiences would serve me well on what to expect with royalties. Once the A&R guys from Instinct Records told me, *"Everything is recoupable, Brian, even the air you breathe!"* In some cases, there are additional recoupments laid out in contracts that cover product damage, which was a leftover charge from the vinyl days for when actual albums were broken in transit. (I wonder if this covered my Kiss album that my dad threw across the room in 1975?)

Having the background of working in the industry enabled me to keep my publishing separate on all of my *Instinct Jazz* releases. I was probably the only artist on the label that ever got paid mechanicals, most other artists signed those publishing rights away, not knowing the value. But it was a constant chase getting those mechanicals, because a lot of labels don't like computing it, or feel they should keep them regardless, because an album did not recoup its entire expenses. See the Exclusive Recording Agreement in Appendix H.

THE HARRY FOX AGENCY

Another way to collect your Mechanicals is by signing up with The Harry Fox Agency, as mentioned earlier, and having them collect on your behalf. But, to be honest, I found them not to be very effective unless you're not a huge, hit songwriter; plus you'd have to pay a fee, which, for the indie artist, makes no sense. No, it's better to align your-self with a good entertainment lawyer and have them write a stern letter requesting accountability for mechanicals for your benefit.

This leads to my next point, having good people on your side is essential, whether it's an agent, manager, or attorney. I've had a few of each through the years and found the attorney to be the best by far, because an attorney is based on work-for–hire terms, meaning you don't have to pay them a percentage of your royalties. So-called "agents" and "managers" base their income on yours and will take 15–20 percent of your earnings, whether they generated the work or not. This does not exclude previous work, before your relationship with them.

MANAGERS

I had one manager back in the '90s who took 15 percent of my advances, royalties, and live performances, and also charged me for her phone calls, Xeroxing costs, postage, and anything else she thought had to do with me. Keep in mind, at that point in my career, I was a struggling artist and she was a wealthy businesswoman. Unfortunately, she never did a damn thing, except take a call from the record company when they wanted me to do a live performance or an interview for a radio station.

As for her husband, he was a frustrated old jazz guitarist who never had much success, so she would take all of my contacts and endorsements and use them for him. Very unprofessional, which backfired on her constantly. The worst thing she ever did was to convince my record label, Instinct, that her husband should produce a few of my tracks. I should add that plans were already made for me to go to London to do the record, but her last ditch effort was a fork in the road. So I played nice and went to her old man's sorry excuse of a studio, which was just a 1920s bungalow in the Los Feliz Hills, just east of Hollywood.

To get to this bungalow I had to climb up the side of a hill, paved with old cement stairs, like something out a 1930s movie. Anyway, I get inside this one bedroom bungalow and all I see is an old Roland keyboard and sampler with some outdated recording gear. I redo my one song for the label, while this guy is on the phone inquiring about buying some Fender amp. It was a complete waste of time and I knew it, but I was too polite to say anything.

So my manager sends the song to the label and it's a big disaster. I get a call from Instinct the next day and they say they hate it. Everything they liked about the song was gone; it was nothing like the original piece. Instinct goes on to say, that if they had gotten demos like this from me in the beginning, they would not have signed me! Thank god they figured out who the culprit was and said not to worry. They had a professional producer waiting for me in London. All was cool, but I knew in my heart it wasn't right, so soon after that incident, I eighty-sixed her and her crusty old husband out as excess baggage. I wish I could say differently, but there are a lot of people out there that fit this description. So be careful with whom you associate and whom you choose as a partner.

OTHER ROYALTY STREAMS

Another great royalty source that I've seen grow in the twenty-first century is the Live Television/Videotape Supplemental Markets Fund (LTVSMF). They collect and distribute residuals for musicians who have worked on live television/video productions. The provision is that you had to have worked on at least one original AFM (American Federation of Musicians) scoring session for a specific live television production. A live television/video production must generate some income or revenue as a result of exhibition in a supplemental market to trigger an obligation on the part of the producer/production company to contribute to the fund.

For example, I get a check each year from LTVSMF for SOAPnet, which is paid for by ABC-TV since they own the cable station. It is for the past union sessions I've produced for *All My Children*, hence, the reruns that are being played on SOAPnet. The important factor is that there must be an AFM session contract filed with the appropriate local musicians union for the original session(s) of the sound recording in order to get paid. If you ever did AFM session work for live television, then this is something you need to look into because they keep a page on their website that lists names of people who have unclaimed checks with the fund.

A few years back, the payment schedule was erratic, but during the past two years the checks have been sent regularly, with an annual amount paid during the month of May. This is attributed to the growing market of SOAPnet and the amount of times they are rerunning the daytime shows.

Now because much of the soaps have been retired from the networks, they have found a new home on the SOAPnet channel as reruns. This a great for the daytime composers like myself, since we all took a big hit when the shows were cancelled.

NEIGHBORING RIGHTS

If you are a music performer/artist or a label that owns the master to commercial releases, then there is another royalty stream that cannot be overlooked called Neighboring Rights. The song is split into two halves, 50 percent equal to the masters, and 50 percent equal to the performer. All of the details and payment parameters were outlined in the 1961 Roman Convention Treaty. They collect from places like radio, TV, theatres, clubs, restaurants, various streaming sources such as web radio, satellite radio, and other digital transmissions. Plus, collections are also made from private copying levies on blank recording media. However not all countries have neighboring rights representation and not all participate in generating royalties.

The following countries participate in the treaty:

Argentina, Australia, Austria, Barbados, Belgium, Bolivia, Brazil, Bulgaria, Burkina Faso, Canada, Chile, Colombia, Congo, Costa Rica, Czech Republic, Denmark, Dominican Republic, Ecuador, El Salvador, Fiji, Finland, France, Germany, Great Britain and N. Ireland, Greece, Greenland, Guatemala, Honduras, Hungary, Iceland, Italy, Jamaica, Japan, Lesotho, Luxembourg, Mexico, Moldova, Monaco, Netherlands, Niger, Nigeria, Norway, Panama, Paraguay, Peru, Philippines, Republic of Ireland, Russia, Slovakia, Spain, Sweden, Switzerland, United Kingdom, and Uruguay.

Since the USA is not included it is a bit tricky.

For an American artist to be eligible for royalties, the music has to be recorded in one of the above countries. Hence, some of my releases on Instinct records are eligible because I recorded them in London, England, which is part of the neighboring rights pact. Complicated, yes, but unfortunately this is the reality. There are ways to get around this—for example, if your release was mastered in a neighboring rights country. I looked into various companies out there to collect these royalties for me, but unfortunately, for obvious reasons, America doesn't have many.

After doing much research I joined the Dutch society, Sena (www.sena.nl), which now collects for me worldwide. Sena grants licenses on behalf of the right holders to companies or organizations that use music, and they collect the associated fees. Sena also monitors and registers where, how, and with what purpose music is played, to get the appropriate license. Does this sound familiar? Well it should, because they are a lot like the PROs, except Sena handles the rights of the master holders and the performers. Very good concept. I wish America had a domestic society like this in place. The closest we have is Sound Exchange.

SUMMARY OF THE ROME CONVENTION FOR THE PROTECTION OF PERFORMERS, PRODUCERS OF PHONOGRAMS, AND BROADCASTING ORGANIZATIONS (1961)

http://www.wipo.int/treaties/en/ip/rome/trtdocs_wo024.html

The Convention secures protection in performances of performers, phonograms of producers of phonograms and broadcasts of broadcasting organizations.

(1) Performers (actors, singers, musicians, dancers and other persons who perform literary or artistic works) are protected against certain acts they have not consented to. Such acts are: the broadcasting and the communication to the public of their live performance; the fixation of their live performance; the reproduction of such a fixation if the original fixation was made without their consent or if the reproduction is made for purposes different from those for which they gave their consent.

(2) Producers of phonograms enjoy the right to authorize or prohibit the direct or indirect reproduction of their phonograms. Phonograms are defined in the Rome Convention as meaning any exclusively aural fixation of sounds of a performance or of other sounds. When a phonogram published for commercial purposes gives rise to secondary uses (such as broadcasting or communication to the public in any form), a single equitable remuneration must be paid by the user to the performers, or to the producers of phonograms, or to both; contracting States are free, however, not to apply this rule or to limit its application.

(3) Broadcasting organizations enjoy the right to authorize or prohibit certain acts, namely: the rebroadcasting of their broadcasts; the fixation of their broadcasts; the reproduction of such fixations; the communication to the public of their television broadcasts if such communication is made in places accessible to the public against payment of an entrance fee.

The Rome Convention allows exceptions in national laws to the above-mentioned rights as regards private use, use of short excerpts in connection with the reporting of current events, ephemeral fixation by a broadcasting organization by means of its own facilities and for its own broadcasts, use solely for the purpose of teaching or scientific research and in any other cases—except for compulsory licenses that would be incompatible with the Berne Convention—where the national law provides exceptions to copyright in literary and artistic works. Furthermore, once a performer has consented to the incorporation of his performance in a visual or audiovisual fixation, the provisions on performers' rights have no further application.

Protection must last at least until the end of a period of 20 years computed from the end of the year in which:

(a) the fixation was made, for phonograms and for performances incorporated therein;

(b) the performance took place, for performances not incorporated in phonograms;

(c) the broadcast took place, for broadcasts. (However, national laws ever more frequently provide for a 50-year term of protection, at least for phonograms and for performances.)

WIPO is responsible, jointly with the ILO and UNESCO, for the administration of the Rome Convention. These three organizations constitute the Secretariat of the Intergovernmental Committee set up under the Convention and consisting of the representatives of 12 Contracting States.

COPYRIGHT BASICS

From an experience point of view, the first time I became aware of the copyright laws was years ago when The Weather Channel started playing my songs on their broadcasts. I had been speaking with the music director of the station at the time and had approved it only if they would supply cue sheets to the PROs and me. So when I say they were playing my music, I mean they were really playing the shit out of my music during every weather report, so my first reaction was to record the programs and keep it as proof if I had problems with ASCAP payments. In actuality, the problem turned out not to be with ASCAP, but with the *Weather Channel itself!*

Lo and behold, I didn't know this at the time, but I was about to be schooled real fast and learn that some broadcasters do not have licenses with the PROs. WHAT!? So here we go, another bumpy ride into the unknown. I called the music director, and guess what? He no longer worked there. He got the hell out of Dodge! So now they were obviously in copyright infringement, because they started playing the music and didn't even bother to get written clearance from me. I owned both the masters and syncs.

So I handed this over to my manager at the time and this is the only thing she ever got right. As you can imagine, The Weather Channel was anxious to settle, but of course offering a low payment of about $500. So we went back and forth and finally settled on $10,000, but looking back on this I bet I could have asked for a hell of lot more if it had been a class action suit. Because you know my music wasn't the only music they were playing; other's copyrights were obviously infringed upon as well. I was young and that seemed like a fair number at the time, even though I had to pay 15 percent to my manager; I still pocketed $8,500.

INTERVIEW WITH JOSHUA GRAUBART—LEGAL ADVICE

Since copyrights have so many different facets to them, I asked my attorney friend, Joshua Graubart, for legal advice on how we can protect ourselves. Josh practices commercial litigation and intellectual property and media law on behalf of numerous corporate and individual clients. His past and present clients include Fortune 500 start-up entities, independent artists, producers, publishers, and distributors. As a litigator, Josh has represented major industrial and consumer goods manufacturers in multi-million dollar intellectual property actions. He has represented several classes of plaintiffs in copyright infringement class actions, as well as defended a major trademark class action suit on behalf of a consumer goods manufacturer. In addition, Josh regularly advises independent artists, publishers, and producers on copyright and other intellectual property issues, and in connection with the entertainment industry generally.

♫

From your experience working as a lawyer in the copyright field, can you explain (to people who are not familiar) the importance of copyrights and how they should be protected?

I'll say it as plainly as I can: if you do not promptly register your works with the Copyright Office, you're setting yourself up for major disappointment. There are few things more frustrating for a copyright lawyer than to have to tell a client that, yes, her work has been infringed, but no, there is no cost-effective remedy. Worse still is having to tell her that it's her fault because she didn't register on time.

New media start-ups in particular are increasingly adopting the stance that it is better to seek forgiveness than permission—that is, infringe now, settle the infringement lawsuit later at pennies on the dollar. The only effective way to make sure you get paid for your work is timely registration, which hands the copyright owner a mighty club with which to beat infringers; without timely registration, the copyright owner may as well be unarmed.

Before the present Copyright Act went into effect in 1978, there was very little protection available for works not registered with the Copyright Office; generally speaking, either you registered when you published or you lost all federal protection. In order to bring the United States in line with the rest of the world, Congress changed the rule in the present Copyright Act: copyright protection now begins at the moment the work is created, without the need for registration.

But that's only part of the story. Lawmakers like the old registration requirement—for one thing, it creates a record of who owns which works, or at least who created them and when, something impossible if no one registers their works. So, to encourage registration, Congress added a carrot and a stick. First, the carrot: copyright owners who register their works before the works are infringed can choose to be awarded "statutory damages"—that is, minimum damages, starting at $750 per infringement and climbing (in certain circumstances) up to $150,000, which a court can award at its discretion without having to weigh tedious and expensively-presented evidence about how much damage the infringer actually caused. The court may also award a victorious copyright owner her attorneys' fees and costs.

Now, the stick: copyright owners who do not register before infringement are barred from all of this; indeed, registration is required in order to bring an infringement suit at all, and delay may in some cases end a suit before it's begun. Once in trial, actual damages must be expensively proved before the court, and a winning copyright owner will still have to pay her own attorneys' fees and costs. Even in clear cases of brazen infringement, copyright owners have spent years fighting and winning court battles, only to receive awards amounting to only a tiny fraction of their expenses.

Happily, copyright registration is simple to do yourself, and the Copyright Office has progressively made registration cheaper and easier. Registration of a work online costs $35 (down from $45 a few years ago), and the completed form and a copy of the work can all be submitted online at www.copyright.gov. Unpublished works, or works all published together as part of a collection (songs on a single album, for example) can often all be registered together under a single fee. Do yourself (and your lawyer) a favor: register your works now and save yourself heartache later.

Can you briefly describe how in the case of the Sirius Satellite Litigation, music copyrights were being infringed upon?

I need to emphasize here that Sirius settled the Sirius Litigation without any admission of liability. Plaintiffs alleged that Sirius both directly infringed the plaintiff's copyrights and indirectly infringed as well, by enabling and encouraging users to download and retain copies of plaintiffs' works. Sirius denied that it had infringed, or encouraged, or enabled its users to infringe. Whether infringement occurred was never adjudicated, as the parties preferred to settle rather than incur the costs and risks of extended litigation. Consequently, I will speak only as to the infringement that plaintiffs alleged.

Under section 106 of the US Copyright Act, copyright owners have the exclusive right to reproduce, distribute, and publicly perform their work. This means that generally, only the copyright owners can authorize copying, distributing, or broadcasting of their work, and so can set the terms and price of the license in negotiation. However, virtually all songwriters and publishers grant public performance authority to one of the performing rights organizations (PROs)—ASCAP, BMI, SESAC—which in turn license broadcasters like Sirius, and the songwriters and publishers receive royalty checks at a standard rate negotiated by the performing rights organizations.

Unlike musical compositions, until quite recently, there was no public performance right for sound recordings in the US. In 1996, Congress added one, but only with respect to digital transmission; analog transmission—that is, traditional broadcast radio (sometimes called "terrestrial radio)—remains exempt. Since there was no existing PRO infrastructure for sound recording public performance, Congress added a "compulsory license" provision to the Copyright Act, which—provided it makes payment for use at a standard rate— permits a digital broadcaster to obtain the right to digitally broadcast. Since 1996, Sound Exchange has been established, and it now collects and distributes royalties collected from the digital broadcast of sound recordings.

Sirius Satellite Radio operated under public performance licenses both from the PROs (for musical compositions) and the compulsory license for public performance of sound recordings. Sirius provided its subscribers with receivers, which, generally, worked like a traditional radio: the receiver received a signal from Sirius and processed it into live audible sound.

However, in 2005—or so the plaintiffs in the litigation argued— Sirius began distributing new receivers which, in addition to working like a traditional radio, also allowed subscribers to record digital copies of the content broadcast by Sirius and store them so they could be replayed on demand for as long as the subscriber continued his Sirius subscription. These receivers had up to 100 hours of recording capacity, and the receiver could be preprogrammed to record particular upcoming songs on any of Sirius's 100+ channels.

The plaintiffs contended that these extra features—the capability to download content, to store that content indefinitely, and to replay it at will—went beyond the scope of the public performance licenses afforded by the compulsory license scheme and acquired from the PROs. Consequently, plaintiffs contended that users' use of the receivers to download and store plaintiffs' works infringed on the plaintiffs' reproduction and distribution rights, and that Sirius was secondarily liable for infringement by its subscribers' use of the receiver equipment.

For its part, Sirius maintained that none of its actions made it liable for infringement.

In the ever-growing digital revolution, how can artists and publishers protect their music from copyright infringement?

You have narrowed this question to define "copyright infringement" as "consumers making unauthorized copies." Limited to that context, "the ever-growing digital revolution" is different only in scale from the world before digitization. In other words, prior to the advent of an Internet capable of quickly transferring substantial quantities of data, consumers made unauthorized reproductions chiefly with cassette tapes, either by copying a friend's record or taping off the radio. These methods were far less convenient than those enabled by file-sharing technologies today, and the quality of such copies were significantly lower, and so this variety of piracy was substantially less of an industry problem than it has become post-Napster, but the problem, and its solutions (or lack thereof), remain the same.

In practice, there is not now, nor was there before Napster, any effective, technological way to prevent "peer-to-peer" copying, nor to prevent recordings of audio transmissions. The major labels experimented with digital rights management (DRM) technology in between the late 1990s and the late 2000s, and ultimately dropped the attempt in the face of consumer resistance, minimal effectiveness, and high cost. Apple attempted to use DRM technology in connection with iTunes, but likewise dropped it in 2009. Even where DRM technology prevented direct copying of the digital files, the so-called analog hole—by which every digital device must ultimately make the content manifest in analog form, so that humans can see and hear it—creates an inevitable opening which DRM technology cannot prevent, though this does entail some level of signal degradation.

Of course, unauthorized copying is still copyright infringement, but in the peer-to-peer context, individual infringers are difficult to find and rarely have the financial resources that make suing them worthwhile. It is not generally cost-efficient to pursue individual peer-to-peer infringers, and the publicity is also bad, which is why both the MPAA and the RIAA have generally stopped pursuing this line. There might be some hope in the form of streamlined copyright infringement suit procedures for smaller claims, an idea floated by the Copyright Office, but this remains a theoretical future development.

There is only one potentially cost-effective way to prevent peer-to-peer copying via the Internet, which is to choke it at the level of Internet service providers; that means (or can mean) both the service providers who provide customers Internet access, and also the hosts of user-generated content sites like YouTube. However, Congress in 1998 enacted the Digital Millennium Copyright Act, which among other provisions, insulates Internet service providers from copyright infringement liability in all but the most egregious of circumstances, provided the content outlet complies with properly formatted takedown requests from copyright holders. As a practical matter, users upload far faster than copyright owners can send takedown requests, so it's a losing battle of whack-a-mole for copyright owners.

Another approach, pursued more aggressively in Europe, but so far inconclusively, is an "X strikes" system implemented by retail-level Internet service providers, by which users who persistently engage in unauthorized copying activity via peer-to-peer systems have access choked or cut-off after a series of warnings. Certain US Internet service providers have very recently subscribed to a fairly weak version of this, a "6-strike" scheme, which, if persistently ignored by a user, will result in throttled Internet speeds, but no cut-off. It remains to be seen how effective any of these schemes will prove. In any event, we're talking here about an industry-wide or government-imposed solution, which is well beyond the independent capability for independent artists or publishers.

Outside the peer-to-peer world, there is some expanded capacity for enforcement against "unauthorized reproduction"-type infringement. We saw this in connection with the Sirius and XM satellite radio cases, where plaintiffs alleged that the radio service, rather than peers, made sound recordings available for download without the appropriate licenses. Here, because it was alleged that the service, rather than its users, made the sound recordings available, it was possible to impute liability to the service. Similar allegations have been made against Grooveshark. In these instances, infringement litigation may be cost-effective. And, of course, there remains infringement, which has nothing to do with the "digital revolution": record labels and film and television producers who simply decline or neglect to obtain licenses. This happened in the past, too, but the explosion in content has meant the entry into the industry of producers and labels (and others) without much experience, and who therefore sometimes fail (willingly or inadvertently) to get their ducks in a row, so to speak.

About the only effective measure that independent artists or publishers can effectively take is to consistently register their works with the US Copyright Office. See my answer to the first question in this interview. This at least allows a meaningful suit to be brought against infringers. Many infringers, such as peer-to-peer sharers, are not worth pursuing, and many more contributory infringers, such as Internet service providers, are insulated from liability by the DMCA, but where there is an available target, failure to have registered the work before infringement will eliminate even the effectiveness of pursuing that target.

♫

COPYRIGHT LITIGATION

This is a convoluted process and there is no one, real answer. I believe it varies from case to case with so many determining factors that I had to get many different attorneys' perspectives. The following is a perspective on how copyright courts determine damages, provided by a copyright attorney who wished to remain anonymous.

In the US (and I'd like to point out that we're talking here only about the US), section 504 of the Copyright

Act governs monetary damages available for infringement. (Note: the current Copyright Act came into force in 1978; certain works pre-dating 1978 may be governed by different rules.) There are two possible forms: (1) actual damages plus profits and (2) statutory damages.

Actual damages plus profits is the default setting. The plaintiff (copyright owner) must prove that he/she suffered a measurable financial loss as a result of the infringement, and the amount of that loss. So, for example, if a musical composition were used in a television program without a license, the copyright holder would be damaged in the amount that he/she would have expected to receive for such a license. To prove this, he/she would need to provide evidence in the form of past licenses (showing what the television producer might normally pay and/or what the copyright owner would normally accept) or testimony from industry "experts" as to what the going market rate for such a license would be.

In addition, the copyright owner is entitled to any additional profits the infringer made (to the extent such profits are beyond the "discount" provided by not getting a license from the copyright holder) from the infringement. In theory, the plaintiff need only show the defendant's gross income from the infringing product, and it is then up to the defendant (infringer) to show how much of that gross income had to go to "legitimate" expenses other than licensing the copyright owner's work. In practice, this can become very complicated—to use our example above, how much of the "profit" of a television program is attributable to the presence of the infringed musical composition?

As may be clear, profits are difficult to nail down, and actual damages are expensive to prove. Where the actual damages plus profit is relatively small, the cost of enforcement by way of a lawsuit is too high to be worth pursuing.

As a result, Congress, when enacting the present Copyright Act, included an option for statutory damages. A copyright owner who has properly registered the infringed work with the US Copyright Office *before* (or in an extremely limited set of cases, very soon after) infringement occurs, may opt instead to be awarded statutory damages, "in a sum of not less than $750 or more than $30,000 as the court considers just," to quote the Copyright Act; where infringement is "willful," statutory damages can stretch as high as $150,000. In other words, the plaintiff copyright holder does not need to show the extent of the damage caused by the infringement, or the profits which resulted; instead, the court (either the judge or, where appropriate, the jury) may intuit the proper amount. A much more cost-effective solution for copyright holders, and as a practical matter, almost all copyright infringement lawsuits pursue statutory damages, for the simple reason that, except in the very rarest of cases, bringing suit for actual damages costs more than the infringement is worth.

Of course, this is where the problem enters: the statute leaves it up to the court to decide what it "considers just" without much in the way of guidance. The honest answer is, *no one knows what statutory damages should be.* Early in my career I asked this question of a particularly eminent senior New York copyright lawyer, and he essentially said the same: it's a mystery.

This is largely because so few infringement matters go all the way through trial. Like all civil matters in the US, the overwhelming majority of cases settle, and those settlements are almost always confidential. I actually undertook some research a few years ago to try to get some hard evidence on this question—and another reason I don't want this attributed to me is that I abandoned the project for reasons you'll see in a moment and therefore don't want to make a canonical statement on incomplete research. I looked for actual infringement cases, which had resulted in court-awarded damages in the last decade or two. Almost all that I found were default judgments (meaning the defendants failed to appear) against clubs or restaurants that had not paid for ASCAP or BMI licenses. The problem is that both ASCAP and BMI operate under heavy regulation by the Justice Department (as a result of antitrust lawsuits in the 1940s) and are either limited or limit themselves to asking for minimal damages for such infringements. Since most copyright holders are not so bound, and would presumably ask for the maximum, the ASCAP and BMI cases aren't very instructive, but they're practically all that's out there.

Even in the rare instances where awards are made outside of the ASCAP/BMI situation, the amount of damages is in serious controversy. Take, for example, the recent high-profile case *Capitol Records v. Thomas*. This was one of the series of lawsuits brought by the major record labels against peer-to-peer file-sharers. The following paragraph is the Wikipedia summary of the damages award saga in that case:

"After declining a settlement offer of $5,000, the defendant, Jammie Thomas-Rasset, was found liable in a 2007 trial for infringing copyright on 24 songs and ordered to pay $222,000 [$9,250 per song] in statutory damages. The court later granted her motion for a new trial because of an error in its jury instructions. In a second trial in 2009, before which she again declined a settlement offer (this time for $25,000) a jury again found against Thomas-Rasset, this time awarding $1,920,000 ($80,000 per song—this jury must have found the infringement willful) in statutory damages, a sum that was later reduced [by the trial judge] to $54,000. The record labels refused to accept the reduced award; so a third trial solely to determine damages was held in November 2010, resulting in a jury award of $1.5 million against Thomas-Rasset. In July

2011, the court [that is, the trial judge] again reduced the $1.5 million jury award to $54,000, or $2,250 per song. The record labels appealed this decision. On September 11, 2012, the Eighth Circuit Court of Appeals reversed the District Court's reduction of the award, and reinstated the award of $222,000, which was the amount awarded by the jury in the first trial."

There has been some argument (rejected by the Eighth Circuit in Thomas, but perhaps still viable elsewhere) that statutory damages on this level may be unconstitutionally severe. Generally, these arguments are presented with respect to peer-to-peer file-sharers, who are admittedly not the target Congress had in mind in creating the statutory damages remedy in the mid-1970s; the intended target was the essentially willful criminal class of bootleggers and counterfeit record presses. Many expect revisions to the Copyright Act in the near future to address this issue.

CONCLUSION

In this chapter we've explored the various types of royalty sources, such as Sound Exchange, Neighboring Rights, Live Television/Videotape Supplemental Markets Fund and royalties based on sales. More importantly we've learned points consisting of the complex copyright laws. Artists should pay close attention to copyright infringements involving their music because, as we've seen, they do occur at a price. Also, it is important to note that a good attorney is worth his weight in gold.

Chapter 8

Selling Your Royalties

In some circles this is sacrilegious to even think about selling your royalties, let alone actually doing it. But in my view, royalty streams, like writers, publishers, mechanicals, digital sales, are great assets, like stocks and bonds, which can be sold. The entertainment industry never follows Wall Street conundrums and is independent from the real estate market. Especially after the 2007–2008 meltdowns of both the markets, people are very skittish about reinvesting into these traditional areas. Because of the huge swings in the stock and real estate markets, more and more investors, both independent and corporate, are venturing into attaining entertainment royalties, which don't fluctuate during recessions.

Everyone seems to know something of the value of selling their publishing, but not everyone recognizes the intricacies of selling their writers' royalties. I must have Googled this topic a hundred times, but there really is very little information out there. I believe it is such a specialized topic, that very few people have traveled down this road. I've done research in the past couple of years and found out some enlightening things. For one, the writer's royalty share of, for example, ASCAP, SESAC, and BMI, can be a very valuable commodity to outside investors. But with the good comes the bad. I want artists to be aware of whom to steer away from and of what is a sensible deal. So here are some tips.

UNDERSTAND BREAKDOWN OF ROYALTIES TO SELL

You should understand that a song has two sides as far as public performance royalties go: those that are collected by what are commonly referred to as PROs (performing right organizations) in the United States—ASCAP, BMI, SESAC. You have writers' and publishers' sides that are valued the same, as far as royalties paid by the PROs. In other words, if a song is placed on a daytime TV show and earns $130 for the writer, then the publisher side of this song for the same placement will earn the same amount.

So from the standpoint of the performance royalties, the writer's share and the publisher's share are basically of equal value (don't confuse this with sync fees or mechanical royalties). Even if you don't control the publishing side of the song or even the copyright, you can still sell your writer royalty stream.

For example, if you have a catalog of songs that have been earning an average of $25,000 per year, the common sales multiple is usually four to five times the average. Hence this catalog would be worth $100–125,000. There are some companies/individuals that may value the catalog a little higher or lower depending on the intrinsic value they put on the catalog; for example, hit songs, television themes, etc. At the end of the day, it really depends on how eager an investor is to acquire the catalog.

KNOW THE SALES BREAKDOWN

Generally there are two ways of earning money on your catalog:
1. An advance against future royalties
2. The actual sales of your royalties

There are a couple of ways the advance works. One way is when a company offers a modest advance, usually no more than the total yearly income. They collect 100 percent of your writer's catalog until the advance is recouped, plus a very high interest rate. Investment bank companies have been known to offer high advances plus high interest rates, and then take 50 percent of the writer's side for life.

I have been offered this type of deal and I advise you to keep clear of it because they are not buying that 50 percent of your writer's side, just giving you an advance/loan and will collect the advance 100 percent until recouped—plus hitting you with a high interest rate (in the 20 percent range) while taking 50 percent of your writer's side. Absolutely ridiculous!

The only way that model would work is considering the large advance as the purchase of the 50 percent writer's and there would be no recoupment at all. Hence from that point, they further collect 50 percent of the writer's.

My advice is the second option—selling the catalog outright. It is the best and quickest way to make money from an old catalog. (For the right price, of course.) Plus, you don't have to sell 100 percent of your writer's either; you may only want to sell 25 percent or even 10 percent, but keep in mind that the purchase price will drop with the smaller percentages. You have no so-called investment partners with the buy-out model, and you are not obligated to pay back an advance via recoupment, which in some cases leaves you liable for the unrecouped amount if you are not paid back within a certain period of time.

WORK WITH PEOPLE YOU CAN TRUST

As you can imagine, there are certainly a lot of scammers out there, so be aware and stay clear of them. I must admit that this was a very scary thing for me when I first investigated the possibility of selling of my writer's royalties. I found out a lot about how little people in general know about royalties (outside of the music community).

Based on my experience, I advise you to stay away from investment bankers, equity companies, oil companies, and "so-called" family trusts. These people are just trying to get a leg in the music business and do not understand the first thing about music royalties. Believe it or not, I found myself explaining to these people how ASCAP, SESAC, and BMI worked and how they collect monies from the various broadcast licensors.

It seems to me that if you are going to invest in a business, you should at least know how the hell it works, even just the basics. I had been offered a few of these deals from companies, and when I accepted them after negotiations, they were abruptly pulled off the table, and believe me it happened more than once. From my perspective, this behavior came across as very shady and dishonest.

The good news is, there is a new company out there that does sell writers' royalties and has had success doing so in the past year. The company is called Royalty Exchange, which is an online auction run by entrepreneur Sean Peace. He has good financial connections that can hook writers up with the right buyers. I must warn you that this is not an overnight sale—it can take months to sell a catalog, and sometimes it may not sell at all—but still, in my particular case, Sean proved to be committed and he closed the deal. What worked for me is that he had the contacts in the money world. I have dedicated my life to all facets of the music industry, from composer to artist to producer, and I have never had ties with the banking "suits" of the world, so Royalty Exchange was the perfect connection for me.

The bottom line is, go with your instincts—do your research before you sign on the dotted line. And, as always, if you're not absolutely sure about something, get a lawyer to look it over.

SKETCHY INVESTORS

This only scratches the surface, as they say. During the process of selling my royalties, I met some sketchy characters out there that made some industry people look like girl scouts. I did my homework and found the going rate for a catalog was four to five times the average yearly income. The first offer I got to buy my writer's royalties was from some guy in California, who offered $125,000, which I knew was low-balling. I came to find out from sources that this guy specializes in buying royalties from desperate old Motown songwriters and putting it into their agreement that he also gets their Gold and Platinum Records! He hangs the awards in his office to give the impression that he actually had something to do with the record industry. Okay, *next!*

Then there was the guy who worked for some Texas oil company who buys drilling rights on people's property throughout the country. Well this guy makes me a buyout offer of $400,000 (that was for everything, Sound Exchange, ASCAP, SESAC, writer and publisher), after months of analyzing my royalties, on a letterhead from some family trust fund. He refused to negotiate; in fact, he kept on playing it off like he had to get permission from his imaginary boss, who never spoke to me directly. I know this was full of red flags, but I had to see if this was on the level, for the amount of money they offered. So finally I said to myself, I'm going to except the offer and see if he is for real or full of it. I bet you know the answer: he backed away, saying no. He couldn't give a reason why and prevented me from discussing the so-called "offer" with his boss. What a bloody waste of time, but not all was lost, as I learned from the experience.

Then there was the corporate raider offer from a New York City investment bank firm, and that should have been warning enough. I speak to this kid on the phone who sounds like he's fourteen years old and knows absolutely *nothing* about the music industry. This asshole has a PhD and here I am explaining to him, call after call, email after email, how the royalty system works! His parents must have bought him that PhD, because this guy couldn't grasp even the basic structure of how the PROs worked. Then it was back to the imaginary boss game. Do all of these idiots have the same boss? Man! This was getting old!

So these guys set up not one, but two phone calls with SESAC so they can explain how the hell the royalty system works. I felt bad for SESAC. He comes back and makes me an offer of $225,000 (excluding the publishing of ASCAP and SESAC), but this offer was really terrible because it wasn't considered a purchase. Theoretically, he was buying half of the writer's royalties, however the money was considered an advance, not a buyout. So I would have had to recoup the $225,000, and he owns 50 percent of the writer's regardless. He called it a partnership; I called it bending me over! Sure, it's a fair deal if they are paying the money for 50 percent of the writer's and there is no recoupment, which means from that point further we split writer royalties 50/50. But he treated it like a recoupable advance, so there is very little risk for them, plus on top of that he was charging right off the top a $50,000 "processing fee"; Come on, give me a break!

I try my previous approach with a past investor, and accept it and see what happens next. Well, once again another company wasn't serious. They came back and said their investors didn't approve the deal. I tell you, I knew it was a lie because, in our earlier phone conversations, he told me they had internal money to make smaller investments without needing investor approval. You see, these guys don't remember anything they say, so they assume you won't either.

I was beginning to think this was not going to happen. I received another offer from some overseas private investor in the Hinterland who wanted to do an advance of $225,000. But again there was a catch, actually a deal breaker for me. It was structured the same as that corporate raider one, but even worse, if that was possible. He would be buying 50 percent of the writer's, but had a clause stating that if the advance didn't recoup by a certain period, the writer's share would revert 100 percent to him. I told him to stick it where the sun don't shine.

TOUGH TIMES

By this point it had been almost six months from starting this crackpot journey and I thought, "At least I tried, no big deal." It was around this time when hurricane Sandy came and battered us all up and down the east coast. The 200-year-old farmhouse that was once my parent's weekend house in the Catskill Mountains caught on fire and half burned (thankfully no one was hurt and all of my studio equipment was safe). The lives of my wife, kids, and me went into a tailspin and became an unbelievable struggle to reach normalcy again. We had to live in an RV in the driveway for a month while we salvaged through the wreckage of our belongings. But God blessed us; I found a great house in New Paltz, NY, ironically where I had once attended SUNY College. I also found a separate commercial space for my recording studio near the new house. Obviously, I put the selling of my royalties on the back burner, because I didn't want to a make a rash decision from my emotional state.

INTERVIEW WITH SEAN PEACE—ROYALTY EXCHANGE

As the New Year broke 2013, I reconnected with Sean Peace who ran the Royalty Exchange and wanted to see if we could really sell my catalog this time. We got an offer within a week to just buy a certain portion of the SESAC writer's catalog for $250,000 from a very rich investor in Monaco, once the home of Princess Grace Kelly. I thought, "Well, this is promising." We closed the deal in two weeks' time and life was better than ever. This was the best way to do it, sell off a certain piece of the catalog and keep the rest.

Royalty Exchange really became a valuable source for selling my royalties. How else would I have gotten a private investor, in Monaco no less, to buy the catalog? A very good source if you are considering this type of sale. Sean Peace started the Royalty Exchange to fill a need in the music industry, to connect buyers and sellers to create the first royalty marketplace. He has started several companies and learned the music business through his last company, SongVest. SongVest is the only marketplace that sells entertainment royalties as high-end memorabilia, with auctions that have included the rights to songs recorded by Aerosmith, Bon Jovi, Carrie Underwood, Ringo Starr, Ozzy Osbourne, and The Monkees.

♫

Why did you start the company Royalty Exchange and can you explain the importance of such a service and how it fulfills a need in the industry?

I started TRE [The Royalty Exchange] because we saw that no one was helping music royalty owners sell their rights, and there was no central place for buyers to come, in which to purchase. I had previously started a company called SongVest that allowed artists to sell a percentage of their song to fans, but ultimately it left out everyone, except for artists, from participating. TRE allows any music royalty owner to sell a percentage of any royalty stream to investors. This is important because normally they can only get a loan on their royalties for twelve to eighteen months of current income. If someone needs more liquidity then, their only option is to call their lawyer or personally find a seller. Same on the buyer's side: if you want to buy royalties, you have to look around and try to find where they are for sale. Additionally there is no way for them to value or understand how to transact these deals. TRE fills that void by creating an online auction marketplace that provides sellers top value for their assets, and buyers with an easy-to–use, transparent way in which to value and purchase royalties.

Can you explain how private investors have become more interested in music catalogs instead of the typical investments of real estate and stocks?

Everyone is looking for alternative investments, which by definition is an investment that is not tied to normal market forces. If the stock market crashes tomorrow, people will still listen to music. The industry might dip, but it won't fall. With bond yields so small, under inflation, people want to invest where they can get some stable yields. It doesn't hurt that music is also something fun to invest in.

What types of catalogs have you found your investors interested in buying?

Of course catalogs with hit songs are always popular, but we have found that "true" investors are just looking for good returns, irrelevant of the popularity of the songs.

It's a very revolutionary idea of selling one's writer's [share] as opposed to the industry standard of selling publishing interests. Do you see this becoming more of an alternative standard for composers who don't control their publishing?

Definitely. People in the industry normally think of selling their writer's share only when they are in the dire straights of financial problems. We are promoting a different reason of "investing in your future." If you can get a large influx of funds by selling a percentage of your royalties, then you can use that income to invest in something else that might give you a better return than your music royalties. If you can do that, then why not sell your works?

Can you explain to composers with catalogs how beneficial this would be for them, as opposed to just sitting on it and earning royalties through the years?

As I just mentioned above, it is about the return on your asset. If you can sell your royalties today and use those funds to invest in something else that has a high value or return, then ultimately you are better off. It also helps that you have flexibility in selling only a percentage or any stream and that it doesn't mean you loose your copyright. Since you also set your reserve price—meaning the minimum price it would sell for—you have additional comfort that you will get what you ask for or more.

♪

SELL YOUR MUSIC TO ASIAN MARKETS

(Courtesy *of Music Connection* magazine) http://musicconnection.com
By **Stefan Broadley**

One would have to be a cave dweller to be unaware that Asia is on the rise, with booming markets such as China and Korea quickly catching up with more established markets like Japan and the "Asian Tigers." Even the markets in Malaysia, Thailand and Indonesia are gathering steam and becoming increasingly attractive to western business interests. But what does that mean for the American music industry, and can western artists and music companies get in on the action?

Avril Lavigne certainly thinks so. She was rewarded with a surprise bonanza of music, merchandise and ticket sales after she sang some lyrics in Japanese. And according to Josh Web from What Culture *blog, Lady Gaga has also cracked the Asian market because "she gets it. What some here (America) feel is over the top and attention-seeking, is totally normal for fans of K-Pop." And even Michael*

Jackson's old producer, Teddy Riley, has switched over to K-Pop (from A-Pop?) and is now based in Korea, riding the wave of Korean artists dominating the charts in Asia.

But those who are making inroads in Asia are not just established artists. "Independent artists, DJs, producers, songwriters can too," says Dan Merlot, an L.A.-based independent music producer who has been visiting Asia for years. Merlot thinks there are significant advantages to operating in Asia because they value Western tastes and creativity so highly.

In fact, all the Asian music professionals we talked to for this article agreed that there are great new opportunities available, due particularly to the Internet. And while the fortunes of "international" music are waning, and interest in homegrown music is rising, our experts also agreed that this trend could work to a WESTERN artist's advantage—if he or she collaborates with native Asian artists and gets representation in those artists' home territories.

Think Global, Act Local

Rob Schwartz, Tokyo Bureau Chief of **Billboard** magazine, says, "The number one thing for any artist trying to break into Asian markets is to get a local partner. Obviously the easiest route to do this is to be on a major label and get the Japanese office to take an interest in promoting you. However, there are other partners who can be equally effective in Japan."

Something Drastic, for example, is a music management and promotion company that, according to CEO **Rob Poole**, is set up to provide its western clients with "long-term connections, help them understand the language, who to market and promote to, and the fundamentals of business."

To anyone interested in penetrating Asia, Dan Merlot suggests researching to find companies that represent foreign music into different regions of Asia (media, management, booking, music sales). He also advises finding out what indie and major acts are selling music, touring or getting media exposure there. "Working with locals is important because they give a face to your music and make it much easier for companies there that willing to work with a foreign artist."

Perform Live

Of course the best way to give a face to your music is to turn up and play it. The Vice President of Village Records in Japan suggests approaching the big concert promoters of cities such as Udo and Kyodo, while Robert Poole suggests targeting the "two big concert promoters, SMASH and Creativeman, who hold the Fuji Rock and Summersonic events respectively. Both support new acts by having extensive stages at their festivals, so submitting material to these two is probably the best way to go these days."

> Working with locals is important because they give a face
> to your music and make it much easier for companies there
> that are willing to work with a foreign artist."
>
> —Dan Merlot

Regarding China, Poole thinks the mainland Chinese market is not yet well developed, but the best ways for new acts to get into the market is to reach out to local city venues directly where acts can easily book gigs, providing they have someone to aid with language.

Korean music sounds much closer to US music than any other country in Asia, so Poole believes it could be a good idea for a US act to collaborate with a Korean act and have a two-way tie-up on tours. And with Southeast Asia growing fast, it should also be possible to find performance slots at festivals in Jakarta, Kuala Lumpur, Bangkok and others.

Asian Markets Vary

By now it should be obvious that there is no singular Asian market. At the moment, "Japan has the biggest market," says **Mr. Aso**, Vice President of **Wondergoo**, a Japanese entertainment retail chain, while "China and other Southeast Asian countries, which have a tendency to get influenced by trends created in Japan, also have potential for growth." So despite all the talk of "awakening the Chinese giant," when it comes to the music industry, Poole reports that "Japan is still the number one target in the region, since the yen is so strong and disposable income is high. Digital sales have largely made up for the decline in CD sales, but CDs do sell well here still."

This obviously doesn't apply in China where there are little to no copyright laws. Although China is fast realizing that in order to grow its domestic markets and encourage local innovation, it needs to put intellectual property laws in place. That is why royalty collection agencies, such as Japan's JASRAC, are starting to make inroads there. But even if copyright laws were in place, the major labels would still find it hard to charge $10 per album when Chinese consumers can barely afford two. This too will improve as

China's economy grows, and its currency gains more purchasing power. But for the moment, independent artists and labels who operate with much smaller overheads are probably the best positioned to make profits off these lower price points.

Interestingly, the Korean market is currently getting the most attention, with acts like **2NE1** dominating Asia, and even America, where they were recently voted best new band in the world by MTV viewers, and their album went to No. 1 on the hip-hop album iTunes chart. "Korea recently has had a pop music explosion dominating the charts in Japan and becoming a popular sub-culture worldwide," Merlot reports. "In 2011, K-pop artists sales increased 22.3 percent. The key to its success is that Korean pop has been collaborating with European and American songwriters, thus giving it a more international sound. South Korean popular culture is today serving as a major driver of youth culture all across the Pacific Rim, particularly China, Hong Kong, Japan, Philippines, Taiwan and Vietnam."

Lost & Found In Translation

Once you have picked your target market(s), the next thing to do is to record translations of your songs. Avril Lavigne now has a huge following in Asia since recording versions of her main songs in eight different languages, paired up with persistent touring there. A VP at Village Records in Japan (who would prefer to remain anonymous) points out that recording foreign language versions also applies to Asian artists. "Taiwanese singers and rockers sing in Beijing (Chinese) words now, because 70 percent of their sales are from China." While the language barrier often seems huge to English speakers, Asians are very used to translating.

New Tech, New Opps

While Asian markets and languages vary considerably, Poole believes "the technology is the same worldwide in terms of social media. Each country has its own; Japan uses Mixi more than Facebook, China has Baidu and Weibo. But since people who are interested in foreign music tend to go to international sites to find it, this is less of a barrier than one might think."

That is not to say America can't import new technologies and business models from Asia. For example, two bands Merlot produced in Japan recently performed at the Tokyo Girls Collection fashion show in Beijing where the audience could use their phones to buy songs on the spot by scanning QR codes on giant screens. And in between performances, they ran fashion shows where the crowds could also impulse purchase the clothes by phone. That's why Asian artists are often funded by fashion labels, not record labels.

Bec Hollcraft: Big In Japan

Bec Hollcraft sings for a band called Stars in Stereo (http://starsinstereo. com) who are currently on a US tour with Foxy Shazam. Before joining Stars in Stereo, Hollcraft was signed to Sony Japan for three years under the name "Becca" (http://beccaofficial.com). She worked out of Japan on and off during that time and released a total of five albums there, including a collaboration album with Japanese band Bennie K. Together they wrote and recorded under the name Bennie Becca, and the album had English as well as Japanese lyrics in the songs.

Music Connection: How did you penetrate the Asian market? How did that come about?

Bec Hollcraft: I was doing a showcase in Los Angeles and my manager at the time invited a few scouts from Sony Japan. He had worked in Japan for years and thought I would be a great fit in the Japanese market. Fortunately the scouts liked me. I was very lucky and it all seemed to happen very quickly. They flew me to Japan when I was 18 in 2007 and I was working immediately.

MC: How did being put in an anime help your Japanese career? How did that opportunity arise?

Hollcraft: Anime is a huge part of Japanese culture and my label worked very hard to get me a placement. That's how bands get out there in Japan; by getting their songs on TV shows or movies. They definitely made fighting for those placements a big part of the process of getting me success in Japan. Because my song was the theme for Kuroshitsuji or The Black Butler, which was a new anime that blew up in Japan, I seemed to have gained most of my fan base from that. Even today, years later, people in different countries, including America, are watching that anime and reaching out to me or finding my music online. Animes can cross over into any culture.

MC: We noticed, in a live video from Japan, that you thanked the crowd in Japanese. You were very well versed! Did you pick up the language from this experience or were you already fluent?

Hollcraft: It was important to me to try to find a way to connect with the fans. What better way than to speak their language? I definitely got help from translators, tutors, and Rosetta Stone, but picked up words here and there. I heard from many different Japanese people that singing and speaking in Japanese is the only way to get truly massive in Japan if you start there, so I tried to do that as much as possible.

MC: What advice do you have for DIY musicians attempting to tap a foreign market?

Hollcraft: Try to understand the culture. Study it, study the music, study what sells out there. Learning the language is extremely helpful. There are always exceptions and I was definitely one of them. I got lucky. All you need is one person in a great position to believe in you and fight for you. . . . Definitely try to work with a rep from that country rather than trying to do it yourself. It is very difficult to try to break into an Asian country without that help. It seems they are very adamant about working with their own people.

MC: Do you have any examples/advice on what NOT to do? Do have any plans of returning to Japan with Stars In Stereo?

Hollcraft: Don't disrespect their culture. Be aware of it and learn about it before you head out there. It will make your experience more enjoyable and you will gain more respect. My band Stars in Stereo and I are dying to play internationally and are doing everything we can to make it out there someday! The most enthusiastic fans I've ever had were in Japan. I am so happy I got to experience that and hope I get to share that with my band soon.

—Andy Mesecher

New Challenges

New technologies also bring new problems, and Merlot reports "the pipelines are more open than ever in terms of the Web. Anyone can follow you and buy your music more easily than ever before using Facebook, iTunes, Twitter, and music videos on YouTube. However, it also makes it harder to stand out among millions of other artists. That's why today's independent artist has to be more hardworking and clever than ever before."

While being a western artist is a great way to stand out in Asia, you will definitely need to work with local companies to target your market.

And collaborating with local artists is another option you would do well to explore.

But what do your potential Asian collaborators, partners and fans want from you? Help with English lyrics is the most obvious need, though the Vice President of Village Records thinks Asian music makers could definitely learn from American music makers and mixing engineers. It is a view echoed by Merlot, who finds Asian artists and music professionals very receptive to international partnerships, especially for help with intangibles like writing songs, cultivating talent, styling, marketing, and getting an inter-national sound and feel.

Most of Merlot's music production work is now coming from Asia for that reason, and his job description increasingly includes cultural ambassador, with his collaborations spread both overseas and back here in the US. In fact, Asian artists often want to come to the US, not only to record and collaborate with American artists, but to experience the Los Angeles scene, clubs, trends and absorb the culture.

This is why **Kathleen Wirt**, Owner/Manager of **4th Street Recording Studios** in Santa Monica, CA, has partnered with Merlot to offer those options as part of her studio's overall recording experience.

Wirt says her facility's most recent client was **Laure Shang Wenjie**, the winner of China's *American Idol* equivalent, who flew to Los Angeles to record a track at 4th Street, "but also to collaborate with L.A. artists and producers," she says, "and soak up the sights, sounds and fashions of Los Angeles.

Just Do It!

Even though the share of international music in Asia is shrinking, Asians still revere western artists and creativity. So while breaking into the Asian music markets has some initial geographic and language barriers for western artists to overcome, those who do are richly rewarded with a receptive audience and enthusiastic collaborators.

Broadley is an L.A.-based producer, composer, mixer and entrepreneur from New Zealand, writing American pop over English dance music, for the Japanese to sell in Asia.

Links: http://stefanbroadley.com (producer site), http://music3.co (music blog), http://emediacircus.com (business site)

Contacts For This Article:

Stefan Broadley
stefanbroadley@gmail.com, 310-621-8889

Dan Merlot
Specialist in representing song placements and co-writes. Also scouting for US-based Asian singers. info@artistsoundsasia.com, http://danielmerlot. blogspot.com

Robert Poole
CEO of Something Drastic, robert@somethingdrastic.com

Rob Schwartz
Tokyo Bureau Chief of Billboard magazine, gangamati@gmail.com

Kathleen Wirt
Owner/Manager, 4th Street Recording Studios, kathleen@4thstreetrecording. com, 310-395-9114

Village Records Japan
village@breeze.biglobe.ne.jp, http://v-again.co.jp/village

CONCLUSION

We've learned in this chapter that selling your royalties can be quite beneficial after years of toil. With this information, you know the basics and how music royalties have become a very valuable commodity to investors. Obviously, you should only work with people you trust and who have your best interest at heart. Most of all, you have to be as informed as possible and know all of the facts before you make that final sales decision.

Chapter 9

Music Composers-Unsung Heroes

Of all of the jobs in the music industry, I believe that for the work involved, the music composer is the least recognized. In fact, I think music is so sorely undervalued in film and television, the productions put more money into craft services than they do into paying composers or licensing music (with the exception of a well known song). Yes, of course there are the exceptions of Hans Zimmer and Danny Elfman, but those are large Hollywood productions. The composers in the trenches, which are most of us, don't get enough credit. We buffer bad acting, the mismatched editing, and add continuity and emotion to the scene.

Just think of the soap operas without music; they would be unbearable to watch, all that dead air and long pauses. Instead, music draws you into a scene, makes you happy, sad, fearful, and an array of other emotions, flowing through the music. Even during the silent era there was a piano or organ in just about every theater for this very reason. Music and pictures just go together naturally, feeding off of each other, elevating an okay scene into an unforgettable one. There is no doubt that a television show or film wouldn't have nearly as much impact if not for the music. Just imagine *Schindler's List* without that haunting solo violin melody, or the 1960s sitcoms without those catchy jazzy themes from *I Dream of Jeanie* and *Bewitched*.

Yes, the composer definitely earns his keep by tantalizing the listener with sonic sounds of deafening musical creativity. Even if the story is not good, the viewers' ears will still be pleased. Though modern technology has made it easier to create music on your iPad or smartphone, the bottom line is, the musical ability of the composer cannot be matched by the most hip, up-to-date gadget. I mean, if a musician can evoke the emotions necessary, whether he plays it on a banjo or a Theremin, it doesn't matter; it's what works for the scene.

GETTING IN THE ZONE

There is more to composing than just buying a computer and a handful of plug-ins! After twenty years composing for television and films, with three Emmys and seven nominations, I've come to rely on instincts and input from producers and music editors around me. It's a team effort, and the sooner you learn this lesson, the better.

1. Get the Vibe. Remember you are composing music for the show, which will be heard by its fans. Understand the viewers and what works between score and picture. In Ken Burns's *Civil War* series, what worked was that beautiful, solo violin melody, not blazing metal guitar. Proper background score is a key to a successful series.

2. Understand exactly what the producer or music supervisor wants. This can be a very tricky thing. It can change from day to day and from moment to moment. I found that it could become confusing if more than one person gives you directions. The best thing to do is ask for musical references from the main person giving the instructions. For example, if they are requesting a vibe like Led-Zeppelin-meets-Metallica, then make sure you get your project's creative team to specify what elements of each band they like and how they want them combined. Ask as many questions as possible to nail the exact vibe they want.

3. Don't rush it; take time and get it right. This really pertains to composing for new clients. Even if you are juggling many projects, as we all seem to do, give it the time it deserves. Clients can sense when you are rushing and not giving it the proper attention. Remember the kids in school who had six weeks to do their final paper, but waited until the night before to do it? By showing the client that you care about their project, it will almost ensure you a continued relationship for future projects.

4. Use real instruments when you can; don't rely on plug-ins and sample CDs. As a guitarist and recording artist for many years, it is annoying to me that there are so many electronic composers today who take the shortcut and substitute talent for computer plug-ins and samples. Instead of getting a real drummer, they use some drum "extraordinaire" plug-in and samples from CDs of horns and bass. It makes no sense—just hire real musicians to make it sound as authentic as possible. Back in the day, I remember laboring through sessions getting musicians to nail the right sound before the digital era and plug-ins; it actually was a great challenge to see if you could achieve the sound for the project, and it was a real feeling of reward when you did.

5. Don't reuse old cues. This is something we are all guilty of—yours truly as well! In all my experience I've found that trying to rework old cues to try to make them sound different for a new client is more time consuming than actually composing from scratch. And trying to pass off an old cue to a new client thinking it's "close enough" is bad business, because nine out of ten times the client will have so many changes that you will be doubling your work. I don't know how many guys do this, but it's a lot like trying to turn a polka song into an electronica tune, and passing it off to the client. Believe me, they will know!

6. Watch the show and understand how the music is used. Believe it or not, there are composers out there who do not bother to watch the show they are composing for, which seems like a recipe for failure. Set your DVR to record a few episodes and see how the music is synced to picture and compose accordingly. Before I even start composing for a new show I always watch a number of episodes, and then go back to the music director and ask what specifically worked for those shows with regard to the music. I also like to throw out ideas to the music director before I proceed, to see if I'm on track.

7. Make sure to send WAV samples (no MP3s) for approval. I've learned not to send MP3s to people, because no matter how many times you explain to them that it's an MP3, they always get bothered about it sounding "too compressed and lacking bottom end." Well, that's because *it's an MP3* and you're listening to it on *computer speakers!* Then of course they look at the file size and say, "Oh, okay then, never mind." So there goes a half-hour of my life I won't get back!

8. Never send a demo sample! Man, this is such a catch-22, you can't believe! Clients always say, just send a demo so I can hear how it's coming along. So you send a rough mix to them and the first thing they say is, "It sounds like a demo!" Well, duh! It *is* a demo. If you are going to play something for anyone for the first time, it should be the final mix of the song. Back in the early days of being a recording artist I remember the record label would always tell me to just send demos or rough mixes of the songs "so we can get an idea of what you are working on." These were the days before I had a nice recording studio; my setup was just a Tascam DA-88 and a cheap Carvin mixer. So off the rough mixes went and the label would come back with, "It sounds like a demo!" Well yeah, that's because they are demos that you said were okay to send.

9. Keep in good communication with the producer or music supervisor. This is one of the most important things to do. Always check in with the client, especially if you have a long lead-time for the final deadline, because ideas can change. For example, that song they told you to emulate at the start of the project may have changed three times and the client might have forgotten to tell you. Of all my advice to you, this is the most crucial. I've been involved in projects that started off as heavy metal, then midway through became techno, and then finally wound up as a punk song that I had to compose from scratch. Yes, it's a lot of work and chasing, but it's all part of the gig.

10. Never say "That's the best I can do!" Many of us have been at the end of our rope with certain clients, for one reason or another—you want to say "I'm done. You do it!" I certainly have been there with a few people, but the best thing to do is ask for an extension if the changes they request become too much. Step away from the project for a few days, if possible, then come back to it with fresh ears and appease the client.

INTERVIEW WITH HAL LINDES—COMPOSER EXTRAORDINAIRE, DIRE STRAITS

Hal Lindes is perhaps best known as the former guitarist of the British rock band, Dire Straits. His distinctive sound and influence can be heard on such landmark albums as, *Love Over Gold* and *Alchemy*. Having been privileged enough to work with Hal, I can say he is one of the most underrated guitarists of our time. His true understanding of the guitar and all it holds in tone and passion is truly remarkable. I have worked with Hal for a number of years on the *Guitar Masters Series* and *Fretworx*. He is always my first choice when I desire a guest guitarist and my first-call man of the hour.

It's no wonder he is in great demand as a musician, arranger, and producer. Hal's talent for writing from the heart is wonderfully evident in his poignant and evocative film score for *The Boys Are Back* starring Clive Owen (dir., Scott Hicks). Hal is currently working on some pre-records and musical arrangements for the Warner Brothers feature film, *The Lucky One*, starring Zac Efron (dir., Scott Hicks). Hal has composed music for a variety of film and TV series and his scores have won many awards including a Royal Television Society award for the BAFTA nominated film, *Reckless*, and a TRIC award for Best TV Theme Music for *Thieftakers*. But beyond all of the accolades, Hal has something that many musicians lack—heart and soul!

♫

Let's go back to the recording of Dire Straits, Brothers in Arms. What was your typical set-up, guitar, amp, pedals, etc.? Were there any particular artists or songs at the time that influenced you?

Unless a song had an obvious call for a certain guitar, I would generally start out with either the early '60s cream strat or one of the Schecter strats through a 1984 Fender Concert RI (2 x 10). If a different amp tonality was required, I would go for either the 1957 Fender Tweed Twin or my stage rig Boogie and Marshall 4 x 12 cab.

My other guitars were the 1980 blue Schecter strat (from Mark with the inscription "Play It Hal, Mark" on the neck plate), the "Alchemy" 1982 Fullerton RI '52 Telecaster with gray top pickups, the 'Twisting By The Pool' 60's Red Gretsch Jet Fire Bird (one of the first production guitars to incorporated active circuitry), a 1955 translucent cream Fender strat, a 1952 blonde Gibson ES-5, a 1974 Sunburst Telecaster Deluxe, and three of my guitars Mark used to play on stage: a 1982 black Fullerton RI '57 strat, a 1972 Black Rickenbacker 425, and a 1968 white Gibson 3 pickup SG.

For effects, I was running through a BOSS SCC-700 Foot Controller system, patching through to a rack-mounted Roland 31 Band Graphic, Roland SRE-555 Chorus Echo Unit, Roland SDE-300 Digital Delay, Yamaha E-1010 Analog Delay, Ernie Ball Volume Pedal, Vox Wah-Wah, MXR Compressor, MXR Phase 90, Boss Digital Delay, Boss Dimension C, and a MXR Micro Amp.

For acoustic work, I would generally use the 1972 Martin D-35, with the "Love Over Gold" 1982 Ovation Classical, 1980 Custom-Legend XII and VI as alternatives to experiment with.

Before starting the rehearsals for *BIA* [*Brothers in Arms*], Fender provided a host of Concert amps to test out, resulting in the selection of a killer sounding tone machine that really stood out from the pack. Mark was also using that Concert initially while in the formative stages of shaping the tone for the "Money For Nothing" riff.

In terms of influences, at the time, I had just finished recording "Private Dancer" and playing some gigs with Tina Turner, which was quite an experience. I was also interested in the guitarist Ted Greene, managing to take some tuition from him after tracking Ted down in his eccentrically disheveled, vintage-gear-strewn apartment in the San Fernando Valley with the freeway flying past his window.

As a band we were listening to ZZ Top's *Eliminator* and Pink Floyd's *The Wall*.

How did the process go? Were the guitar parts written in the studio or already laid out between Mark and you? How were your guitar parts juxtaposed to those of Mark's?

Prior to making *BIA*, all band rehearsals used to take place at Wood Wharf Rehearsal Studios in Greenwich, South London, situated next to the Cutty Shark overlooking the River Thames: a rough and tumble place, with an organic vibe that was highly conducive to the creative process. At low tide, the banging of hammers against barges in need of repair were heard between the pauses of the band's music, and at day's end the red sun would set like a fireball over the river. This changed with *BIA*, with the initial rehearsals taking place at Phil Manzanera's studio in Virginia Waters in Surrey.

As with the past albums, the pre-recording routine process remained pretty much the same, with Mark running down a tune, usually on his Ovation Adamas, while the rest of us would scribble down the chord changes. If Mark had a specific part in mind, he would spend some time with the player and craft the part. At some point, the song would be played by the band and Mark would usually hear something in a part one of the musicians was working on and spend time with that player, refining it. My goal was to find a guitar part that would support and compliment Mark's guitar performance.

Little by little the songs would get shaped and fine-tuned before the band relocated to Air Studios in Montserrat, where engineer/

co-producer, Neil Dorfsman first heard the songs performed live by the band. The line up at the time was Mark and myself on guitars, John Illsley on bass, Terry Williams on drums, Alan Clark, and newcomer, Guy Fletcher, on keyboards.

What microphones were used to record the guitar parts? Do you remember the studio gear and producer? Was it recorded and mixed at the same studio?

The main microphones were mostly Neumann U67s, AKG 451s, and Shure SM57s. The amps were mic'd with an SM57 on the speaker, a U67 slightly back, and one or two overhead mics to capture the room ambience.

For the acoustic parts, I would use the 1972 Martin D-35 I've owned since my school days and still very much in use today. (This D-35 and a 1975 Martin D-28 were prominently featured recently on the musical score for the Scott Hicks film, *The Boys Are Back*).

As far as I can remember, the acoustic was mic'd with an AKG 451 pointing towards the 12th fret, and a Neuman U-67 pointing between the bridge and the sound hole, with both mics positioned a foot or two away from the guitar.

Air Montserrat had a gorgeous sounding Neve 8078 console, custom ordered and specifically built for Sir George Martin, who was around at the time of recording *BIA*, visiting the studio.

The music was recorded on a Sony 3324 Digital 24 track recorder, which the band had purchased specifically for the project. Additional recordings and mixing took place at The Power Station in New York. The building was originally a Consolidated Edison power plant, then a sound studio where the television game show *Let's Make A Deal* was filmed, and by the early '80s became the Mecca of recording studios.

Since the Dire Straits days you have been a very successful and active film composer. Can you tell us how the guitar is incorporated into your scores?

When used against moving images, the guitar is a unique and powerfully evocative voice with a direct emotional connection, which is honest in an un-manipulative way.

When appropriate, I strive for the guitar to drive the musical piece, utilizing more traditional orchestral instrumentation to support underneath the guitar, giving weight and scale to the music that feature films require.

I tend to lean more towards the acoustic aspects of the guitar scoring, incorporating four- and eight-string ukuleles, dobro, mandolin, charango, three-quarter size acoustics, classical nylon and twelve-string guitars into the mix.

What is your typical recording set-up and how do you go about recording your guitar tones today in our digital world?

My acoustic guitar of choice for film scores is a 1975 Martin D-28 with its fat, baseball-type of neck and sustain that is somewhat reminiscent of a grand piano.

An old Gefell UM-70 microphone is positioned between the bridge and soundhole about a foot or two away from the Martin. The mic goes to a vintage Neve 1272 mic pre, then through to an Apogee Rosetta 800 converter running at 48k/24 bit.

While screening the film on a 55" LED monitor, I record a number of performances, usually without a click. I look for the performance that helps the image just pop off the screen, which surprisingly, may be the performance with a few imperfections in it, like loose timing, uneven velocities, or a razzing note. There is something about an imperfect performance that can sometimes bring out the vulnerability and character of a film scene.

As a film composer, the one rule I've learned over the years is that there are no rules to film scoring. Each film has its own particular quirks attached to it, and if the composer can remain open enough, then the film image will create the music for him.

Do you have a favorite can't-live-without guitar processor/effects that you used on your scores?

Good question. The mantra is big, clean, and warm, which the Gefell UM-70 and the Neve 1272 certainly help to achieve, but that's not to say that another combination of mics and mic pres won't yield an unexpected, but equally desirable result.

In my case, it's probably more about the tools that are needed to help inspire and create a film score than the actual make and manufacture of the individual item. Apart from the mic and mic pre, things like capos, slides, soft, hard, felt and finger picks, bows, hammers, and a variety of acoustic instruments are essential items.

What projects are you working on currently?

I'm currently working on some pre-records and musical arrangements for the Warner Brothers film, *The Lucky One*, starring Zac Efron and directed by Scott Hicks.

I'm also putting the finishing touches onto an acoustic guitar CD for EMI called, *Guitar Heart*.

Anything you'd like to add, any guitar recording tips or advice?

Shake it up, get inspired, be adventurous and most importantly, enjoy yourself. After all, it's only rock 'n' roll . . .

♫

BRIAN TARQUIN LAUNCHES TVFILMTRAX.COM, RELOCATES JUNGLE ROOM STUDIOS

By Matt Gallagher (Courtesy of *Mix* magazine)

Emmy Award–winning guitarist, composer and producer Brian Tarquin parlayed more than 20 years of experience in producing original music for libraries such as FirstCom, Megatrax, Sonoton, One Music, Killer Tracks and 5th Floor Music (ABC-TV) into creating TVFilmTrax.com, his new online production music library offering downloadable tracks to media professionals for licensing. The TV Film Trax catalog encompasses a variety of contemporary genres, plus Tarquin's Classic Rock series of cover tunes (including Led Zeppelin, ZZ Top and Eric Clapton) and Guitar Masters series featuring the likes of Jeff Beck, Allan Holdsworth, Steve Morse, Joe Satriani, Steve Vai and more.

Tarquin designed the TVFilmTrax.com service for music supervisors, editors, producers and directors who often need new production music immediately. It uses the Soundminer audio search engine to facilitate quick, efficient searches that accommodate a broad range of terms, such as BPM, genre, style, instrument, sound type, key and composer.

"What's wonderful about broadcasters is that they're constantly looking for new music because they always have new productions," Tarquin says. "I thought the whole scenario of an iTunes for the TV/film industry would work out quite well."

In addition to launching TVFilmTrax, Tarquin also spent 2011 relocating his Jungle Room Studios from Nyack, NY, to a 200-year-old farmhouse about 100 miles northwest of New York City. "I grew up in this house," Tarquin says. "My parents sold it a decade ago and we just bought it back from the person they sold it to." Tarquin has owned and operated Jungle Room Studios as his private facility for more than 20 years—first in Los Angeles, followed by Nyack, and now in The Catskills—where he has produced music for a long list of major television shows (*All My Children, Bones, CSI Miami, CSI New York* and *NUMB3RS,* to name just a few), most recently *Extra* and *TMZ.* He also produces his albums as well as for artists such as guitarists Zakk Wylde, Billy Sheehan and Jeff Beck.

Mix recently caught up with Tarquin to ask him about his latest endeavors.

When did you launch TVFilmTrax?
I launched it in the last quarter of this year [2011]. We've been putting together all of the data and everything. It requires a lot of publishing information and metadata, so I have to get all that together before I can launch it because it has to be registered with ASCAP, BMI and SESAC.

You've gone from being an independent composer to owning a company through which you can sell and distribute all of your products. Right. And through all those years, I made a lot of contacts, I know a lot of the music supervisors, so it helps. And it helps to have worked for a lot of these music libraries, too, because you understand it and you know how it works, and to know the [performance rights] societies and how it works, and obviously the people who run the music supervision and music editing.

What inspired you to develop and launch your own production music service?
I've written for so many different libraries, and I always realized what a great [service] a library can deliver to TV and film, and through technology it's gotten to be a lot easier because, quite simply, everything is downloadable now. With TV and film, especially TV, they need [music] so quickly and

immediately that being able to log into a portal that they can search quickly and take what specific tracks they need and download [them] immediately is better than mailing any CD overnight.

I thought, 'Well, this is a great [time] to come out with a library that would be just downloadable.' It could be [searched by] typing in a style of music, like "hard rock" or putting in a description of music like "adventurous" or "comedy" or even "greed." The software is so flexible that immediately it will pop up so many different songs. And you're not dealing with a large library where you would have tens of thousands of CDs to go through. What producer has the time to go through 15 CDs with 99 tracks on them each? In a matter of minutes, they can find what they need, download it and off they go.

A lot of the larger companies will have CDs that go back into the '70s, which probably a lot of people are not using; for TV, they want to be on the cutting edge of what's new and hip, and what's just been released. Many people are just looking for the newest thing, so for them an old catalog probably becomes a moot point. I think if somebody's looking out for a real Honduras heritage song, they'll obviously go to Sonoton or something like that, but we can supply a lot of the contemporary tracks.

We have a classic rock series, too. A lot of times, a production company won't have enough money to get a Led Zeppelin song because Atlantic is going to want so much for the masters. In this case, we own the masters so that particular scenario would [involve] a special license. We have everything from chill and the Asphalt Jungle [electronic music tracks] to basic blues, jazz, acid-jazz, to drama and comedy, and things like that.

Did you feel that now is a good time to launch your own library?
I think for me it was a good time because I wound up having this huge catalog of thousands of songs that I have done through the various styles through all these years. And then through having the [BHP Music] label, we have gotten so many submissions with product and so forth that it seemed like it would probably be a good time to be able to launch something like this, because when you think about it, even just five years ago, you would have to press all these CDs and that gets costly. I thought I'd wait until the time is right where we can launch something online. I was able to get everything together this year to be able to launch it.

I'd like to ask you about moving Jungle Room Studios. How did that come about?

My parents had a house up in The Catskills in New York. It was like a weekend getaway house that we had for 35 years, because I grew up in the city and we came up here on the weekends and summers. It was a 36-acre farm and a 200-year-old house. It was fun. [When I was] a kid, we'd always come up here and actually we had band practices here. So I was able to get it back from the woman who bought it from my mom when my dad died about 10 years ago. We just got it, and I thought, 'Wow, this would be great for a studio space.'

So I came back here earlier in the year and basically set up the studio and started around that same time with working on tracks for the library and also for the album I'm currently doing, *Guitar Masters Vol. 5.*

There was a large area of one side of the house that's kind of like a sun porch, and I put the control room in there. I have another room with a glass in between the rooms where I made the live room.

It's a pretty big house. There are 16 rooms altogether. They're not huge rooms because back then it was a farmhouse, so they made the rooms a little smaller. But still, it's enough space for the kids and everybody to wander around, and we've got a lot of acres so they can run around and tackle each other [laughs], so it's cool.

Did you face any special challenges?

The one room with the control room, they probably put that in in the '40s or the '50s, so that's not quite as old. The other part of the house, the living section, is much older. It actually all worked itself out pretty easily; I didn't have to do too much other than the glass and address some reflection [issues]. But all in all, it's a great workspace. It's nice because you have these huge windows in here. You're so accustomed to working in the dark in studios. [Laughs] So during the day when the light's out, it's nice to have a little light instead of being a studio rat locked up in the dungeon. I had to get the electrical done and get everything isolated. That's always the first thing I do with a studio. It's clean electricity; I can turn it way up and there's nothing in there, no hiss at all, so everything's isolated pretty well.

So you have a control room and a live room, and an amp room?

It's an isolation booth that I built. I put all the amps in there. I have a Marshall cabinet in there and a few legacy cabinets, and some Fenders and things. I have an amp switcher in the control room so I can have eight amps that go to any eight cabinets or speaker enclosures. It's so convenient in that you don't have to get out and rewire things, because you lose that momentum of creativity when you mess around with all of that. I can just choose whatever amp I need for a session and just be able to lift two switches and go wherever I need to go. I try to keep all the amps together so I can listen to what I have.

I've got a Trident 70 Series mixer; it's a 32-input with a TT patchbay and everything. For records and the *Guitar Masters* series, I always record everything on 2-inch. I have an Ampex MM 1200, a 2-inch/24-track. I record everything on there; I'll do all the basic tracks, like drums, guitars. I'll try to leave it in that [analog] format, and if I get a track from another guitarist, I'll fly it in and that's when I'll dump it down to Logic or Pro Tools. From there, I'll mix to half-inch.

I write for *Extra* and *TMZ,* and I'm actually in the middle of doing a session for them, a bunch of rock cues. I'll do everything in Pro Tools, and then once I get everything approved, I'll do all the final mixes down to quarter-inch and I'll back it up on disk. I'll put that down and it makes that much more of a [sonic] difference: There's a fatter 3-D kind of tape sound. So I even do that with the cues; I'll just punch that down to quarter-inch and then I'll put that on their FTP site.

So you strongly prefer an analog sound.

Yeah. It even makes a big difference if you're just doing Pro Tools with Logic and you're going through an analog desk, as opposed to just mixing all in the box.

With Pro Tools it depends. If I do some album tracks and I'm going to track them all on analog and bounce them down to Pro Tools, I'll probably just clean [them] up, and the only thing I'd really be doing is flying in a track that somebody sent me. So if Zakk Wylde sends me a track, I could fly it in that way. Other than that, I'll try to leave everything on. If they come to the studio, then I'll just mix it right down from 2-inch to half-inch. But sometimes it's nice to track it all, as much as you can, onto 2-inch, bring it into digital format and be able to clean it up, and then you can mix them there. So it's kind of the best of both worlds. With a lot of the TV stuff, I'll just do it in Pro Tools because I know that there will be changes. I find that with TV cues, it's best to stay in the digital domain because I can have endless tracks, and I can also edit anything I need to.

How are things going with *Guitar Masters Vol. 5?* Is that in progress? Yeah. We're in progress right now. We have a Joe Satriani track scheduled on that one. We have Hal Lindes from Dire Straits, Gary Hoey, Billy Sheehan, Zakk Wylde. So we're going to have some fun tracks on this album. I'm recording all the basic tracks here and then I have them come here or I send them a rough mix of the song and they'll put their parts down, and they send it back to me and we'll fly it in. Like I was saying, we'll take it off the 2-inch, all the tracks, and put them into Logic and then I'll fly in their parts.

That's a similar process to the previous album we talked about, the **Les Paul tribute (Guitar Masters, Vol. 4).** Yeah. Some of them are out on tour and can't come here. Then the guys that come here, they can lay down the tracks themselves, like Randy Kovins, Leslie West. And I think Hal Lindes might be here, and Andy Timmons. It will be a fun project. It'll be released at the beginning of the year, in the first quarter. We're just cutting the tracks now.

INTERVIEW WITH STANLEY CLARKE—COMPOSER/BASS LEGEND

Stanley Clarke was referred to as a legend by the age of twenty-five years old. He is also a noted music composer, orchestrator, conductor and performer for such films as *Boyz n the Hood, What's Love Got to Do with It, Passenger 57*, and *Poetic Justice*, to name a few. He has been quoted as saying, "Film has given me the opportunity to compose large orchestral scores and to compose music not normally associated with myself." Sony has even released a CD entitled *Stanley Clarke at the Movies*, which showcases his true diversity as a musician.

In the 1970s he redefined and reshaped the way bass players approached their instruments. He took Larry Graham's (Sly and the Family Stone) slap-funk technique and pushed it to the next level. He's one of the renowned members of the progressive jazz-fusion band, Return to Forever, with Chick Corea. He is also the inventor of the piccolo bass and tenor bass. I had the pleasure of speaking with Stanley and asking him about the Larry Graham song, "Hair," which he covered with Joe Satriani on the *Guitar Masters, Vol. 1* compilation.

He shared the story of how he stumbled upon that particular song.

"I think it was before they even recorded it. I was standing in a club in San Francisco with Carlos Santana. Carlos had on this trench coat with all these tape recorders underneath his coat – he's a real fan of music and loved to make recordings of live shows. He said, 'Man, you have to check out Graham Central Station.' It was in this little club. I knew Larry with

Sly and thought he was an amazing bass player. When I heard 'Hair,' I said 'Oh, Shit!'"

So as homage to Larry, he recorded the song with Joe Satriani.

Stanley has a home studio where he does most of his solo projects for albums and film and television scoring. For the recording of "Hair," Stanley told me that he used his famous Alembic basses and F2 preamps. He recorded using two SWR amps and cabinets. One cabinet had 2" x 15" speakers and the other cabinet housed 4" x 10" speakers. He then mic'd each cabinet separately and took a direct signal out of the amps themselves. This gave him the flexibility to blend during mixdown.

Stanley recorded using the Fairlight hard disc recorder, which at the time was similar to ProTools. Interestingly enough, he used an analog mixer to monitor and EQ the signal. During mixdown, his engineers still liked having something physical to work with and used the analog board. When mixing on digital hardware, such as ProTools, many old school engineers like the feel of actual faders underneath their fingers to control the mix and utilize the onboard EQs. I have a vintage Trident 32 x 16 console and the EQs are so musical I want to be able to physically turn the frequency knobs to affect the tracks. It also allows me to bus certain tracks and use vintage outboard effects processors, like the Eventide H3000 and the Lexicon PCM70.

As far as outboard gear, Stanley told me he is a fan of the Fairchild limiter, which he used on his first four solo albums. But with the new technology of today, there is a current Fairchild plug-in that Stanley feels gets 95 percent of the sound of the original hardware. He explained that because of the Alembic's wide dynamic range, you need a really nice limiter to control the sound when recording. This also affects Stanley's choice of mics; when choosing a mic, he considers not only the source, but the room ambience too. For instance, when he wants a really big bass sound, he uses an outside studio. In the past, he's used studios that housed separate rooms for each instrument, and he really likes the feel and sound of each instrument being physically separated.

With his new release, *The Toys of Men*, he discussed the present state, or rather the lack of instrumental music on the radio, saying, "The airplay thing is really tough—there is really nothing out there. I do have some faith in satellite radio. They have so many more possibilities and programs. All of my friends who have XM are musicians and are into the technology.

As for the average guy, satellite radio just needs to figure out how to reach them and build up their listenership. Not until cars come with satellite-ready radio will it catch on."

It was a rare pleasure getting tips from the man who revolutionized the sound of the bass. I can only look forward to what lies ahead for this ever-evolving artist.

OUTTAKE
Tony Verderosa (Courtesy of *Music Connection* magazine)
http://musicconnection.com

President, KBV Music

E-mail: info@kbvrecords.net
Web: http://kbvmusic.com
Most Recent: *Beware the Gonzo*

It is easy for an artist to get lost in the shuffle of a music library, KBV Music President Tony Verderosa points out. Like being signed to a major label, an artist or song can easily become overlooked when the model calls for holding a vast selection just in case something there fits a particular project.

Verderosa set up KBV Music, a hybrid company established to produce, provide and release soundtracks and scores for the TV and film industry, and the newly launched KBV Records as a distinct philosophy change. "We've gone back to basics," Verderosa explains. "We're not interested in having 50 million pieces of music. KBV is client and artist focused."

The company's philosophy leads to Verderosa and the team he leads being very selective in which artists find a home at KBV. "I have good sense of whether a song will stand the test of time," says the hands-on executive. "If someone is playing in front of me, I have a good sense of whether there's something there. We have to be really careful about quality."

As someone who has worked as a musician with such big names as Katy Perry, Joe Perry, and Dream Theater, Verderosa feels he has developed a solid commercial ear. Though KBV puts most of its emphasis on the still-growing world of film and TV, Verderosa notes that finding a song for placement isn't all that different from recognizing a good pop hit. "For the types of productions we work, there's no difference," he says. "We're very adept at editing a 4-minute hit down to a 30-second hit."

Despite their success with multimedia placements, KBV Records is first and foremost a label. As Verderosa says proudly, "We're moving our emphasis back to the studio where I can work with the musicians I love."

OUTTAKE
Michelle Crispin (Courtesy of *Music Connection* magazine)

http://musicconnection.com

Sr. Creative Director, Film & TV

E-mail: michelle@mightygen.com
Web: http://mightygen.com
Most Recent: Katie Costello

"Music supervisors are the new A&R," says Michelle Crispin, Sr. Creative Director, Film & TV at Mighty Generation Music, a full-service music licensing and publishing company specializing in the placement of artist's songs in all media. As with label A&R, those in film & TV take just anything that comes across their desks.

No one knows this better than Crispin who brings to Mighty Generation a wealth of experience in the music business. The original lead singer for Fem 2 Fem, as a solo artist Crispin subsequently worked with the development team behind Christina Aguilera. Like every career artist, she eventually felt that she needed to know the administrative side of the music business. That led to the music major's work with Mighty Generation Music, a job Crispin describes as "So much fun."

Crispin has learned what every musician should know. "Format can hurt a song's chances for placement if the hook is not immediate," she says. Songs need to have short intros, and long fade outs are no help to a good song either.

"Certain songs are easier to place than others," she confirms. "The sky is the limit for source music. For that, the music needs ambiguous language. Still, the hook has to come in quickly."

Certain artists are easier to work with as well. "Some will do whatever is necessary to get a placement," Crispin says. "Others are totally offended by it."

While Crispin's desk at Mighty Generation is already overloaded with music, that doesn't mean she's not open to submissions. However, she is just as strict about format as are the productions she services. All submissions need to be able to stream. She warns new artists, "If I have to download, I won't."

CONCLUSION

This chapter reveals the music composer in true light. The cardinal rule for a composer is to do the right thing for the scene, whether it's playing bagpipes or viola. Also the chapter highlights working with the music supervisor closely and building a trustworthy relationship. Keeping open communications and high production values is the best way to be first on call for shows.

Chapter 10

Industry Insiders

The best advice is always from the people who work in the field. They will give you the shakedown on what to expect and how to brace yourself for unexpected situations. I remember going to audio engineering school in the late '80s, and they would give lectures about the signal flow and all of this audio theory, but what good is it if you don't put your hands on the equipment and really use it practically? It wasn't until I had my own studio, working in it everyday, that I truly understood how the audio signal flowed. So read on and gather some important information from these interviews, but also go out there practice the advice given.

INTERVIEW WITH AARON DAVIS—MUSICBOX/OLE MUSIC PUBLISHING
http://olemusicbox.com

Aaron Davis, VP of Music Licensing for MusicBox was in the right place at the right time when he moved to Los Angeles in 1996 as a cocky guitarist/vocalist with dreams of making it big as a songwriter/performer. Davis went on to build a top-notch sales team at MusicBox, where the focus is on customer service through quality creative. "It's not just lip service," he stresses. "We inject some creative input into nearly every project we take on. Andrew Robbins and Alex Gershwin were both born into the music business, and are musicians as am I. We don't have any widget sales guys here. We're all in it because we love music and film and the marriage of the two." Another area where Davis has been instrumental in guiding MusicBox has been expansion into representing outside catalogs, and the intelligent use of in-house production resources. "Our competitors were growing through amalgamation and I could see that if we were going to survive we had to start representing other boutique catalogs, and producing the music styles we were hearing on the charts. If you're not big enough, you can't be heard. Today we're close to thirty libraries and 50,000 tracks, and it's absolutely fantastic to have Ole [Music Publishing] on our side. They are continually expanding our repertoire, hunting down fresh, unique catalogs that matter to our clients, and financing original production so we can sound just like what's happening on the Billboard charts."

♫

From your experience working at music production libraries can you describe (to people who are not familiar with them) the importance of such libraries and how they fulfill the need in the industry?

Production music is an often-misunderstood strata of the music for media business. Thirty or forty years ago, "canned music" as it was called then (definitely a negative connotation), was notoriously poor quality, and used mostly "when necessary due to budget constraints." However in the last thirty or so years, the quality has risen considerably as recording technology has become more and more affordable to the common musician, and production music users find there is safety and value in being able to hear the track you're buying, before you buy it, which is impossible when hiring a composer. Furthermore, [using] production music is typically less expensive than hiring a composer, but the trade off is that the purchasing client/music user does not get to retain ownership of the publishing or copyright. Provided you can negotiate all required media clearances necessary at the onset of the project, production music is a great value and very convenient,

Working in sales, what types of shows and films tend to use libraries, and have you seen an increase in usage from the industry through the past years?

Literally anything can use production music. Having been in the music-for-media biz for about half my life, I can say that there is no content type that production music can't compliment—might be broadcast network primetime dramatic series; could be a PBS documentary; a movie trailer. You really never know. More generally, high-volume users of production music are reality, doc, and factual programming producers, ad agencies, on-air promo departments at cable and broadcast networks, and productions where owning all content in the show isn't an absolute must. The budget for a show often dictates this decision, which is why you see a ten-to-one disparity in the use of production music when comparing cable TV series with broadcast net series.

One of the most important things I think budding musicians want to know is how to get placement. What is the best way for composers/songwriters to get their music into productions?

Well, I can tell you that giving it away for free isn't the answer, and I am not kidding. The more often music is given away; the less all music is worth, in the collective consciousness. There's no magic to it really. You need to do your research. Know who you're calling, know what show they are working on, know about the musical needs of that show, and present your material concisely (don't ramble), and make sure you say something that shows your music is being sent with a creative idea already in mind. For example, "Hey Mr. Music Supervisor, I'm noticing a ton of country crossover talent being used in ABC's Nashville, so I wanted to present my artist, Lindi Ortega, and her new single, 'Cigarettes and Truckstops' for your consideration. Attached is an MP3. Please let me know if you'd like the .WAV file. She is also available for on-screen performances/features in support of the release of her new record. If you'd like to learn more about her, here's a link: http://lindiortega.ca/."

Aside from a strong, to-the-point, and creatively intelligent pitch, the other avenue is relationships. Move to Hollywood, and immerse yourself in the culture of music for media, and if you can't do that, get in on every blog, and music-for-media related website you can and participate in the discussions regularly. There are mixers, organizations, parties, websites, seminars, etc., all geared towards making connections between artists and the business at large. Show up often, be friendly, and things will start happening for you too!

What are some critical things your clients look for in compositions/songs for their particular productions?

For promo, the editors want lots of flourishes, audio "events," hits, and building sections around which they can edit video. Same goes for trailers, they just want it all bigger. For TV, being playable beneath dialog and not getting in the way of it is most important. For commercials, they are often looking for evolving tracks that have a Question/Answer, or "call-to-action" moment, but these are all generalizations and ultimately it comes down to the unique needs of that piece of content.

Finally what advice can you give people who want to become involved in composing for music libraries? How can they get the edge over all of the other composers out there?

Be patient, but consistent. I don't mind receiving your email every couple of months, so long as you're not upset that I don't respond. It's never personal, and I don't mean to avoid you or your correspondence, but composers need to be understanding that people in my position, much like the music supervisors themselves, are bombarded all day long with folks trying to get their foot in the door. Another tip is to deliver polish in everything you do. Don't send me links to your MySpace page. I don't know what tracks you want me to hear, and which you don't, so I'm not going to go exploring on my own. Spoon feed the right material to me, and explain what you believe it's useful for. Example, "Hey Aaron, I saw your credits on Pawn Stars, so I'm sending you these twenty bluegrass tracks because it seems like you could never have enough of them."

TUNESAT
By Albert Vega (Courtesy of *Music Connection* magazine)
http://musicconnection.com

"Tracking down when and where your music is being used, and getting paid for those uses, is a full-time job in itself. TuneSat is there to support the music community by making this task easier through near real-time detection data, providing the where and when automatically." —Chris Woods

Launched in 2009 by co-founders, CEO Scott Schreer and COO Chris Woods, TuneSat is an audio monitoring service designed to detect uses of musical works across the television and Internet spectrum. In its few years of existence, the company has lined up clients as notable as Universal Music Publishing Group and Sony Entertainment because of its ability to locate and track unauthorized performances, which in turn, can lead to the collection of unpaid royalties.

And it isn't only major publishers enlisting the assistance of the New York-based company. TuneSat's client list runs the gamut, from independent recording artists and legacy acts to record labels, attorneys, and managers. As Woods puts it, "[Our client list] is anybody with an interest in the revenue stream of a master recording." Traditionally, the duty of tracking musical performances on television and online, in order to collect rights royalties, is the job of Performance Rights Organizations, such as ASCAP and BMI. PROs detect a musical use and then go about collecting royalties on behalf of the songwriters and publishers they represent. The problem, as Woods sees it, is in the process used to track performances. "The issue that everybody knows about," says Woods, "is that PROs use a manual process. It's literally pen and paper, and this causes a lot of inaccuracies in what's reported to those societies and rather large discrepancies in the royalty distributions."

TuneSat's solution to this is a development known as "audio fingerprinting," whereby TuneSat's technology analyzes the distinct characteristics of a music file and scours broadcast television content and Internet files looking for a match. It also has the capability of detecting musical matches if the content is buried underneath other audio such as crowd noise, sound effects or even other music (such as a sample).

Schreer introduced Woods to fingerprinting technology, shortly after becoming a songwriting team in the early 2000s. In the interest of testing the technology and confirming what they suspected were royalty discrepancies; Schreer and Woods conducted case studies with their catalog as publishers and writers over a two-and-a-half year period. After comparing their data to the royalty statements they received, Woods concluded, "We found that as much as 80 percent of music on television goes unreported. We always knew it was quite large, but we didn't know it was that big." And as Woods points out, television has only gotten bigger since then and the data did not even include Internet uses.

Currently, TuneSat is monitoring television in 13 European countries (in addition to the US) and launched its Internet monitoring service earlier this year. "Our area of expertise is music on television performances, but we've learned a lot over the past decade about performances outside of TV. Basically, what we're doing is crawling the Internet looking for multimedia files embedded, or made available, on websites. We're not listening to streams, such as something on Pandora, but actual files." Examples of what TuneSat detects are instances such as a blogger posting a client's music, or a video or podcast using a client's music. Not only does TuneSat report the use, but it also provides a date of when the work was used, the duration of the performance, the URL where the link was found and the content URL where the content actually exists. "We also let our clients know where the use can be found within the file. So think of a podcast that could be an hour long. We tell our clients exactly where in the podcast the use is located."

And while Woods emphasizes that TuneSat is not a collection agency, it has also launched an Administrative Services Department designed to help music rights holders take further action should they decide to. "Administrative services will be a big help to those who don't have the time or the resources to maximize their revenue stream with the TuneSat data." Woods adds, "Tracking down when and where your music is being used, and getting paid for those uses, is a full-time job in itself. TuneSat is there to support the music community by making this task easier through near real-time detection data, providing the where and when automatically. Our mission is to provide a simple and transparent solution, enabling [our clients] to get the money they deserve."

As for the cost of working with TuneSat currently, the quoted rate is as little as ten dollars for ten tracks. There is a one-time setup fee, then a monthly rate depending on what countries are being monitored and the amount of tracks being monitored. Clients with less than 10,000 tracks can subscribe and upload files online, while clients with larger catalogs can contact TuneSat directly for account setup.

For those interested, go to www.tunesat.com and be sure to read its thorough FAQs page.

THE NEW PARAMETERS OF FILM & TV
by Dan Kimpel (Courtesy of *Music Connection* magazine)
http://musicconnection.com

Can you visualize your music in a film or on a television show? For an independent artist, a new band or a rising songwriter, contributing music to a show is entrée to new audiences and industry credibility, and in a universe of evaporating record sales, a lucrative pursuit in its own right. Indeed, many working musicians attest that they can potentially earn more from one strategic placement than they might realize after months of grinding gigs.

That said, there are parameters governing what makes music work for a show—and what does not. For independent and feature films, these demands are even more specific and exacting because the musical choices made by a music supervisor must mirror the plot and the characters, and also match the director's vision.

While the playing field has become increasingly level in terms of affordable digital technology and Internet outreach, the competition has become much greater for placements. Now, music can be pitched from anywhere in the world. Music publishers, record labels and companies who can anticipate the trends and maneuver accordingly have the inside track. In this exclusive feature, *MC* speaks with a cross section of industry sources about what the film and television industries know about using music that those who create it often do not.

Lyrical Litanies

"A good lyric for film and TV is universal enough to allow the song to be used in a variety of scenes while still maintaining integrity, originality and focus," writes author and songwriter **Robin Frederick** in her indispensable book, ***Shortcuts to Songwriting for Film & TV***. "Of course, no song will work for every scene, but some themes and situations occur more frequently than others—falling in love, breaking up or overcoming adversity, for example. If you choose one of these, you're more likely to be successful. Imagery, emotional detail and a fresh approach to your theme will all add muscle to a universal lyric, making it more appealing to film and TV. On the other hand, too many specific physical details, like place names, proper names and dates, will limit the uses."

Frederick also advises that while music supervisors often seek out tracks that sound like the current charts, all genres of music are welcome. "Songs are very effective at evoking a time period or location. From delta blues to big band jazz to Seattle grunge, films and TV shows use them all. And yes, a flashback to Studio 54 will require a really hot disco track to set the scene. If you've got it, they need it."

David Scheffler, whose company **Drama King** works with a variety of shows and productions for Fox, ABC, CNN, Discovery Channel, Animal Planet, Hallmark and Court TV, adds a musical counterpoint to this information. "Harmonic simplicity is very important; no linear melodies unless it's a theme or there's no dialogue; don't even think about noodling or soloing; it's all about supporting the visual with a vibe, feeling and emotion. Less is more." But, he adds, "You can break every rule I just laid out, depending on the individual situation."

Empathic Envoys

Mason Cooper founded **Songrunner Entertainment, LLC**, a music supervision and music rights firm that serves as the independent music department and music solutions specialist for film producers and directors. Songrunner client network includes production companies Ten/Four Pictures, Mythic Films, Vitamin A Films, Sunset Pictures and other projects. Cooper has worked on television shows that have aired on Showtime, MTV Networks, and features for Sony and MGM.

A music supervisor and soundtrack consultant, Cooper is adamant that he is not in the music business, but the film business. "Just like someone who is pitching to me has to answer to someone internally—a boss, a department head—I answer to a director or producer. Most often, what goes into a decision isn't just, 'I like your song.' We're not here to find the best song or the most gorgeous melody. We are here to find what fits the scene and the film as a whole: action, emotional storyline and personality."

Cooper advises that someone pitching to a film would do well to consider the film's overall dramatic arc, and to use their resources to find out what scenes, settings and emotions will be revealed within the drama. "Read between the lines and the subtext. For example, if a film is about two race car drivers who grew up in competition and one of them wins in the end, we don't need songs about that. The rest of the movie is the dinner party, the night club, picking up girls, a flash back—30 out of 33 scenes will not be racing scenes."

"Source" refers to a song used in the background, i.e. a party, dinner or club scene, or maybe playing on the radio, and this is often where an independent song will find a home. "Is that piece of music in there going to make more people buy tickets to the theater?" asks Cooper. "No. Will it sell more DVD's? No. Someone already bought the ticket, or the DVD. Now it has to work creatively for the scene. Famous songs are more expensive, so why spend money on a song that isn't economically helping the film? Also, if a famous song is playing, it date-stamps the film, and it also might pull the viewer's attention away. I prefer to use unknown songs in source uses; they can become part of the atmosphere. The lyrics should be general."

Refrain from saying a song is perfect if you haven't seen the film, and remember that timing is of the essence. "Don't pitch songs to a busy music supervisor that are not targeted to his or her exact needs," Cooper cautions. "Ask permission."

Heavy Hitter Head Cindy Badell-Slaughter

A quick perusal of **Heavy Hitters'** comprehensive website reveals musical styles from rock to reggae, sensitive songwriters to "stripper rock," and virtually every style in between. **Cindy Badell-Slaughter**, who heads up the company along with husband and co-owner **Bill Slaughter**, was Director of Music Operations for CBS Broadcasting Inc. for ten years. Prior to that, she worked as Director of Music Clearance for EMG Inc., Warner Bros. Television and Lorimar Productions. Over the years, Cindy handled music administration and/or music clearance for soundtrack albums, movies and mini-series, countless highly rated television shows such as *CSI, CSI NY* and *CSI Miami*, plus on-air promotion for three networks, FOX, CBS and UPN.

"One of the fundamental things I learned was that what you hear performed live, what you enjoy in your car or at home, and what moves picture are three different things," says Badell-Slaughter. "When you hear a CD from your favorite indie band, out of 12 songs there might be two songs that work to picture. Each song has to have a great intro; the music has to have movement in it because scenes are not static. There needs to be a building and ebbing of intensity, and it has to transition. Film and TV requires the music to have a hook, a message or the drive to move someone else's picture."

"What you hear performed live, what you enjoy in your car or at home, and what moves picture are three different things."

—Cindy Badell-Slaughter • Heavy Hitters Music

Multiple versions, vocal and instrumental, can increase chances of usage, says Badell-Slaughter. She also references what she calls "vocal down" versions; with the lead vocal mixed slightly lower in the track so as to not interfere with on-screen dialogue. And the song has to be intriguing from the onset. She references the crucial first on screen seconds of a crime drama like *NCSI*. "There's so much movement in the opening song: attitude, sass, badness, joy. The music is establishing the mood in five to 10 seconds."

Her body's responses to the rhythms of music often are often the most accurate barometer of the music's applicability for a scene, she says. "When you listen to a song and your body moves to the beat, it has entered your chemistry. If you're just sitting there, you are not going to listen to it again. Someone gave me a song I thought was bland, with repetitive lyrics. But I was bobbing. It was 130 beats per minute. I played it to a scene where models were walking down a runway, and it totally changed the whole thing. Music supervisors can hear in the first seconds."

When Heavy Hitters Music was founded in the '90s by Barbara Jordan, who subsequently sold the catalog to its current owners, there were far fewer companies representing independent artists. Back then, it was a business of physical compilation CDs delivered by mail to music supervisors. Today, with immediate online access to quality song files, Badall-Slaughter notes that the process is much less time-intensive, but much more competitive.

"It's international: there are no borders. Everyone has to pull out his or her best game. Back in the '90s, I was so happy when I would get demos, and a CD would say 'female rock,' that the quality didn't matter. Now, with high definition, the quality of everything has to be really well mastered. And there's so much to choose from. There might be 20–30 other songs waiting to fill that one spot."

Placements: Do's And Don'ts

For independent artists and songwriters aspiring to network place-ments, **David Quan, Director, Music Services, NBC/Universal,** offers these quick tips:

- "I don't care how great your song is; if it doesn't fit the show it's not going in. Maybe you think your song is the best ever; we're not going to write a show around your song."
- Doing research, essential. "I work on weekly series with 22 episodes per season: you should at least watch one. There's no excuse for not doing your homework."
- Realize the dramatic needs of the show, and how a song might work. "The music must play a character; you need to know which one."
- Wild pitches are highly ineffective and off-putting. "For example, if the show is high action intensity, don't send me some melancholy female singer-songwriter."

What Is The Hype About

In a recent Industry Profile in *MC*, **Extreme Music's Russell Emanuel** dis-cussed Extreme's immense roster of talent, a list that includes composers and artists like Quincy Jones, Timbaland, Snoop Dogg and Hans Zimmer.

While Extreme, the production music library arm of Sony/ATV Music Publishing, deals mainly with major hitmakers, another Emanuel-run com-pany, **Hype Music,** operating in conjunction with MTV, creates opportuni-ties for emerging artists and bands with placements, including shows created by the network. "A remarkable talent-incubating, hybrid, music licensing company fueled by some of the world's hottest, emerging, independent art-ists," touts the company's website.

Among the Hype artists is Wallpaper, whose "#STUPiDFACEDD" was heard over the end credits on the recent MTV Video Music Awards. Wallpaper's next capitalized single, "F*CKING BEST SONG EVERRR," aired immediately following a new episode of MTV's *Jersey Shore* and was again shown partially during this show's credits. An animated music video of the song, created by Christy Karacas (*Super Jail, Cartoon Sushi*), is the first content to be commissioned by MTVX for the animation showcase *Liquid Television,* and is available on liquidtelevision .com The music video will go into rotation across MTV's channels, including AMTV, AMTV2, MTV2, mtvU and MTV Hits, and be featured on MTV.com and MTV Mobile.

"Great talent is great talent," says Emanuel. "We always look for music that shines. Wallpaper has such a unique sound—he's a hall of famer in my opinion. We're in a good situation: a lot of great artists cross our desks. We're seen as the crossover music library. Also, our partnership with MTV puts us in the sights of the high-end managers. With talent like that in the room, it's a no-brainer."

> "When we select material, we talk about titles. If a song is called 'I Love Cocaine,' it's only going to be used very occasionally. The more upbeat the lyrical concept, the easier it will be to use."
> —Russell Emanuel • Hype Music, Extreme Music

While music libraries in the past relied on bland, non-descript sounds, Extreme prides itself on featuring the artistry of real music creators. "It depends on the creativity of the editor of the show," says Emanuel. "There are types of shows that still need music that blends into the background. If shows are a little more adventurous, then the more adventurous the music. Consider a show like *Jersey Shore*, where the background music isn't featured, but it becomes a part of the show."

Emmanuel agrees that specific titles are limiting. "When we select material or we're talking to an artist, we talk about titles. If a song is called 'I Love Cocaine,' it's only going to be used very occasionally. The more upbeat the lyrical concept, the easier it will be to use."

The Special K's, the Nick Tree Band, Reachback, Theft, Heavy Young Heathens: not household names yet, but Emanuel is optimistic about their futures. "With all of those Hype Music artists, what we bring is a way for them to accelerate their careers. We have 40–50 thousand music supervisors worldwide: TV shows, films, Internet and advertising campaigns. Russia is an emerging market, and always the UK, France, Italy—everywhere is active at the moment."

Emanuel says that a dedicated staff helps discover the music. "In most territories we have representatives. The job of that team is to know what's going on in the marketplace, and aggressively pitch people. Our role is to place great music in as many places as possible."

He understands that the cycles of music continue to drive the need. "Pop music and solid, atmospheric orchestral cues are generally always needed.

It's pretty obvious; it mirrors what is on the commercial charts." And don't dump that Syndrum track from the late '70s quite yet. "It probably worked then, it probably works 30 years later, and it will work again in the 2030s," says Emanuel. "But everyone wants the '80s. I have no idea why. They want the Prophet 5, the Moog sounds, the Linn Drum, particularly."

Emanuel observes that the trend-setting *Glee* can dictate musical trends. "When a show like that comes out, it breaks the mold and redefines everything. It's not unusual that pop culture follows it. It's not rocket science here—we'll all go where the money is."

Valuable resources: *Music Connection's* Annual Directory of Film/TV Music Supervisors (in this issue); the ASCAP "I Create Music" EXPO (ascap.com); The Music Business Registry *Film & Television Music Guide* (musicregistry.com) and the *Hollywood Reporter: Film & TV Music Special Issue*. Meet music supervisors at: the monthly Hunnypot events in Hollywood, CA; The Taxi Road Rally (for Taxi members only, taxi.com); and The Billboard/Hollywood Film and Television Music Conference (billboardevents.com/billboardevents/filmtv/index.jsp).

CONTACTS FOR THIS ARTICLE:

Mason Cooper: songrunner.com
Cindy Badell-Slaughter: heavyhitters.com
Robin Frederick: robinfrederick.com
David Quan: NBC/Universal, nbcuni.com
David Scheffler: dramaking.com

CONCLUSION

Hopefully you will have a better understanding of the process of music licensing through the stories and experiences I have shared in this book. It is impossible to digest all of the book's information in one sitting, but this book can serve as a reference guide when needed. Of course, the only way to fully understand the many complexities of music licensing is to dive in and experience it firsthand. In the early '90s I did exactly that, learning from my mistakes and becoming wiser with each license that I secured for each piece of my music.

There are many legal books out there like Donald Passman's *All You Need to Know About the Music Business*, which serves as a good reference for law, so I encourage you to read that, as well as consulting with a good entertainment lawyer. But at the end of the day, you will have to familiarize yourself with the procedures and the legal contracts so you will know the ins and outs of how your music is being licensed.

One important thing to remember is to become friends with people on the other side of the business, like the music supervisors, editors, directors, producers, post-production editors, and publishers, as they can help you in your quest for licensing. Another large consideration to keep in mind is avoiding free licenses, like the many MTV productions offer. Of course, it's a great way to build your resume when you are starting out, but it's very detrimental to the rest of the licensing community. You've heard the old saying, "Why pay for the cow when you can get the milk for free?" This way of getting free music lowers the standards for other entities that want to license their music. I have spoken to countless people who open "fly by night" music companies who tell me, as if they have just discovered the Ark of the Covenant, that licensing music for free will get them more airplay. That is just plain wrong, because the truth of the matter is, giving it away does not guarantee a production will use it. In fact, many people who give their music away always seem to have an inferior catalog in production and are grasping at straws to get their music used, even if it means throwing it at people for free.

It is very important to know your field! For how much money is a song being licensed? It all depends. Is it for in-show use, promo, network, cable, local, vocal, instrumental, etc.? There are many variables and you better know them all. The best thing to do is get familiar with what other companies are charging and know the needle drop rates. If this is going to be your career, then treat it as such and know all aspects of licensing. I actually had one struggling composer buy the music programs Stylus and Atmospheres for the magic cure. So he sends me these terrible compositions that have no beginning, end, or middle, and then wonders why no company has hired him as a composer. If it was that easy to become a composer, don't you think everyone would be doing it? Unfortunately there are so many novices out there clouding up the industry who think the pickings are easy for extra cash.

As Judas Priest said "You've Got Another Thing Comin"!

Appendix A

Music Library Guide:
(Courtesy of The Music Registry)

1. APM Music
6255 Sunset Blvd # 820,
Hollywood, CA 90028–7403
PHONE: (323) 461–3211
FAX: (323) 461–9102
info@apmmusic.com
www.apmmusic.com

Adam Taylor
PRESIDENT
ataylor@apmmusic.com

Sharon Jennings
VP MUSIC & MARKETING
sjennings@apmmusic.com

Steven Stern
*VP CUSTOM MUSIC
SERVICES*
sstern@apmmusic.com

Colleen Oscarson
VP OPERATIONS
coscarson@apmmusic.com

Johnnie Blankenship
VP SALES
gblankenship@apmmusic.com

Mark Gibbons
MUSIC DIRECTOR
mgibbons@apmmusic.com

Brian Brasher
*KEY ACCOUNT DIRECTOR,
TRAILERS*
bbrasher@apmmusic.com

Edwina Travis Chin
MUSIC DIRECTOR
etravischin@apmmusic.com

Giselle Vasconez
KEY ACCOUNT DIRECTOR
gvasconez@apmmusic.com

Marsha Sill
KEY ACCOUNT DIRECTOR
msill@apmmusic.com

George Maloian
MUSIC DIRECTOR
gmaloian@apmmusic.com

Georgia Robertson
MUSIC DIRECTOR
grobertson@apmmusic.com

2. Extreme Production Music
550 Madison Ave # 552

New York, NY 10022–3211
PHONE: (212) 833–4900
FAX: (212) 833–4977
info@extrememusic.com
extrememusic.com

Leslie Cribbs
SR SALES MARKETING
EXECUTIVE
leslie@extrememusic.com

Cindy Chao
DIRECTOR SALES &
MARKETING
cindy@extrememusic.com

Tyra Elder
SALES & MARKETING
EXECUTIVE
tyra@extrememusic.com

3. FirstCom Music
1325 Capital Parkway # 109
Carrollton, TX 75006–3645
PHONE: (800) 858–8880
FAX: (972) 242–6526
info@firstcom.com
firstcom.com

4. Getty Images Music/Pump Audio
75 Varick St.
New York, NY 10013–1917
(646) 613–4000
www.gettyimages.com/music

Robert E. Vasquez
MUSIC DEVELOPMENT
MANAGER

PHONE: (646) 613–3962
robert.vasquez@gettyimages.com

5. Heavy Hitters Music
440 Western Ave # 101
Glendale, CA 91201–3539
PHONE: (818) 246–1250
FAX: (818) 246–1299
heavyhittersmusic.com

Bill Slaughter
CO-OWNER
bill@heavyhittersmusic.com

Cindy Badell-Slaughter
PRESIDENT
cindy@heavyhittersmusic.com

Rich Kiersnowski
CREATIVE FILM&TV
rich@heavyhittersmusic.com

Kristin Summers
MUSIC COORDINATOR
kristin@heavyhittersmusic.com

6. Killer Tracks
9255 Sunset Blvd # 200
Los Angeles, CA 90069–3308
PHONE: (800) 454–5537
PHONE 2: (310) 865–4455
FAX: (310) 865–4470
sales@killertracks.com
www.killertracks.com

Anna Maria Hall
VP SALES
ahall@killertracks.com

Carl Peel
VP PRODUCTION
cpeel@killertracks.com

Mark Rome
SR MUSIC SUPERVISOR
mrome@killertracks.com

7. MasterSource/First Com
28030 Dorothy Dr # 201
Agoura, CA 91301–2682
PHONE: (818) 706–9000
FAX: (818): 706–1900
info@mastersource.com
mastersource.com

Marc Ferrari
PRESIDENT
marc@mastersource.com

8. MusicBox/Ole Music Publishing
9000 West Sunset Blvd., Suite 806
West Hollywood, CA 90069
PHONE: (866) 269–0900
FAX: (310) 402–0547
www.olemusicbox.com

Aaron Davis
VP MUSIC LICENSING
PHONE: (310) 402–0308
FAX: (310) 402–0547
aaron@musicboxmx.com

Andrew D. Robbins
DIR FILM/TV MUSIC
PHONE: (310) 402–0310

FAX: (310) 402–0547
robbins@musicboxmx.com

9. MusicSupervisor.com
3209 Tareco Dr.
Los Angeles, CA 90068–1525
PHONE: (310) 738–3800
FAX: (323) 878–2765
support@musicsupervisor.com
www.musicsupervisor.us

Barry Coffing
FOUNDER
barry@musicsupervisor.us

Cindi Avnet
DIRECTOR MUSIC PLACEMENT
PHONE: (818) 766–0877
FAX: (818) 506–1529
cindi@musicsupervisor.us

Julius Robinson
DIRECTOR CREATIVE OPERATIONS
PHONE: (818) 766–0877
FAX: (818) 506–1529
julius@musicsupervisor.us

Gael MacGregor
CONSULTANT/MUSIC SUPERVISOR LIAISON
PHONE: (818) 845–1197
FAX: (866) 364–2522
gael@musicsupervisor.us

10. Non-Stop Music
3400 W. Olive Ave., 4th Floor

Burbank, CA 91505–5538
PHONE: (818) 752–1898
FAX: (818) 752–1899
www.nonstopmusic.com

Tim Arnold
VP
tim@nonstopmusic.com

Sean Johnson
DIR TRAILERS
PHONE: (818) 636–0200
FAX: (818) 752–1899
sean@nonstopmusic.com

Micki Peel
DIR BROADCAST SALES
micki@nonstopmusic.com

Collin Perry
DIR FILM TRAILER MUSIC
PHONE: (717) 979–8977
collin@nonstopmusic.com

Veronica Garcia
DIRECTOR LATIN AMERICA
PHONE: (310) 487–2368
veronica@nonstopmusic.com

Kari Lasser
LOCAL TV & CABLE
PHONE: (818) 421–1406
kari@nonstopmusic.com

11. Sonoton
Schleibingerstr 10 Munich, 81669
Germany
PHONE: 49–89–4477–8211

FAX: 49–89–4477–8288
sonoton@sonoton.com
www.sonoton.com

Rotheide & Gerhard Narholz
FOUNDERS/OWNERS
narholz@sonoton.com

12. TAXI
5010 N Parkway Calabasas # 200
Calabasas, CA 91302–2556
PHONE: (800) 458–2111
FAX: (818) 888–8811
memberservices@taxi.com
www.taxi.com

Michael Laskow
PRESIDENT/CEO
PHONE: (818) 222–2464

Andrea Torchia-Alford
VP A&R
PHONE: (818) 222–2464
andrea@taxi.com

**13. TunEdge Music
Services**
16350 Ventura Blvd # 224
Encino, CA 91436–5305
PHONE: (800) 279–0014
FAX: (877) 886–3343
www.tunedge.com

Brandon D'Amore
CEO
PHONE: (818) 783–9400
FAX: (818) 784–3066
bd@tunedge.com

Rod West
CO-OWNER
PHONE: (818) 783–9400
FAX: (818) 784–3066
rw@tunedge.com

14. TV Film Trax/MusicBox
PO Box 1232
New Paltz, NY 12561
PHONE: (917) 449–8841
www.tvfilmtrax.com

Brian Tarquin
OWNER/HEAD OF
PRODUCTION
PHONE: (917) 974–0039
info@tvfilmtrax.com

15. 5ᵗʰ Floor Music/ABC
4151 Prospect Ave.
Los Angeles, CA 90027–4524
PHONE: (323) 671–5211
FAX: (323) 671–3311
www.abc.com

Sylvia A. Webster
EX DIR CREATIVE
SERVICES
ASSISTANT JENNIFER DRAKE
PHONE: (323) 671–4767
FAX: (323) 671–4557
sylvia.a.webster@abc.com

Caitlin Hill
DIRECTOR MUSIC
PHONE: (323) 671–5335
FAX: (323) 671–4557
caitlin.hill@abc.com

Appendix B

Performance Rights
Organizations
(Courtesy of The Music Registry)

1. AMRA
149 S. Barrington Ave., #810
Los Angeles, CA 90049–3310
PHONE: (310) 440–8778
FAX: (310) 440–0059
info@amermechrights.com
amermechrights.com

Sindee Levin
PRESIDENT
PHONE: (310) 440-8778
FAX: (310) 388-0762
lalaw90049@aol.com

2. ASCAP
7920 W. Sunset Blvd., 4ᵗʰ Fl.
Los Angeles, CA 90046-3355
PHONE: (323) 883-1000
FAX: (323) 883-1049
info@ascap.com
ascap.com

Shawn LeMone
VP FILM/TV VISUAL MEDIA
PHONE: (323) 883-1000
FAX: (323) 883-1047
slemone@ascap.com

Michael Todd
SR DIRECTOR FILM & TV
PHONE: (323) 883-1000
FAX: (323) 883-1047
mtodd@ascap.com

Charlyn Bernal
ASSOCIATE DIRECTOR FILM
& TV
PHONE: (323) 883-1000 x245
FAX: (323) 883-1047
cbernal@ascap.com

Jennifer Harmon
ASSOCIATE DIRECTOR FILM
& TV
ASSISTANT MAX ESPINOSA
PHONE: (323) 883-1000
FAX: (323) 883-1049
jharmon@ascap.com

Jeff Jernigan
ASSOCIATE DIRECTOR FILM
& TV
PHONE: (323) 883-1000
FAX: (323) 883-1049
jjernigan@ascap.com

Alisha Davis
ASSOC MEMBERSHIP REP /
FILM/TV

PHONE: (323) 883-1000
FAX: (323) 883-1049
adavis@ascap.com

Nancy Knutsen
CONSULTANT FILM & TV
MUSIC
PHONE: (323) 883-1000
FAX: (323) 883-1047
nknutsen@ascap.com

3. ASCAP
One Lincoln Plaza, 6ᵗʰ Fl.
New York, NY 10023-7097
PHONE: (212) 621-6000
FAX: (212) 724-9064
info@ascap.com
ascap.com

Sue Devine
SR DIRECTOR FILM/TV
ASSISTANT RACHEL PERKINS
PHONE: (212) 621-6227
FAX: (212) 621-8453
sdevine@ascap.com

4. BMI
8730 Sunset Blvd., 3ʳᵈ Fl.
West Los Angeles, CA 90069-2210
PHONE: (310) 659-9109
FAX: (310) 657-6947
losangeles@bmi.com
bmi.com

Doreen Ringer Ross
VP FILM/TV RELATIONS
ASSISTANT REEMA IQBAL

PHONE: (310) 289-6306
FAX: (310) 657-2850
dross@bmi.com

Ray Yee
EX DIR FILM/TV RELATIONS
ASSISTANT REEMA IQBAL
PHONE: (310) 289-6361
FAX: (310) 657-2850
ryee@bmi.com

Lisa Feldman
SR DIRECTOR FILM & TV
PHONE: (310) 289-6312
FAX: (310) 657-2850
lfeldman@bmi.com

Anne Cecere
DIRECTOR FILM/TV
ASSISTANT CHAD IRVIN
PHONE: (310) 289-6300
FAX: (310) 657-2850
acecere@bmi.com

Philip Shrut
ASSOC DIRECTOR FILM/TV
PHONE: (310) 289-6305
FAX: (310) 289-2850
pshrut@bmi.com

Taviana Shabestari
ASSOC DIRECTOR WRITER/
PUB RELATIONS
PHONE: (310) 289-6369
FAX: (310) 657-6947
tshabestar@bmi.com

5. BMI
3340 Peachtree Rd. NE, # 570
Atlanta, GA 30326-1059
PHONE: (404) 261-5151
FAX: (404) 261-5152
atlanta@bmi.com
bmi.com

Liz Van Graafeiland
OFFICE MANAGER
PHONE: (404) 261-5151
FAX: (404) 261-5152
lvangraafeiland@bmi.com

6. CMRRA
56 Wellesley St., West, #320
Toronto, ON M5S 2S3 Canada
PHONE: (416) 926-1966
FAX: (416) 926-7521
inquiries@cmrra.ca
cmrra.ca

David A. Basskin
PRESIDENT
ASSISTANT DENISE BENNETT
PHONE: (416) 926-1966 x222
FAX: (416) 926-7521
dbasskin@cmrra.ca

Gail O'Donnell
FILM/TV SYNCHRONIZATION
PHONE: (416) 926-1966 x248
FAX: (416) 926-7521
godonnell@cmrra.ca

Angela Angeli
FILM/TV SYNCH

PHONE: (416) 926-1966 x249
FAX: (416) 926-7521
aangeli@cmrra.ca

7. SESAC
6100 Wilshire Blvd., # 700
Los Angeles, CA 90048-5107
PHONE: (323) 937-3722
FAX: (323) 937-3733
sesac.com

Erin Collins
VP FILM/TV & DEVELOPING MEDIA
ASSISTANT MANECA
LIGHTNER
PHONE: (323) 937-3722
FAX: (323) 937-3733
ecollins@sesac.com

Mario Prins
COORDINATOR WRITER/PUB RELATIONS
PHONE: (323) 937-3722
FAX: (323) 937-3733
mprins@sesac.com

8. SESAC
55 Music Square East,
Nashville, TN 37203-4324
PHONE: (800) 826-9996
FAX: (615) 329-9627
sesac.com

Shannan Hatch
SR DIRECTOR WTR/PUB RELATIONS

PHONE: (615) 320-0055
FAX: (615) 329-9627
shatch@sesac.com

John Mullins
DIRECTOR WTR/PUB
RELATIONS
PHONE: (615) 320-0055
FAX: (615) 329-9627
jmullins@sesac.com

9. SESAC
67 Upper Berkeley St.

London, W1H 7QX England
PHONE: 44-207-563-7028
FAX: 44-207-563-7029
sesac.com

Wayne Bickerton
MD
PHONE: 44-207-563-7028
FAX: 44-207-563-7029
rights@sesac.co.uk

Appendix C–Music Library Contract

Composition and Production Agreement

This Agreement is entered into as of the 21st day of September, 2006, by and between
(hereinafter referred to as "Company") and (hereinafter referred to as "Composer").

The parties hereby agree as follows:

1. SUBJECT MATTER

(a) Company hereby specifically commissions Composer to render his services as writer, composer, arranger, programmer, orchestrator and producer under the direction, control and supervision of Company in connection with the creation of musical compositions (hereinafter referred to as the "Compositions") and master recordings embodying said Compositions (hereinafter referred to as the "Masters") enumerated on Exhibit "A", attached hereto, for use in, without limitation, audio-visual works sometimes collectively referred to herein as "Musical Works."

(b) Composer agrees that from time to time additional Musical Works may be incorporated into this agreement by an Amendment to be signed by both parties. All such services and Musical Works shall be subject to the terms and conditions set forth herein, as may be modified by Company from time to time. Further, all such Musical Works shall be set forth in successive addenda to Exhibit "A" (i.e., Exhibit "A-1", Exhibit "A-2", etc.), (hereinafter the "Exhibits"). Each such additional Exhibit shall set forth the number of Musical Works to be delivered to Company, a deadline date for the delivery of the Musical Works, the musical style and duration(s) of the Musical Works, the amount of the advance or fee (if any) to be paid, and the format in which each of the Musical Works shall be delivered. Company shall be under no obligation to accept delivery of any such Musical Works unless and until Company approves the same. As to any such additional Musical Works, if Composer fails to execute the Amendment, the Amendment will be deemed executed by Composer upon delivery of the Musical Works to Company, and in this event, Composer hereby designates Company as their limited purpose attorney in fact to execute in Composer's name or on Composer's behalf, all assignments, copyright applications and other documents that Company may deem necessary in its sole and absolute discretion to effectuate the purposes of this Agreement.

2. GRANT OF RIGHTS

(a) Composer and Company agree that, from their inception, the Compositions and Masters shall be considered works made for hire as contemplated and defined in Section 101 of the United States Copyright Act; and all rights pertaining thereto, including without limitation the copyrights and all extension and renewal terms thereof, the performances embodied on the Masters, other intellectual property rights, and any ancillary rights arising therefrom, are entirely the property of Company, its successors and assigns, absolutely and forever, for all uses and purposes whatsoever, whether now known or hereafter created throughout the world and free from the payment of any royalty or compensation whatsoever other than as herein provided. Company shall accordingly have the sole and exclusive right to register for copyright the Compositions and Masters under Company's name as the sole owner and author thereof. In the event and to the extent Company may for any reason not be considered the owner of any rights of any kind in the Compositions and Masters as an employer for hire, then and to that extent Composer hereby assigns, sells, transfers and conveys to Company, its successors and assigns, in perpetuity and throughout the world, all right, title and interest in the Compositions and Masters, including without limitation, all copyright interests and all extensions or renewals thereof for the entire world.

Without limiting the foregoing, Composer expressly grants to Company the following rights:

(i) To perform the Compositions and Masters for profit or otherwise, including without limitation, by radio and television broadcast, Internet (whether by streaming or downloading or otherwise), podcast, ringtones, videogames, or any other medium, whether interactive or noninteractive, whether now known or hereinafter devised.

(ii) To (in Company's sole discretion) substitute a new title or titles for the Compositions, prepare derivative works, including without limitation, the right to make changes, arrangements, adaptations , translations, and transpositions of the Compositions, in whole or in part, to add new lyrics to the music of the Compositions or new music to the lyrics of the Compositions or to add lyrics to the Compositions in instrumental form in any media and in connection with any other musical, literary, dramatic, or other material. Composer hereby waives any claim that Composer may have under any doctrine of "moral right" as that term is generally known in the field of literary, artistic and musical endeavors, or any other similar doctrine existing under the laws of any country.

(iii) To make and license others to make traditional format phonorecords, digital phonorecords, tapes, compact discs, CD-Roms, DVD-Roms and any other reproductions of the Compositions and Masters in whole or in part, for distribution in any manner and media (including any and all forms of electronic media) whether now known or which may hereafter come into existence, and the right to manufacture, advertise, license and sell such reproductions for any and all purposes whatsoever;

(iv) To synchronize, or license others to synchronize, the Compositions and Masters with motion pictures, television, videogames or any other audio visual material ("Audio Visual Material") and to distribute such Audio Visual Material via any manner and means, whether now known or hereafter devised, including without limitation via any Audio Visual Device

(v) To exploit any and all rights of every kind and nature now or hereafter existing, whether or not now recognized under common law or any statutory scheme, including, without limitation, any copyrights (and renewals and extensions thereof) in the Compositions and Masters, in whole or in part and to secure registration of same in Company's name as author thereof.

(vi) To print, sell, advertise, reproduce, record, exhibit, manufacture, distribute and otherwise use and license others to do same, the Compositions and Masters, in whole or in part, in any manner and for any purpose, whether now known or which may hereafter come into existence.

(vii) To exploit all digital rights in and to the Compositions and Masters or either; and to exploit any and all rights of every kind and nature now or hereafter existing under common law or any statutory scheme.

(b) Company reserves the right to determine, at its sole discretion, the manner, extent and means of exploiting the Compositions or Masters. Notwithstanding the foregoing, Company shall not be obligated to exploit the Compositions or Masters.

(c) Company and its designees shall have the worldwide right in perpetuity, and may grant to others the right to, at no cost, use, reproduce, print, publish and disseminate in any medium, Composer's name, portraits, pictures and likeness or biographical materials concerning Composer (hereinafter "Composer's Image"), as news or information, or for the purpose of trade or for advertising purposes in connection with Compositions and Masters produced hereunder.

(d) Composer expressly releases Company, its agents, employees, licensees, and assignees from any and all claims which Composer has or may have for invasion of privacy, publicity, defamation, or any other cause of action arising out of the production, distribution, performance, broadcast, or exhibition of the Composition or Master or use of the Composer's Image in connection therewith.

(e) Composer shall, upon Company's request execute and deliver any and all instruments and documents which Company deems necessary to vest in Company the rights granted by Composer hereunder. If Composer fails to execute any such document, Composer irrevocably authorizes and appoints Company as Composer's attorney in fact in Composer's name and in Composer's place and stead to execute and deliver such documents,

Composition and Production Agreement   Page 2

including but not limited to documents required to secure to Company copyrights to the Compositions and Masters (and extensions and renewals thereof) throughout the world.

3. DELIVERY

Composer shall deliver the Compositions and Masters on or before the Delivery Date(s) set forth on Exhibit "A" (the "Delivery Date"). The Compositions and Masters shall be delivered in the versions and format(s) set forth on Exhibit "A" (the "Delivery Format"). The musical style of the Compositions shall be determined by Company, or by Composer at Company's request, prior to the start of Composer's services. All Compositions shall first be submitted in demo form for Company's review and approval prior to final production. Company shall be under no obligation to accept delivery of the Compositions and Masters unless and until Company approves the same. Each of the Masters must be commercially and technically suitable, in Company's sole discretion. In the event that Company desires changes, modifications or additions to the Compositions and/or Masters either before or after such have been delivered to Company, Composer shall make such changes, modifications or additions in the time and manner as may reasonably be required by Company.

4. COMPENSATION

(a) Conditioned upon Composer's full and faithful performance of all the terms and provisions hereof, and subject to section 4(c) below, Composer shall be paid the sum as set forth on Exhibit "A" (the "Compensation") in accordance with the payment schedule set forth on Exhibit "A" (the "Payment Schedule"). It is understood that Company is engaging Composer to compose and produce the Compositions and Masters and to furnish all of Composer's services hereunder as a package (hereinafter the "Package Fee"), and that this Package Fee is inclusive of all fees for Composer's services and all costs and expenses in connection therewith, including but not limited to musician fees (for Composer's performance and the performance of any other musicians hired by Composer), demo fees, preproduction costs, recording costs, recording studio fees, sequencing, programming, engineering charges and arrangements. Composer shall not employ any musicians, vocalists, arrangers, engineers, etc. to perform on the Masters unless such persons execute an employment agreement to be provided to Composer by Company upon Composer's request, acknowledging that such performances are works made for hire on Company's behalf.

(b) If and to the extent the public performance rights in the Compositions are licensed in any territory of the world, by way of a "blanket license" or otherwise, by a performing rights licensing organization which accounts separately to writers, Composer shall retain the right to collect the so-called "Writer's Share" of any such performance fees or royalties directly from such licensing organization. Composer shall not be entitled to receive any portion of the so-called "publisher's share" of public performance royalties. Company shall index the Compositions accordingly with the applicable performing rights organization(s). Accordingly, Composer shall have no claim whatsoever against Company for any royalties received by Company from any performing rights society which makes such direct payments. In the event there is no performing rights society able to issue such public performance licenses or Company's licensees elect to forgo participation in such performing rights societies, Company shall have the right to license directly the public performance rights in the Compositions to third parties and collect all sums therefrom. Composer shall not be entitled to any royalties or other moneys collected by Company in connection with the direct licensing of performance rights by Company.

(c) The term "Composer" shall be understood to include all writers of the Compositions. In the event that one or more other writers, composers and/or lyricists are writers together with Composer of any of the Compositions (including persons employed by Company to add, change or translate the words or to revise or change the music), then the covenants herein shall be joint and several and the payments herein shall, unless a different payment is specified in Exhibit "A", be due to all writers collectively and paid in equal shares to each.

(d) Composer shall not be entitled to any portion of any advance payments, guarantee payments, or minimum royalty payments which Company may receive in connection with any subpublishing agreement, collection agreement, licensing agreement or any other agreement that includes the Compositions or Masters.

Composition and Production Agreement   Page 3

(e) Except as expressly provided herein, no royalties or other moneys or consideration shall be payable to Composer for the exercise by Company of the rights granted hereunder. Furthermore, Composer expressly acknowledges and agrees that Composer shall not share in any licensing fees collected by Company, including but not limited to synchronization fees and blanket license fees.

(f) Composer acknowledges and agrees that Composer's services are being provided hereunder as an independent contractor; accordingly and pursuant to Composer's request, Company shall not withhold, report or pay withholding taxes with respect to the compensation payable hereunder. Should Company be subjected to any expense or liability by reason of such failure to withhold report or pay such taxes, Composer agrees to indemnify and hold Company harmless therefrom.

5. DEFINITIONS
(a) "Compositions" will mean any musical work, including titles, lyrics, if any, libretto, music, musical scores and all arrangements (including public domain arrangements), adaptations, translations and other versions thereof and all other words derived from the foregoing, including all interpretations regardless of duration. Different arrangements, adaptations, translations, recordings or other versions of a musical work will be considered, collectively, one Composition.

(b) "Masters" will mean every form of recording but not limited to, a compact disc, digital audio tape, digital audio files, analog audio tape, or any other contrivance, appliance or device whatsoever, whether not known, developed or discovered at anytime hereafter, bearing or used for emitting or transmitting sound derived from recordings of the Compositions, whether or not the same also bears or can bear visual images.

(c) "Phonorecord" will mean all forms of audio reproduction, including but not limited to, discs, mini-discs, tapes, digital audio files, CD's, CD-Roms, DVDs, DVD-Roms, DAT's, DCC laser devices, devices now or hereafter known.

(d) "CD Rom" will mean a compact disc interactive software embodying a multi-media software program for simultaneous interactive presentation of video, audio, graphics, text and data.

(e) "Audio Visual Device" will mean any form of audio reproduction or distribution in conjunction with images whether via Videogram, CD-Rom, DVD, DVD-Rom, mobile phone, iPod, videogames, the Internet or any other type of multimedia devices or the like, whether now known or hereinafter devised.

(f) "DVD Rom" will mean a read only DVD disk used for storing data and interactive sequences as well as audio and video to be run without limitation in DVD-Rom or DVD Ram drives.

(g) "Digital Audio File" will mean "any electronic data file containing audio in any digital format whether now known or hereinafter devised."

(h) "Digital Rights" will mean any and all forms of distribution and exploitation of the Compositions or Masters in digital format whether or not specifically set forth herein including without limitation streaming, downloading, podcasting or otherwise.

(i) "Internet" means a global computer network.

6. WARRANTIES AND REPRESENTATIONS
(a) Composer is presently a member of or affiliated with, or shall, within one month of the date hereof, become a member or an affiliate of the following performance right society: SESAC

(b) Composer hereby promises, warrants, represents, and covenants that: (i) Composer has full right, power and authority to enter into and perform this Agreement and to assign, convey, grant and transfer to and vest in Company all rights hereunder, free and clear from any and all claims or other encumbrances by any person, firm or corporation; (ii) the Compositions are new and original (or based on material in the public domain, if so requested by Company) and capable of copyright protection throughout the world; (iii) neither the Compositions or Masters, in whole or in part are an imitation or copy of, or infringe upon any other material, or violate or infringe upon any common law, statutory or other rights of any person, firm or corporation, including, without limitation, contractual rights, copyrights and rights of privacy; (iv) Composer has not sold, assigned, leased, licensed or in any other way disposed of or encumbered any rights in the Compositions or Masters granted to Company; (v) Composer shall not take, authorize or permit to be taken any action in derogation of Company's rights hereunder; and (vi) The Musical Works have been or shall be prepared, performed and recorded on a non-union basis and accordingly there are no obligations of any sort or nature, financial or otherwise, to any union in respect to the Musical Works.

(c) Composer shall not employ any musicians, vocalists, arrangers, engineers, etc. to perform on the Masters unless such persons execute an employment agreement, to be provided to Composer by Company upon Composer's request, acknowledging that such performances are works made for hire on Company's behalf.

(d) Composer agrees to provide, upon request, written documentation confirming any of the foregoing warranties and representations, including, but not limited to, work-for-hire agreements for all composers, arrangers, musicians, and/or vocalists utilized in the Musical Works.

7. CREDIT
Conditioned upon Composer's full and faithful performance of all of the terms and conditions hereof, Company shall use reasonable efforts to accord a credit to Composer in the liner notes on all Phonorecord(s) embodying the Compositions which are manufactured and distributed by Company and as and if appropriate, in Company's sole discretion, in any other device or form of distribution. All characteristics of such credit shall be at Company's sole discretion. The casual or inadvertent failure by Company to comply with the foregoing credit provision shall not constitute a breach of this Agreement.

8. INDEMNIFICATION
Composer hereby indemnifies, saves and holds harmless Company from all damages, liabilities, costs, losses, expenses and attorneys' fees arising out of or connected with any claim, demand, action or proceeding by a third party that is inconsistent with any of the warranties, promises, covenants or representations made by Composer in this Agreement if such claim, demand, action or proceeding is either (a) reduced to a final judgment adverse to Company in which it has been adjudicated that Composer has breached any of the warranties, promises, covenants and representations in this Agreement, or (b) settled with Composer's written consent, such consent not to be unreasonably withheld. Pending the determination of any such claim, demand or action, Company may withhold payment of any or all royalties or other moneys payable hereunder.

9. NOTICES
All notices hereunder shall be in writing and shall be deemed received five (5) business days after they are mailed by registered or certified mail, return receipt requested or one (1) business day after faxed with follow-up oral confirmation of correct and complete reception of said fax and shall be addressed as follows:

Company:

Composer:

10. ASSIGNMENT
Company may, at its election, assign the Compositions, Masters, this Agreement or its rights hereunder or any of its obligations hereunder, in whole or in part, to any other entity. Company may also assign its rights hereunder to any of its Licensees to the extent necessary or advisable in Company's sole discretion to implement the license granted. Composer may not assign this Agreement or any of Composer's rights hereunder but Composer may assign Composer's right to receive royalties.

Composition and Production Agreement   Page 5

11. REMEDIES

The rights and remedies of Composer in the event of any breach of the provisions of this Agreement shall be limited to the right, if any, to recover monetary damages in an action at law and in no event shall Composer be entitled by reason of any such breach to a reversion of the rights granted in this Agreement or to terminate this Agreement or to seek to enjoin or restrain the exhibition, distribution, broadcast or marketing of any uses of the Compositions and/or Masters hereunder. Notwithstanding the above, Company shall not be in breach of any of its obligations under this Agreement unless and until Composer notifies Company in writing in detail of its breach or alleged breach and Company fails to cure that breach or alleged breach within thirty (30) days after its receipt of that notice from Composer.

12. ENTIRE AGREEMENT

This Agreement sets forth the entire understanding of the parties hereto relating to the subject matter hereof and supersedes all oral and written prior and contemporaneous negotiations, understandings and discussions. No modification, amendment, waiver, termination or discharge of this Agreement or any of its terms or provisions shall be binding upon either party if not confirmed by a written instrument signed by Composer and Company unless otherwise provided for herein.

13. JURISDICTION

This Agreement has been entered into in the State of California, and the validity, interpretation and legal effect of this Agreement shall be governed by the laws of the State of California applicable to contracts entered into and performed entirely within the State of California. The California State and Federal Courts will have exclusive jurisdiction of any controversies regarding this Agreement and any action or other proceeding which involves such controversies will be brought in Los Angeles County.

IN WITNESS WHEREOF, the parties have executed this Composition and Production Agreement on the day and year first written above.

Exhibit A

The Compositions and Master Recordings listed below (including all versions and alternate mixes) shall constitute the subject matter of the Composition and Production Agreement dated the 21st of September, 2006, between   ("Company") and   ("Composer"):

Album Project: (working title):

Number of Works commissioned: Twenty (20)

Musical Work(s) (working titles):   List of final titles to be annexed upon completion

Musical Style: Contemporary high energy club electronica styles

Duration: :60+

Mixes: Full mix, No Vocal mix (if applicable), Narration mix and Groove mix to be provided for all Compositions

Edits: :30 edits to be provided for all mixe⁻

Delivery Date: January 2, 2007

Delivery Format: As per annexed Composer Delivery Instructions

Compensation:

Payment Schedule: upon commencement of Composer's services and   upon delivery to and acceptance by Company of the Compositions and Masters

Writers: All titles to be credited to   100% unless otherwise indicated in writing by Composer

Exhibit B

Composer Delivery Instructions

1. **Deliver a Data Disc with 24-bit_48kHz audio files**
   a. Deliver uncompressed stereo WAV or AIF files.
   b. SDII files are also acceptable if WAV or AIF are unavailable.
   c. Delivery via FTP is also acceptable.
   d. 96kHz files are also acceptable.
   e. Do not compress the files using any type of Zip or Stuff utility.
   f. All cues should have natural fade endings. Do not truncate beginnings or endings.
   g. Include at least 3 seconds of space before and after each music cue.
   h. Record & mix at the highest possible sample rate, without upsampling or downsampling.
   [Give us whatever sampling rate the multitrack session was recorded at. For example, do not give us 44.1kHz/16-bit mixes if the songs were recorded at 48kHz/24-bit. NEVER convert the mixes to another sampling rate for Megatrax. When mixing, use the same sampling rate as the session. If mixing analog, please try to print the mixes at 96KHz/24bit].

2. **Label the audio files according to the following convention:**
   Songname+Mix
   Examples:
   Full mix: Song1-Full Mix
   No Vocal mix: Song1-NoVocal
   Narration mix: Song1-Narr
   Alt. mix: Song1-AltFull
   :30 edit: Song1-30FullMix
   etc.

3. **NO mastering, NO premastering, NO watermarking.**
   Never use any type of mastering effects/plug-ins on the mixes before delivering to Megatrax. No TC Finalizers, No WAVES L2/L3, etc. Our projects are mastered at professional mastering houses. Putting any type of mastering effects or plug-ins will just compromise the finished product by limiting what the mastering engineer can do. If you or your mixing engineer know how to use a stereo bus compressor (not Limiter) that is OK. Just don't use any "brick wall" limiters or digital "mastering" devices when printing mixes for Megatrax.

4. **Check and fix all multitrack sessions for digital clicks and pops**
   Clicks and pops may occur as a result of poor edits, missed crossfades, clipping or incorrect word clock settings.

5. **Provide a document (MS Word, Excel or text file) with working titles, BPM and descriptions for all tracks**
   a) Do not reference the names of existing artists or bands in your song titles.
   b) If any alternate mixes are provided, be sure to indicate clearly how it is different from the main mix.

- **Deliver STEM mix-outs as follows:**

   a) Pro Tools session format preferred

   b) The following stems should be provided:

      i.   drums/percussion/loops [no isolated loops]
      ii. bass

   Composition and Production Agreement   Page 8

    iii.   rhythm keyboards

    iv.   rhythm guitars

    v.   melody/lead/solos

    vi.   vocals

    vii.   strings

    viii.   brass

    ix.   sound design/fx

c) Do not isolate any samples taken from sampling CDs – blend/combine any samples into other tracks]

d) Stems should be prepared in such a way that when all Stems are playing, the sound is identical to the Full Mix.

Additional Notes:

1. **Demos must be provided for Company review and approval prior to final production**

2. **All Compositions must be 100% original (except if based on material in the public domain) and not infringing in any way upon any existing musical work.**

3. **Use cleared samples only.**
   a) Read the dislaimers on all sample libraries. If production music library use is prohibited, don't use them.
   b) Sampling of any existing recording or portion thereof is strictly prohibited.

Appendix D

TVFilmTrax.com PO Box 453, Neversink, NY 12765 • 917-974-0039 • tvfilmtrax@gmail.com

TVFILMTRAX.COM Non-Exclusive Licensing Agreement

AGREEMENT made as of this _____ day of _____, 2012, by and between www.tvfilmtrax.com at PO Box 453, Neversink, N.Y. 12765 (referred to herein as the "COMPANY") and _____, at _____ (collectively referred to herein as "ARTIST") (COMPANY and ARTIST are collectively referred to herein as the "Parties" and each as a "Party").

WITNESSETH:

TVFilmTrax.com, (TFT), is involved in the online licensing, marketing and sale of "Tracks" to their registered "Customers" (as each of the foregoing are hereinafter defined) via the URL www.tvfilmtrax.com, which for the avoidance of doubt includes without limitation, any and all sub-URL's of www.tvfilmtrax.com, or authorized or powered by TFT and any third party sites featuring Tracks and/or using any TFT web properties or assets ('the Site').

WHEREAS, ARTIST has at the request of the COMPANY, and upon the COMPANY'S special order and commission, made and composed the musical compositions, arrangements and musical materials described on Schedule A, annexed hereto and hereby made a part hereof (hereinafter referred to as the "Compositions"); and WHEREAS, ARTIST has at the request of the COMPANY, and upon the COMPANY'S special order and commission, made and produced the master recordings set forth on Schedule A, annexed hereto and hereby made a part hereof (hereinafter referred to as the "Masters"); and WHEREAS, ARTIST and the COMPANY acknowledge and agree that this Agreement is a contract for services and each considers the results of the services, namely, the Compositions and Masters (hereinafter collectively referred to as the "Work").

THEREFORE, the Parties, intending to be legally bound, hereby agree, as follows:

1. GRANT OF RIGHTS

1.1 Rights granted herein are in perpetuity. Subject to the terms of this Agreement, Licensor hereby grants to Licensee for Film/TV Placement, Sound Track Commercial

CDs and Ringtone Distribution on a non-exclusive basis, one hundred percent (100%) control of the Licensed Works, including, but not limited to titles, lyrics and music thereof,
and performances and recordings embodied therein, in any and all forms. At Licensee's request, in order to effectuate Licensee's rights with respect to the Licensed Works, Licensor, and any and all other third parties holding rights in and to an Original Composition or Original Master Recording, will execute assignments as Licensee may deem necessary at any time to evidence, establish, maintain, protect, enforce or defend its right in such Licensed Works. Licensor acknowledges and agrees that, included within the rights granted to Licensee herein, and, notwithstanding anything to the contrary herein contained, is Licensor's irrevocable grant to Licensee, its successors, licensees, sub-licensees and assigns, of the right, license privilege and authority, throughout the entire world with respect to the entirety of the Licensed Works, whether now in existence or hereafter created as follows:

(i) All rights of control, publication, printing, performance, mechanical or other reproduction, synchronization, sale, exploitation, arrangement, adaptation, translation, use and disposition, now or hereafter known;

(ii) The right to register the Licensed Work with the appropriate performing rights society i.e. ASCAP, BMI or SESAC, upon confirmation of Licensed Use, as 100% publisher of the Licensed Work in perpetuity, and to collect any and all monies accruing or earned there from (other than so-called "writer's share") generated by the Licensed Work, through the Licensed Use from the appropriate performing rights society. It is expressly understood and agreed that Licensor has no music publishing rights whatsoever in the Licensed Works, through the Licensed Use, and unless expressly stated to the contrary under the terms of this Agreement is not entitled to any participation in any portion of the publisher's share of any proceeds derived from the exploitation of such publishing rights. Licensor and any co-writers will receive their "writers" share of public performance royalties directly from the society. In addition, the right, at Licensee's option, to register each Licensed Work with Sound Exchange (or any other organization authorized to collect digital performing rights income) and to collect all applicable digital performing rights income on behalf of the owner of such Licensed Work. Licensee shall submit 50% of the income so collected to Licensor as part of Licensor's share of Gross Receipts

(iii) Pursuant to (b) Licensee will register the License Work with the appropriate performing rights society under each and every writer. Should a writer not be affiliated with any performing rights society, Licensee will register the track with the writer identified as "no affiliation". It will be the writer's responsibility to become a member of the performing rights society of his/her choice, inform Licensee of affiliation, alert such society of the Licensed Works affected, and pursue collection of the writers share of performance income as a result of the Licensed Use. Licensee will not be held responsible for any loss of income on behalf of any writers, who have failed to become registered members of a performing rights society.

(iv) The right to use the name, photograph, likeness, and/or biographical material of the writers of the Original Compositions, the artists, musicians, instrumentalists, mixers and producers of the Original Master Recordings, and biographical material concerning all of the foregoing for the purposes of the trade or otherwise in connection with the Licensed Works.

(v) All rights to publish, record, produce, reproduce, transmit, perform, broadcast, telecast, otherwise communicated (in any version or versions thereof by any means), license, assign and enter into agreements to or with any person or entity with respect to all or any rights or part of the rights granted hereunder including, but not limited to, the sub-licensing of the Licensed Works to a third party for exploitation; provided, however, Licensee must receive the written consent of Licensor prior to licensing a Licensed Work for use other than through Film/TV Placement, Sound Track Commercial CDs and Ringtone Distribution

(vi) The right to exercise any right Licensee deems reasonably necessary or desirable in connection with the administration, exploitation, or protection of the Licensed Works in accordance with this Agreement.

(vii) Licensee desires to add a unique catalog identifier to the Original Compositions and Original Master Recordings in order to create Licensed Works (as hereinafter defined), for exploitation and distribution to third parties; to issue License(s) (as hereinafter defined), administer and collect all revenues from each Licensed Use (as hereinafter defined); and compensate Licensor for such Licensed Uses.

1.2 Original Compositions/Original Master Recordings. Licensor shall deliver (as defined below) the agreed upon Original Compositions and Original Master Recordings to Licensee who shall then assign a new title to such works i.e. Licensed Works, which shall thereafter be listed on Exhibit A, attached hereto and incorporated herein by reference. Licensing, sub-licensing, registration with performance societies and all other uses of the Licensed Works shall be made solely in the name of the new titles listed on Exhibit A. The writers' credits of the Licensed Works shall remain the same as those for the Original Compositions.

1.3 Performing Rights. Performing rights in the Licensed Works shall be licensed by the performing rights society to which Licensee and the writer(s) of the Original Compositions belong. Said society is hereby authorized and directed to collect and receive all monies earned from the public performance of the Licensed Works, and shall be directed to pay to Licensee the 100% publisher's share of public performance fees for the Universe. Licensor agrees to execute any documents necessary to effectuate this assignment.

2.   WARRANTIES AND REPRESENTATIONS

ARTIST warrants and represents as follows:

(i) ARTIST is the sole author, composer, creator and producer of each of the Compositions and Masters; the Compositions and Masters are ARTIST'S own original work and creation; the Compositions and Masters, and any and all parts thereof including any music "samples" used or contained therein, are not copies of any other copyrighted work; and, each of the Compositions and Masters has not been previously published or exploited and is capable of copyright and other protections throughout the Territory.

(ii) No adverse claims exist or will exist in respect of any of the Compositions or Masters and none of the Compositions or Masters, or any materials contained or used therein including any music "samples", infringe upon or violate any rights whatsoever (whether at law, in equity, by statute, regulation or treaty, or otherwise) of any person or entity.

(iii) To the extent that the Compositions and Masters are held not to be "works made for hire," ARTIST owns and controls all rights in each of the Compositions and Masters on an unencumbered and beneficial ownership basis throughout the Territory prior to the assignment thereof to COMPANY.

(iv) ARTIST has not sold, assigned, leased, licensed or in any way deposed of or encumbered any of the rights herein granted to COMPANY. (iv) ARTIST has the full and exclusive right, power and authority to enter into this Agreement and make the grants contained herein.

3.   *Compensation*

(a) ARTIST shall be entitled to the entire so-called "Writer's share of public performance income" and COMPANY shall be entitled to the "Publisher's share of public performance income" payable in each case, so called by any performing rights society. In any filing accomplished by either Party with any performing rights society, ARTIST shall be listed as the entire owner of the writer's share and COMPANY shall be listed as the entire owner of the publisher's share of any performance royalties.

(b)   Artist shall receive 50% (fifty percent) of all profits actually received by company from the license, use or other exploitation of the related Master and Song hereunder. These monies will be paid on an annual basis in January.

(c)   It is understood and agreed by and between all of the Parties hereto that if ARTIST consists of more than one person, all sums payable hereunder shall be divided between such persons as ARTIST determines, and COMPANY shall have no responsibility or liability in connection therewith.

(d) Except as specifically provided in this Agreement, ARTIST shall not be entitled to any other compensation, fees or payments, and COMPANY shall not be required to make any other payments of any kind or nature to ARTIST or to any third party (including any union, guild, society, club or association, or any international, federal, state or local government, agency, authority, bureau, office or organization), for, as a result of, or in connection with the acquisition, exercise or exploitation of rights by the COMPANY pursuant to this Agreement.

4.   *DEFINITIONS*

(a) As used herein, "Compositions" shall mean any musical work, including titles, lyrics (if any), libretto, music, musical scores and all arrangements (including public domain arrangements), adaptations, translations and other versions thereof and all other works derived from the foregoing, including all interpretations, regardless of duration. Different arrangements and adaptations, translations, recordings or other versions of a musical work will be considered, collectively, one "Composition". A musical Composition that would otherwise be a Composition shall not be deemed a Composition unless it is acceptable to the COMPANY, as commercially satisfactory, in the COMPANY'S sole discretion.

(b) As used herein, "Masters" shall mean every form of recording, including but not limited to, a compact disc, digital audio tape or any other contrivance, appliance or device whatsoever, whether now known, developed or discovered at anytime hereafter, bearing or used for emitting or transmitting sound derived from recordings of the Compositions, whether or not the same also bears or can bear visual images. Each of the Masters must be fully mixed and edited and delivered simultaneously in audio CD-ROM format and as complete Pro-Tools files in data CD-ROM format, and all necessary licenses and applicable approvals and consents shall be obtained prior to delivery to COMPANY.

5.   *RECORDING COSTS*

ARTIST shall pay any and all costs, fees, royalties and expenses, and shall be solely responsible for any and all duties, obligations or liabilities (including to any union, guild, society, club or association, or any international, federal, state or local government, agency, authority, bureau, office or organization), incurred for, as a result of, or in connection with the composing, production or recording of the Compositions and Masters, and COMPANY shall incur no costs, fees, royalties or expenses, and shall have no responsibilities, obligations or liabilities therefore.

6.   *NAME AND LIKENESS*

COMPANY and any licensee of COMPANY each shall have the right and may grant to others the right to reproduce, print, publish or to disseminate in any medium, ARTIST'S name, portrait, picture and likeness and all other persons performing services in connection with the Compositions and the recording of the Masters, and biographical materials concerning them, as news or information, for the purposes of trade, or for advertising purposes.

7.   *ASSIGNMENTS*

COMPANY shall have the right to assign this Agreement in whole or in part, or to grant licenses hereunder. ARTIST may only assign the Agreement or ARTIST'S share of income here from with COMPANY'S prior written consent.

8.   INDEMNITY

Artist shall defend, indemnify and hold TFT harmless from and against any and all liabilities, suits, claims, losses, damages, costs or judgments, and shall pay all costs, including reasonable attorney's fees, and damages arising from or in any way related to:

(a) Any breach or alleged breach by Artist of any warranty or representation under this Agreement;

(b) Any failure or inadequacy by or on behalf of Artist with respect to any registration or filing of any right or entitlement related to any tracks;

(c) Any claim by any person or entity for any royalty or other compensation arising from use or licensing by TFT, consistent with this Agreement, of any Represented Tracks;

(d) The Parties hereto shall promptly provide each other with written notice of any claim or threatened claim and the indemnified Party may, at it's own expense, assist in the defense of any claim provided that the indemnifying Party shall control such defense and all negotiations in settlement thereof provided that any settlement intended to bind the indemnified Party shall not be final without the indemnified Party's written consent, which shall not be unreasonably withheld or delayed.

9.   Legal Action

(a) Any legal action brought, or any enforcement of its rights undertaken by COMPANY against any alleged infringer of the Compositions and/or Masters will be initiated and prosecuted at the COMPANY'S sole expense and in its sole discretion, including the right to settle any such action. In the event of a recovery by the COMPANY of any monies as the result of a judgment or settlement, such monies shall be the property of and retained entirely by the COMPANY, and ARTIST shall have no rights and shall make no claims thereto. If requested by the COMPANY, ARTIST shall cooperate with the COMPANY in the prosecution of any such action.

(b) If a claim is presented against the COMPANY in which it is asserted that the Compositions or Masters infringe upon or violate or interfere with the rights of any person or entity, COMPANY shall notify ARTIST of such claim, and ARTIST at ARTIST'S sole expense, may participate in the defense of such claim; but COMPANY shall have the absolute right to control the defense and to settle or otherwise dispose of such claim in any manner which COMPANY shall determine.

10.   AUDIT

ARTIST shall be entitled to conduct an audit of COMPANY'S records and statements of accounts relating solely to the matters set forth herein, during normal business hours at COMPANY's place of business, upon ten (10) business days written notice to COMPANY. The Audit notice shall state the identity of the person or persons to attend the audit on ARTIST'S behalf and the proposed duration of the audit. Each such audit undertaken in accordance with this Agreement shall be accomplished at ARTIST expense, except that in the event such audit reveals a discrepancy resulting in an under-accounting to ARTIST of more than ten percent (10%) of the total sums due to ARTIST during the accounting periods audited, then the amount of such discrepancy and interest thereon shall be paid to ARTIST by COMPANY.

11. MISCELLANEOUS

(a) This Agreement is binding upon the Parties hereto, their respective successors-in-interest, heirs and assigns, and represents the entire understanding between the Parties and cannot be terminated or amended except by a writing signed by all of the Parties hereto. It shall be construed in accordance with the laws of the State of New York applicable to contracts to be wholly performed herein. If any part of this Agreement shall be invalid or unenforceable it shall not affect the validity of the balance of this Agreement.

(b) All notices and payments hereunder will be sent to the Parties at the addresses indicated above, unless either Party changes such mailing address by giving written notice to the other Party. All notices shall be in writing and shall be delivered either by registered or certified mail, return receipt requested, postage prepaid, or by telegraph, all charges prepaid. The date of mailing or of deposit in a telegraph office whichever shall be first, shall be deemed the date of service. ARTIST shall send a copy of all notices directed to the COMPANY to Ben McLane, Esq. 11135 Weddington Street, Suite #424 North Hollywood, CA 91601.

(c) Any process in any actual proceedings commenced in the courts of the State of New York or elsewhere arising out of any claim, dispute or disagreement relating in any way to this Agreement may, among other methods, be served upon ARTIST by delivering or mailing the same, via registered or certified mail, addressed to ARTIST at the address first above written. Any such delivery or mail service shall be deemed to have the same force and effect as personal service within the State of New York or the jurisdiction in which such acts or proceedings may be commenced.

(d) ARTIST shall not, without the prior written consent of COMPANY, disclose or permit or authorize the disclosure of any of our affiliates or licensees confidential information.

(e) The Parties acknowledge and agree that ARTIST is an independent contractor and not COMPANY'S employee or agent.

(f) The term "COMPANY" as used throughout this Agreement shall be deemed to apply to the Company and its designees, successors and assigns.

(g) The headings to the Sections in this Agreement have been inserted for convenience of reference only and shall not be deemed a part of or affect the construction or interpretation of any provision of this Agreement.

IN WITNESS WHEREOF, the Parties hereto have executed this Agreement on the date and year first above written.

By: _____ *Brian Tarquin-Owner*
         WWW.TVFILMTRAX.COM

_____ _____   _____
Date   Artist   SS#

_____

Address

_____

Email

_____

Telephone

Schedule A

Date: _____
Writer(s): _____ Performing
Rights Society Affiliation: _____ List of Compositions and
Masters Description of titles:

_____
_____
_____
_____
_____
_____
_____
_____
_____
_____

Schedule C

MUSICIAN(S) AND PRODUCER(S) FORM

I hereby confirm so far as the same concerns me, that for good and valuable consideration, the receipt and adequacy of which I acknowledge that neither TV Film Trax nor any of its affiliates, licensees, customers or any person, company or corporation deriving any rights from TV Film Trax will have any obligation to make any payments of whatsoever nature to me or anyone claiming rights through me or on my behalf as a result of any use of the Compositions and/or Masters:

Composition(s)/Master(s)

_____
_____
_____
_____
_____
_____

Session Date: _____

Musician's Name: Musician's Name:

Musician's Name: Musician's Name:

Recording Producer's Name: Recording Producer's Name:

Appendix E

WORK FOR HIRE AGREEMENT

AGREEMENT made as of this 1st day of May, 2009, by and between
having an office at
(referred to herein as the "COMPANY") and
(collectively referred to herein as "ARTIST") (COMPANY and ARTIST are
collectively referred to herein as the "Parties" and each as a "Party").

WITNESSETH:

WHEREAS, ARTIST has at the request of the COMPANY, and upon the
COMPANY'S special order and commission, made and composed the musical
compositions, arrangements and musical materials described on Schedule A, annexed
hereto and hereby made a part hereof (hereinafter referred to as the "Compositions"); and

WHEREAS, ARTIST has at the request of the COMPANY, and upon the
COMPANY'S special order and commission, made and produced the master recordings
set forth on Schedule A, annexed hereto and hereby made a part hereof (hereinafter
referred to as the "Masters"); and

WHEREAS, ARTIST and the COMPANY acknowledge and agree that this
Agreement is intended to be a contract for services and each considers the results of the
services, namely, the Compositions and Masters (hereinafter collectively referred to as
the "Work"), to be works made for hire for the COMPANY as contemplated and defined
in Section 101 of the United States Copyright Act;

NOW, THEREFORE, the Parties, intending to be legally bound, hereby agree, as
follows:

1. GRANT OF RIGHTS

(a) It is understood and agreed that the Compositions and Masters, and all copyright and
other intellectual property rights therein and performances thereon, are the exclusive
property of the COMPANY throughout the world (the "Territory"), and each is prepared
by ARTIST as a work made for hire as part of collective works and compilations. Such
collective works and compilations include, but are not limited to, a collective music
library belonging to COMPANY and various compilation sound recordings (in compact
disc and other formats) belong to the COMPANY.

(b) Without limiting the generality of the foregoing, the COMPANY shall be the sole,
absolute and exclusive owner and author of all copyright and other interests in the
Compositions and the Masters (including all notices, recordings, and other derivatives
thereof) and shall have the sole and exclusive right to publish, sell, exploit, use,
reproduce, distribute, perform, and otherwise depose of the Compositions and the
Masters, and any of them, and all rights therein, by any methods now or hereafter known,
or to refrain from doing any of the foregoing acts, and to retain any and all benefits,

revenues, money or income accruing therefrom, subject only to the payment of the amounts equivalent to the share of performance royalties referred to in Subparagraph 3(b) of this Agreement.

(c) Without limiting the generality of the foregoing, COMPANY'S rights shall include the right to reproduce copies of the Compositions; the right to authorize the reproduction of the Compositions in the form of phonograph records, compact discs, and audio cassette tapes; the right to prepare or cause the preparation of derivative works in dramatic or dramatico-musical works based on the Compositions; the right to distribute copies of the Compositions to the public by sale, rental, lease, loan or otherwise; the right to publicly perform and to cause or authorize the public performances of the Compositions; the right to display and to cause or authorize the display of the Compositions to the public by all means now known or to become known in the future; the right to adapt, change, add lyrics to or otherwise modify the Compositions in any manner; and any and all rights in and to the Compositions, whether now known or to become known in the future; and the sole and exclusive right to convey the rights set forth in the preceding Section in whole or in part to third parties.

(d) Without limiting the generality of the foregoing, COMPANY'S rights shall include the right to reproduce the Masters and the performances embodied thereon in all formats and in any mediums now or hereafter known; the sole and exclusive right to distribute reproductions of the Masters and their performances embodied thereon in any manner whatsoever; the sole and exclusive right to perform records derived from the Masters publicly and to permit the public performance thereof by any method now or hereafter known; the sole and exclusive right to permit others to use the Masters in timed synchronization with visual images; and the sole and exclusive right to convey the rights set forth in the preceding Section in whole or in part to third parties.

(e) If for any reason the Work, or any part or element thereof, should not be considered a work made for hire under applicable law, ARTIST does hereby sell, assign and transfer to COMPANY, its successors and assigns, the entire right, title, and interest in and to the Work, including but not limited to any registrations and copyright applications relating thereto and any renewals and extensions thereof, whether listed on Schedule A or written or composed during the term. COMPANY'S rights shall include all rights of authors under 17 U.S.C. Section 106, including but not limited to those rights set forth in Sections 1(b),(c) and (d), above.

(f) ARTIST shall execute all papers, assignments, registrations, forms, instruments, deeds and other documents, and perform such other proper acts as COMPANY may deem necessary to secure for COMPANY or its designee the rights herein set forth, including the Assignment of Copyright annexed hereto as Schedule 2 and made a part hereof. In the event ARTIST shall fail to timely execute such documents or perform such acts, COMPANY shall have the right, but not the obligation, to sign such documents and perform such acts in the name of ARTIST and make appropriate dispositions relating thereto, and ARTIST hereby grants COMPANY a limited power of attorney for that purpose.

2. WARRANTIES AND REPRESENTATIONS

ARTIST warrants and represents as follows:

(i) ARTIST is the sole author, composer, creator and producer of each of the Compositions and Masters; the Compositions and Masters are ARTIST'S own original work and creation; the Compositions and Masters, and any and all parts thereof including any music "samples" used or contained therein, are not copies of any other copyrighted work; and, each of the Compositions and Masters has not been previously published or exploited and is capable of copyright and other protections throughout the Territory.

(ii) No adverse claims exist or will exist in respect of any of the Compositions or Masters and none of the Compositions or Masters, or any materials contained or used therein including any music "samples", infringe upon or violate any rights whatsoever (whether at law, in equity, by statute, regulation or treaty, or otherwise) of any person or entity.

(iii) To the extent that the Compositions and Masters are held not to be "works made for hire," ARTIST owns and controls all rights in each of the Compositions and Masters on an unencumbered and beneficial ownership basis throughout the Territory prior to the assignment thereof to COMPANY.

(iv) The payments set forth in Section 3, below, are inclusive of and in complete consideration for any and all services rendered by ARTIST or a third party (including other musicians and recording producers) in respect of the Compositions and Masters, and COMPANY will not have any obligation to make payments to anyone other than ARTIST as herein set forth.

(v) ARTIST has not sold, assigned, leased, licensed or in any way deposed of or encumbered any of the rights herein granted to COMPANY.

(iv) ARTIST has the full and exclusive right, power and authority to enter into this Agreement and make the grants contained herein.

3. PAYMENT

(a) As full and complete consideration and in full payment, per track for the services rendered and Work delivered by ARTIST hereunder, and for the rights granted to COMPANY hereunder by ARTIST, COMPANY shall pay ARTIST as follows:

(i) 50% upon execution of this Agreement;

(ii) 50% upon complete delivery and acceptance of the Compositions and Masters.

3

(b) ARTIST shall also be entitled to the entire so-called "Writer's share of public performance income" and COMPANY shall be entitled to the "Publisher's share of public performance income" payable in each case, so called by any performing rights society. In any filing accomplished by either Party with any performing rights society, ARTIST shall be listed as the entire owner of the writer's share and COMPANY shall be listed as the entire owner of the publisher's share of any performance royalties. In the event that COMPANY collects a separate fee for the direct granting of so-called public performance rights, including the writer's and publisher's share, COMPANY shall pay to ARTIST fifty percent (50%) thereof after the deduction of an administration fee of ten percent (10%) of such fee. But in the event that no such separate fee is collected, then no more than one-third (1/3) of the total fee shall be deemed to be in respect of public performance rights, and of that, one-half (1/2) shall be in respect to the so-called "Writer's share of public performance income" and will be accounted to ARTIST in accordance with the Agreement.

(c) Notwithstanding the provisions of Section 3(c), above, in the event COMPANY shall adapt, change, add lyrics to or otherwise modify any of the Compositions, then ARTIST shall be entitled to only one-half (1/2) of the so-called "Writer's share of public performance income" and COMPANY shall be entitled to one-half (1/2) of the so-called "Writer's share of public performance income" in respect of any such Compositions.

(d) It is understood and agreed by and between all of the Parties hereto that if ARTIST consists of more than one person, all sums payable hereunder shall be divided between such persons as ARTIST determines, and COMPANY shall have no responsibility or liability in connection therewith.

(e) Except as specifically provided in this Agreement, ARTIST shall not be entitled to any other compensation, fees or payments, and COMPANY shall not be required to make any other payments of any kind or nature to ARTIST or to any third party (including any union, guild, society, club or association, or any international, federal, state or local government, agency, authority, bureau, office or organization), for, as a result of, or in connection with the acquisition, exercise or exploitation of rights by the COMPANY pursuant to this Agreement.

4. DELIVERY
(a) ARTIST shall deliver the finished Masters containing recorded versions of the Compositions to COMPANY no later than May 15, 2009.

(b) Simultaneously with the delivery of the Masters, ARTIST shall submit a fully executed Musician(s) and Producer(s) Form as annexed hereto as Schedule C and made a part hereof, together with a brief description (identifying genre, tempo, orchestration, etc.) of each Composition appearing on the Masters. Upon the request of COMPANY, ARTIST shall supply COMPANY with written sheet music and orchestrations for each Composition.

5. DEFINITIONS

4

(a) As used herein, "Compositions" shall mean any musical work, including titles, lyrics (if any), libretto, music, musical scores and all arrangements (including public domain arrangements), adaptations, translations and other versions thereof and all other works derived from the foregoing, including all interpretations, regardless of duration. Different arrangements and adaptations, translations, recordings or other versions of a musical work will be considered, collectively, one "Composition". A musical Composition that would otherwise be a Composition shall not be deemed a Composition unless it is acceptable to the COMPANY, as commercially satisfactory, in the COMPANY'S sole discretion.

(b) As used herein, "Masters" shall mean every form of recording, including but not limited to, a compact disc, digital audio tape or any other contrivance, appliance or device whatsoever, whether now known, developed or discovered at anytime hereafter, bearing or used for emitting or transmitting sound derived from recordings of the Compositions, whether or not the same also bears or can bear visual images. Each of the Masters must be fully mixed and edited and delivered simultaneously in audio CD-ROM format and as complete Pro-Tools files in data CD-ROM format, and all necessary licenses and applicable approvals and consents shall be obtained prior to delivery to COMPANY. A Master that would otherwise be a Master shall not be deemed a Master unless it is acceptable to the COMPANY, as commercially and technically suitable and satisfactory, in the COMPANY'S sole discretion. COMPANY will not hold unreasonable approval.

6. RECORDING COSTS
ARTIST shall pay any and all costs, fees, royalties and expenses, and shall be solely responsible for any and all duties, obligations or liabilities (including to any union, guild, society, club or association, or any international, federal, state or local government, agency, authority, bureau, office or organization), incurred for, as a result of, or in connection with the composing, production or recording of the Compositions and Masters, and COMPANY shall incur no costs, fees, royalties or expenses, and shall have no responsibilities, obligations or liabilities therefor.

7. NAME AND LIKENESS
COMPANY and any licensee of COMPANY each shall have the right and may grant to others the right to reproduce, print, publish or to disseminate in any medium, ARTIST'S name, portrait, picture and likeness and all other persons performing services in connection with the Compositions and the recording of the Masters, and biographical materials concerning them, as news or information, for the purposes of trade, or for advertising purposes.

8. ASSIGNMENTS
COMPANY shall have the right to assign this Agreement in whole or in part, or to grant licenses hereunder. ARTIST may only assign the Agreement or ARTIST'S share of income here from with COMPANY'S prior written consent, which consent may be withheld for any reason or no reason. COMPANY agrees to pay direct licenses when applicable to ARTIST or estate.

9. INDEMNITY

ARTIST shall indemnify and hold COMPANY free and harmless from any and all loss, claim, damage and liability (including, but not limited to, court costs and actual attorney's fees) arising out of or in any way inconsistent with any of the warranties, representations or agreements made by ARTIST herein. ARTIST agrees to reimburse COMPANY on demand for any payment made by it at any time after the date hereof with respect to any liability or claim to which the foregoing indemnity applies.

10. LEGAL ACTION

(a) Any legal action brought, or any enforcement of its rights undertaken by COMPANY against any alleged infringer of the Compositions and/or Masters will be initiated and prosecuted at the COMPANY'S sole expense and in its sole discretion, including the right to settle any such action. In the event of a recovery by the COMPANY of any monies as the result of a judgment or settlement, such monies shall be the property of and retained entirely by the COMPANY, and ARTIST shall have no rights and shall make no claims thereto. If requested by the COMPANY, ARTIST shall cooperate with the COMPANY in the prosecution of any such action.

    (b) If a claim is presented against the COMPANY in which it is asserted that the Compositions or Masters infringe upon or violate or interfere with the rights of any person or entity, COMPANY shall notify ARTIST of such claim, and ARTIST at ARTIST'S sole expense, may participate in the defense of such claim; but COMPANY shall have the absolute right to control the defense and to settle or otherwise dispose of such claim in any manner which COMPANY shall determine.

11. AUDIT

ARTIST shall be entitled to conduct an audit of COMPANY'S records and statements of accounts relating solely to the matters set forth herein, during normal business hours at COMPANY's place of business, upon ten (10) business days written notice to COMPANY. The Audit notice shall state the identity of the person or persons to attend the audit on ARTIST'S behalf and the proposed duration of the audit. Each such audit undertaken in accordance with this Agreement shall be accomplished at ARTIST expense, except that in the event such audit reveals a discrepancy resulting in an under-accounting to ARTIST of more than ten percent (10%) of the total sums due to ARTIST during the accounting periods audited, then the reasonable costs of such audit shall be paid to ARTIST by COMPANY, together with the amount of such discrepancy and interest thereon.

12. MISCELLANEOUS

(a) This Agreement is binding upon the Parties hereto, their respective successors-in-interest, heirs and assigns, and represents the entire understanding between the Parties and cannot be terminated or amended except by a writing signed by all of the Parties hereto. It shall be construed in accordance with the laws of the State of California applicable to contracts to be wholly performed herein. If any part of this Agreement shall be invalid or unenforceable it shall not affect the validity of the balance of this Agreement.

(b) All notices and payments hereunder will be sent to the Parties at the addresses indicated above, unless either Party changes such mailing address by giving written notice to the other Party. All notices shall be in writing and shall be delivered either by registered or certified mail, return receipt requested, postage prepaid, or by telegraph, all charges prepaid. The date of mailing or of deposit in a telegraph office whichever shall be first, shall be deemed the date of service. ARTIST shall send a copy of all notices directed to the COMPANY to

(c) Any process in any actual proceedings commenced in the courts of the State of California or elsewhere arising out of any claim, dispute or disagreement relating in any way to this Agreement may, among other methods, be served upon ARTIST by delivering or mailing the same, via registered or certified mail, addressed to ARTIST at the address first above written. Any such delivery or mail service shall be deemed to have the same force and effect as personal service within the State of California or the jurisdiction in which such acts or proceedings may be commenced.

(d) ARTIST shall not, without the prior written consent of COMPANY (which consent may be withheld for any reason or no reason), disclose or permit or authorize the disclosure of any of our or our affiliates or licensees confidential information.

(e) The Parties acknowledge and agree that ARTIST is an independent contractor and not COMPANY'S employee or agent.

(f) The term "COMPANY" as used throughout this Agreement shall be deemed to apply to the Company and its designees, successors and assigns.

(g) The headings to the Sections in this Agreement have been inserted for convenience of reference only and shall not be deemed a part of or affect the construction or interpretation of any provision of this Agreement.

IN WITNESS WHEREOF, the Parties hereto have executed this Agreement the date and year first above written.

Schedule A

Date: _____

Writer(s): _____

Performing Rights Society Affiliation: _____

List of Compositions and Masters
Description of titles:

_____

_____

_____

_____

_____

_____

_____

_____

_____

_____

_____

Schedule B

ASSIGNMENT OF COPYRIGHT

_____ hereby assign(s) to   its designees, successors and assigns, the worldwide copyright and all other rights in and to the musical composition(s) and master recording(s) entitled:

Title(s): _____

See Attached Schedule A, dated _____
Music by:

_____

Recorded by:

_____

Copyright registration number (if any): _____

(Hereinafter referred to as the "Work") including the title, music and lyrics thereof together with all copyrights and all other rights in and to the Work throughout the world under any law, statute, treaty or regulation heretofore, now or hereafter existing, enacted or promulgated, together with all claims, demands and causes of action heretofore, now or hereafter existing, for the use of the Work or infringement of the copyright therein or any other legal or equitable right to the use and ownership thereof in all fields of use now or hereafter existing throughout the world and otherwise throughout the universe by any means or technology now known or hereafter existing.

_____ has caused this assignment to be executed as of the __day of

_____, 200__.

_____

(Name, Company, Title)

<u>Schedule C</u>

MUSICIAN(S) AND PRODUCER(S) FORM

I hereby confirm so far as the same concerns me, that for good and valuable consideration, the receipt and adequacy of which I acknowledge, I assign to _____ all rights that I have or may have in and to the following Compositions and Masters, including the copyrights therein, for all uses of whatsoever nature whether now known or hereafter devised, throughout the universe. I acknowledge that neither _____ nor any of its affiliates, licensees, customers or any person, company or corporation deriving any rights from _____ will have any obligation to make any payments of whatsoever nature to me or anyone claiming rights through me or on my behalf as a result of any use of the Compositions and/or Masters:

Composition(s)/Master(s)

_____

_____

_____

_____

_____

_____

Session Date: _____

Musician's Name: _____   Musician's Name: _____

Musician's Name: _____   Musician's Name: _____

Recording Producer's Name: _____   Recording Producer's Name: _____

Appendix F

DISTRIBUTION AGREEMENT

The following will constitute our agreement:

1. You appoint us as your exclusive distributor throughout the United States, its territories and possessions and Armed Forces Post Exchanges ("Territory") of your audio record and video catalogues ("Records") through Normal Retail Channels and Electronic Transmissions during the period covered by this Agreement. ("Term")

2. (a) The Term will commence on _____ and will continue until _____.

(b) We will have the option to extend the Term for two (2) additional years by giving you written notice to that effect at any time prior to the date the Term would otherwise have expired; provided, however, we may not exercise the option unless Net Sales of Records prior to the date the Term would otherwise expire is at least Two Hundred Thousand ($200,000.00) Dollars.

3. During the Term and in the Territory our services will include the following:

(a) Solicit and process orders, and distribute Records on your behalf through Normal Retail Channels (as hereinafter defined).

(b) Bill and collect from customers.

(c) Monitor and control inventory of Records.

(d) Process returns of Records in accordance with our customary policies and practices. You acknowledge that we sell Records to our customers on an unlimited return basis.

(e) Administer advertising for Records at your request up to an amount approved by you. You agree to reimburse us on demand for all costs incurred by us on your behalf in connection with advertising and marketing for your Records. We may, at our option, elect to deduct such amounts from any sums payable to you hereunder.

(f) Accept and store Records at our warehouse and/or distribution center. Accept, subject to a reasonable allowance for shrinkage, not to exceed five (5%) percent, risk of loss for Records, including Records in transit to customers and Records returned to us by customers. The risk of loss accepted by us is limited to the actual manufacturing cost and shall not apply to any Records which you were obligated to remove from our warehouse prior to the date of the loss. We will not be liable for prospective profits or special, indirect or consequential damages.

(g) With respect to the loss of Records shipped via limited liability carriers, the claim settlement made by us with the carrier will constitute full payment to you;

(h) Fulfillment of orders, by picking, packaging and shipping Records to our customers from our warehouse and/or distribution center:

4. (a) You will be responsible for the manufacture of Records and components and the delivery of all finished goods f.o.b. to our warehouse and/or distribution center. All Records will be delivered to us in all respects ready for sale to the public and in full compliance with industry standards.

(b) You will deliver to us simultaneously with delivery to us of Records, sufficient marketing and promotional elements for use at retail (i.e. one sheets, postcards, posters, etc.).

(c) We will mutually determine the size of all manufacturing orders.

5. (a)YouwilldeterminetheretaillistpricecategoryforeachRecordfroma mongtheretail list price categories offered by us to our customers, subject to our reasonable approval. With respect to a Record for which we do not have a standard retail list price category (such as a box set), you and we will mutually determine

a retail list price.

(b) We will determine the selling price of Records to our customers, based upon the retail list price category designated by you after consultation with us, and will be consistent with our selling prices for other records in the same retail list price category.

(c) You and we will mutually determine the release date of each title hereunder.

(d) You will provide Records to us on a consignment basis and remain the sole owner of the inventory of Records until sold. You lose title to Records upon sale by us and we are the sole owner of the proceeds of your consigned goods (receivables). You solely own the inventory of Records and will maintain adequate insurance coverage at all times.

6. You will pay us and we will have the right to deduct from all proceeds hereunder a Distribution Fee equal to twenty-three (23%) percent of Gross Sales ("Distribution Fee").

7. (a) We will have the right to deduct from any amounts payable to you hereunder, the following charges:

(1) All costs incurred by us in connection with the co-op advertising of Records. We will be under no obligation to advance such costs, and may do so only with your prior written approval;

(2) Two (2%) percent of the amount invoiced by us to our customers during such billing month representing the allowance for cash discounts;

(3) All costs incurred by us in connection with other discounts and special sales programs approved in writing by you;

 (4) The following service charges:

(i) Drop-shipping charge per unit.

(ii) Ten (10¢) cents per CD unit for any LP title for each six (6) month period for excessive inventory. The term "excessive inventory" means any LP title with annual Net Sales of less than Two Thousand ($2,000) dollars.

(iii) One thousand ($1,000) dollars per twenty (20) pages of your catalogue included in our retail mailings.

(iv) Five hundred ($500) dollars per page for advertisements and flyers provided by you for our retail mailings if we print such materials; three hundred ($300.00) dollars per page as an insertion fee if you supply us with such materials.

standards, as follows: CD unit.

(v) Non-compliance charges with respect to variations from industry (A) Ten (10¢) cents per each UPC barcode, shrink wrap, or sticker per

(B) Twenty (20¢) cents per each re-boxed CD;

(C) Fifty (50¢) cents for each box-set barcode or refurbished CD.

(vi) A handling charge of seventy-five (75¢) cents for each Record returned to us, provided, we will have the right, on notice to you to increase the handling charge in an amount reasonably related to the increase in our actual costs for handling returns.

(b) We will compute Net Sales for each two (2) month billing period ("Billing Period"), and provide you with a written accounting, together with any payments due you hereunder, within thirty (30) days after the end of each Billing Period during the Term. In the event that you fail to have aggregate Net Sales of at least one thousand ($1,000) dollars during a Billing Period, then we shall not be obligated to render a statement to you for that Billing Period, and we will suspend rendering statements until you shall have accrued Net Sales of at least one thousand ($1,000) dollars. All accountings will be in accordance with our customary procedures and will be binding unless you object thereto within one (1) year after the date the statement is rendered. You have the right to audit our books and records once with respect to any statement within one (1) year after such statement is rendered to you. Such audit will be conducted in our offices during normal business hours, on reasonable notice to us.

(c) Twenty (20%) percent of the amount invoiced by us during each Billing Period will be retained by us as a reserve against anticipated returns and credits. The reserve established with respect to each Billing Period, to the extent not reduced for actual returns and credits, will be liquidated and paid over to you within fifteen (15) months. If at any time during the Term, returns exceed initially established reserves for sales, then we, in our reasonable business judgment, may establish a longer liquidation period. If your returns exceed thirty-three (33%) percent of the

previous six (6) months' gross sales or if you are "upside down" with us and a current (excluding returns reserves to be liquidated in the future) balance is due us, we are entitled to retain your inventory as collateral, refuse you access to the inventory and liquidate your inventory.

8. (a) Within fifteen (15) days following the expiration or termination of the Term, you will remove all inventory of Records from our storage facilities; provided, however, you will first deface such Records and packaging to our reasonable satisfaction in order to insure that they will not be returned to us. Notwithstanding the foregoing, you will not be required to deface Records if you (i) notify all of our customers to send all returns of such Records to a third party distributor who has agreed to accept all such returns; and (ii) take all other steps which we deem reasonably necessary to insure that such returns are sent to such third party distributor. You will be responsible for any freight and other charges in connection with removal and defacement of Records. In the event removal is not completed as set forth above, we will charge you fifty (50¢) cents per CD unit as an inventory disposal fee.

(b) Records returned will be scrapped in accordance with our then-current policy unless you give us prior written instructions to the contrary. Any and all costs and expenses paid or incurred by us in complying with your instructions (including storage and shipping) will be your responsibility. Following the termination of this Agreement for any reason, we will not be obligated to process returns and such processing will be your sole responsibility.

(c) Any successor distributor of Records will be required by us to accept all returns tendered to such successor distributor, and for our benefit or that of our customers, such successor distributor will give a credit or refund, whichever is requested by our customers, in the amount such customers paid us for such Records. You and any successor distributor will notify our customers in writing of the provisions hereof and shall hold us harmless from and against all costs, expenses and liability arising out of returns of Records. You will cooperate fully and in good faith with us to achieve a smooth transition at the end of the Term.

(d) Upon the termination of this Agreement for any reason whatsoever, we may, at our sole election, have the exclusive right to distribute, sell, promote, advertise and market the then existing inventory of Records for a period commencing on the date of such termination and continuing until six (6) months thereafter ("Sell-off Period").

(e) Within sixty (60) days after the end of the Sell-off Period, you will give us instructions concerning the delivery to you or your designee of all inventory of Records then in our warehouse and/or distribution center. Any such delivery will be at your sole expense and subject to the payment of all outstanding debts or monies due us by you hereunder. If you have not given delivery instructions to us with such sixty (60) day period, you will be deemed to have authorized us to destroy such inventory on your behalf at your expense.

9. (a) You warrant and represent that: (i) You have the right and power to enter into and fully perform this agreement.

(ii) The compositions, Records, names, likenesses, performances, trademarks and logos, and other musical, literary and intellectual properties embodied in the Records (including

packaging) hereunder will not violate any law or infringe upon the rights of any third party, and you have the full right to exploit all of the foregoing in the Records.

(iii) You own the exclusive right to exploit the Records and to authorize us to distribute the Records hereunder.

(iv) You are and will at all relevant times continue to be a signatory to and will comply with the rules and regulations of any union or guild having jurisdiction thereof, and all Records will have been recorded in accordance with applicable union and/or guild agreements.

(v) Prior to our distribution of any Records, you will have obtained at your sole expense, all necessary consents, permissions and licenses in connection with the Records, and the packaging therefore (including without limitation, mechanical licenses, artwork licenses, so-called "sample" clearances and musician clearances).

(vi) Youwillbesolelyresponsibleforallrecordingandproductioncosts,andforany claim of non-payment of recording and production costs in connection with the Records, and fully indemnify us in accordance with the terms hereof. You will make all other payments necessary in order to enable us to distribute Records. You will pay all mechanical, artist and producer royalties, and all other sums or royalties due third parties in connection with Records.

(vii)You will be responsible for and will pay all sales and property taxes (including any taxes on inventory) which may be applicable to the transactions hereunder. Notwithstanding the foregoing, if we become liable for any such taxes, we will have the right to charge you for the amount thereof from proceeds hereunder.

(viii) We will not be responsible for the payment of any costs, expenses, charges, fees or royalties to any persons whatsoever except as specifically provided herein.

(b) You hereby indemnify and save us and our employees and agents harmless from and against any and all claims, damages, liabilities, costs and expenses (including reasonable attorneys' fees) arising out of any breach or alleged breach of any warranties or representations made by you herein or your failure to perform in accordance with this agreement. You will reimburse us on demand for any payments made by us in respect of any claim or liability to which the foregoing indemnity applies. We may withhold sums payable to you hereunder in any amount reasonably related to our potential liability and cost pending the resolution of any claim or action as to which this indemnity applies.

(c) We will have the right, without liability to you, to decline to distribute any Record which we deem patently offensive or which, in the judgment of our attorneys, might subject us to unfavorable regulatory action, violate any law, violate the rights of any person or entity, or subject us to liability for any reason.

10. For purposes of this agreement, the following terms will have the following meanings:

 (a) Normal Retail Channels - Normal retail distribution channels in the record industry, specifically including sales to record stores, book stores and distributors, one-stops, rack jobbers

and other wholesalers, mail order and other direct-to-customer sales, Electronic Transmissions, and any other sales to our customers.

(b) Records - Any device, now or hereafter known, on or by

which sound or sound coupled with visual images (whether or not also incorporating graphic material and/or text in any interactive format) may be recorded and reproduced which is manufactured, created or distributed primarily for home and/or consumer use, including, without limitation: (i) audio cassettes, vinyl records, compact discs, digital tapes and other audio formats; (ii) video-cassettes, video-discs, DVD and other so-called "home video" devices; (iii) so-called "interactive" devices such as CD-ROM; and (iv) devices created or recorded by the consumer or other remote receiver from a digitally or electronically transmitted signal.

(c) Net Sales - Gross Sales less the Distribution Fee, reserves, returns, credits, rebates, discounts and adjustments.

(d) Gross Sales - The dollar amount invoiced to and paid by our customers for your Records distributed hereunder.

11.(a) We will not be deemed in breach hereof if we are unable to perform our obligations due to a so-called "force majeure" event. If any such event occurs, we will have the right to suspend the running of the Term until the passage of such event.

(b) No failure to perform will be deemed a breach hereof unless the other party gives the party in default written notice of such failure and same is not cured within thirty (30) days thereafter.

(c) This agreement contains the entire understanding of the parties relating to the subject matter hereof and cannot be changed or terminated except by an instrument signed by the party to be charged.

(d) In the event of the dissolution or the liquidation of the assets of either of us, or the filing of a petition in bankruptcy or insolvency or for an arrangement or reorganization, by or for either of us, or in the event such petition is filed against either of us and is not dismissed within thirty (30) days, or in the event of the appointment of a receiver or a trustee for all or a portion of the property of either us, or in the event that either of us makes an assignment for the benefit of creditors or commits any act for, or in, bankruptcy or becomes insolvent, the other party may terminate the Term hereof upon written notice.

(e) All notices required to be in writing hereunder will be sent to the addresses set forth above via Certified Mail, Return Receipt Requested. Copies of all notices to us will be sent to

 (f) We may assign this agreement to any parent, subsidiary or affiliate, or to any entity that merges its assets with ours or to any entity which hereafter acquires all or substantially all of our stock or assets.

(g) This agreement has been entered into in the State of New York, and its validity and legal effect will be governed by the laws of the State of New York applicable to contracts entered into and performed entirely therein. All claims, disputes or disagreements which may arise out of this agreement will be submitted to the jurisdiction of the Courts of the State of New York or the Federal District Courts in the State of New York.

Appendix G

Foreign Distribution Contract XXXXXXX / MP MEDIA GERMANY e.K.

1 Object of this Agreement

Object of this contract is an exclusive distribution agreement for one or more selected sound recordings within the territory as stated in the annexed Schedule A

2 Assignment of Rights

2.1 Supplier possesses full right, power and authority to enter and perform this agreement on behalf of its own or/and distributed labels.

2.2 All necessary permissions for the recording, reproduction, licensing and distribution have been obtained by the Supplier. This refers to all kind of necessary authorizations, as from: Licensors, Authors, Co -Authors, Composers, graphic designers of artwork, author-collecting societies (ASCAP, Harry Fox, MCPS) etc.

2.3 As by this agreement, Supplier assigns to Distributor exclusive distribution rights. Such rights are granted exclusively, but limited to the terms and territory stipulated hereunder.

2.4 Supplier assures that he has not assigned the above mentioned distribution rights and will not assign these rights to anybody during the period of this contract.

2.5 Products have been produced and manufactured in accordance with all applicable laws and regulations and all contracts, rules and regulations of all unions and guilds having jurisdiction, if any.

2.6 The Supplier shall indemnify, defend and hold harmless Distributor as well as customers, dealers, directors from and against all claims, costs, liability, obligations, judgments and costs

Distribution Contract XXXXXXX / MP MEDIA GERMANY e.K.

(including court and attorney fees), arising out of or incurred for the purpose of avoiding any suit, proceeding, claim or demand or settlement thereof, which may be brought against Distributor for breaching any rights mentioned in 2.1, 2.2, 2.4, 2.5.

3 Territory

3.1 Supplier assigns to Distributor rights within the territories specified in annexed Schedule A (named .Territory.hereafter)

3.2 Within the territory, Supplier shall distribute product exclusively through Distributor. 3.3 Distributor shall not export product outside territory without written consent of Supplier.

4 Manufacturing and Delivery

4.1 The Distributor himself will determine, according to his best judgment, the quantities of the Supplier's stock to be delivered to his warehouse. It is understood that the Distributor will make all efforts to avoid overstocking the Supplier's product and will welcome any suggestion the Supplier cares to make but the final decision regarding any purchase must remain exclusively with the Distributor.

4.2 The Supplier shall forward in advance by e-mail or CD-Rom the following details of any Product that the Distributor shall distribute on behalf of the Supplier:

a) Bar Code Number – b) Artist Name – c) Title of the Album/single – d) Catalog No. – e) Cover as JPG-FILE

4.3 Supplier shall manufacture the product and deliver it free from defects and ready to sell to distributors warehouse stipulated in Schedule B annexed to this agreement.

4.4 Supplier will be solely responsible for declaration and payment of all artist royalties (or royalties for licenses) and all mechanical copyrights due to copyright proprietors arising out of manufacture, sales, distribution and promotion of the product at the country of origin. Mechanical copyrights of delivered products shall be paid to copyright proprietors or their legal representatives (such as publishers, collecting societies (ASCAP, MCPS etc.)) at the country of origin; price settings are quoted .all in..

5 Warehouse and Ownership

5.1 Distributor shall stock Supplier's product in his warehouse.

5.2 During the time of storage, Distributor shall take out insurance against loss or damage of the Supplier's product.

2/8

Distribution Contract XXXXXXX / MP MEDIA GERMANY e.K.

6 Price Structuring of Distributor

6.1 Product will be sold to retail markets based on the price list set up by the Distributor. Distributor may decide price categories at his own discretion and market policy.

6.2 In case of sell outs, low price or budget price settings Distributor shall consult Supplier.

7 Distributors Services

7.1 Distribution within the territory, which includes activities such as: - Storage of Suppliers stock

- Listing of Suppliers titles in Distributors catalogues and sales sheets - Acquisition of sales by telephone or through distributors sales representatives - Processing of orders - Packaging, shipping - Invoicing - Collecting from accounts - Handling of returns - Listing in computerized ordering systems (such as Phononet)

7.2 Distributor shall assure distribution to all major retail stores and store chains within the territory. He may also supply important Mail Order Companies and Clubs.

7.3 Distributor shall support Suppliers promotional activities. However, if certain activities provide further costs, both parties shall mutually decide about a cost split or other cost compensation.

8 Supply Price and Compensation Supplier will charge prices listed in annexed Schedule B (Supply prices).

For his services Distributor shall be compensated through the margin between Supply Price and the Net Sales Revenues, which Distributor achieves through sales to his accounts (such as retail clients)

9 Returns and defective Product

9.1 Distributor has the right to accept returns from his retail clients according to his sales policy.

9.2 However, it is mutually agreed that Distributor shall do his best effort to avoid returns and to keep the percentage of returned goods as low as possible.

9.3 Distributor shall restock the returned goods and keep proper records of all returns.

9.4 Distributor can return any unsold material 2 times a year to Supplier at Supplier's expense. A return request will be presented, in writing, to the Supplier who will then give his written authorization of return to the Distributor within a period not to exceed 30 days of his receiving

3/8

any such request.

Distribution Contract XXXXXXX / MP MEDIA GERMANY e.K.

9.5 If product is returned as defective, it shall be stored separately. Supplier and Distributor will jointly decide if defective goods are to be returned to Supplier or destroyed by Distributor.

10 Statements and Payments

10.1 Payment of Supplier's invoice shall be done within 90 days end of month after product enters the Distributor's warehouse.

10.2 The Supplier has provided the Distributor with the following banking information; Name of Bank:

Address: Postal Code / City: Account Nr.: IBAN: SWIFT: VAT Nr.:

11 Promotion

11.1 The Supplier will be in charge of organizing basic promotional activities (such as mail outs, advertising, retail promotion, printing of flyers or catalogues).

11.2 The Distributor shall be allowed a minimum of 5 CDs of each Product of the Supplier to be used for promotion to the Distributor's Sales-Staff within the Sales Territory. Distributor will also receive 10% of the first order of each title as copies free of charge. In addition, the Supplier will provide 30 promotional copies of each release as material to be used in support of the Distributor's Dealer Promotion. In case the Distributor needs more items for mail outs, retail promo, or other promotional purposes, he shall ask Supplier for authorization. Supplier will then grant more promotional items for current, back-catalogue titles or non priority releases according to Distributor's estimation of when the state of the market is receptive to such activity.

11.3 The Supplier agrees to provide the Distributor with a budget in the amount of US$ 5000 (five thousand) per year which the Distributor will use to conduct a basic media promotion (excluding advertising) for those titles the Distributor chooses to release in the territory. Payment for the promotional budget should be arranged in advance of the initial release of any of the Supplier's material made available to the Distributor for sale in the Territory and is non- refundable.

12 Term and Termination

12.1 This agreement shall continue for a term of twenty-four (24) months commencing from the date indicated on Schedule A of this agreement. If not cancelled by either party hereto per registered letter three (3) months before expiry date, agreement will continue for next twelve (12) months.

4/8

Distribution Contract XXXXXXX / MP MEDIA GERMANY e.K.

12.2 Extraordinary termination is possible if one of the parties filed entered in insolvency or liquidation or filed for bankruptcy. Upon extraordinary termination due to the Supplier's isolvency, the Distributor is entitled to settle any open invoices with the return of any of the Supplier's material in the Distributor's possession at the time of termination. It is further accepted that any costs related to the shipping of this material will be the responsibility of the Supplier or his appointed Agent only (See 9.4).

12.3 Should the Supplier elect to an early termination in order to sign an Agreement with a major label, the Distributor shall receive the following extra consideration: 25% of the nonrecoupable foreign portion of any advance received by the Supplier pro-rated over a period of three years following the beginning of said new Agreement.

12.4 Distributor has the right to accept returns of Suppliers product from his customers and charge their returns to Supplier until six (6) months after termination of the contract.

12.5 After any kind of termination or expiration of this distribution agreement, Distributor shall provide to Supplier a final accounting at the end of the six month period in which he may accept returns. Consequently, the returns shall be shipped to Suppliers warehouse at the Supplier's expense.

12.6 In any case both contracting parties shall fulfill all pending obligations resulting on this contract also after termination of this contract.

13 Severability and Waiver

13.1 Should any part of this agreement be held unenforceable or in conflict with the applicable laws or regulations, the invalid or unenforceable part or provision shall be replaced with the provision which accomplished, to the extent possible, the original business purpose of such part or provision in a valid and enforceable manner, and the remainder of the Agreement shall remain binding upon the parties.

13.2 Waiver by either party of a default or breach or a succession of defaults of breaches, or any failure to enforce any rights hereunder shall not be deemed to constitute a waiver of any subsequent default or breach with respect to the same or any other provision hereof, and shall not deprive such party of any right to terminate this Agreement arising by reason of any subsequent default or breach.

13.3 No modification, alteration, waiver or change in any of the terms of this Agreement shall be valid or binding upon the parties hereto unless made in writing and duly executed by both parties hereto.

14 Governing Law and Interpretation

This Agreement shall be governed by and interpreted in accordance with the laws of the Federal Republic of Germany, without regard to principles of conflicts of laws. The parties hereby consent to and submit to the jurisdiction of any state or federal court located in Berlin, Federal Republic of

Germany. In case of litigation the prevailing party will get compensated for attorney fees.

5/8

Distribution Contract XXXXXXX / MP MEDIA GERMANY e.K.

In witness hereof, the parties hereto have entered into this Agreement as of the day and year first written above.

XXXXXX,

Supplier XXXXXXX

Represented by:

XXXXXXX - (Position) -

Berlin,

Distributor MP MEDIA GERMANY e.K.

Represented by

Uwe van Straten - Owner -

6/8

Schedule A

A) Distributed Titles

Distribution Contract XXXXXXX / MP MEDIA GERMANY e.K.

Exclusive distribution rights as stipulated in the body of this contract are granted for the following titles, series, label or catalogues: "XXXXXX"

B) Territory

Exclusive distribution rights as stipulated in the body of this contract are granted for the following territory: Germany, Austria, Switzerland

C) Term

This agreement shall commence by:

XXXX X, 2007

Further terms and termination clauses as stipulated in number 12 of the contract body

D) Delivery and Shipping

All prices are quoted: Freight paid by the Supplier

Distributor will name freight forwarder of his choice and communicate address and phone number of the local freight agent at Suppliers location. Indicated shipping address for all shipments is: MP

MEDIA GERMANY e. K., Flottenstrasse 28 – 42, 13407 Berlin, Germany

Approved

Supplier Distributor

7/8

Schedule B

Distribution Contract XXXXXXX / MP MEDIA GERMANY e.K.

a) Supply Prices Formats Full price full length album (CD Format) Euro XXXXX Full price full length album (2-CD Format): Euro XXXXX Full price full length album (DVD Format): Euro XXXXX

Prices per item sold and not returned Different prices on titles or series can be mutually changed at short notice (in case of promotional activities, special discounts etc.) Inco terms of price setting: Freight paid

Approved

Supplier Distributor

Appendix H

Effective date: _____

Between _____ [company address] ("Company") and _____ [artist or band member name(s)], p/k/a "_____" c/o _____ [artist address] ("Artist"), for Company to have the exclusive recording rights of Artist under the binding terms set forth below.

1. Delivery Commitment/Term: As of the effective date, Company shall have the exclusive right to release and record Artist's next 2 albums (minimum of 10 songs per album), and any related singles and/or videos, on a 1 album + 1 option basis. The 1st album shall be due to Company within 3 months from the Effective Date of this agreement. Company shall have right to pick up options for the 2nd album within 15 months after delivery and acceptance of the immediately preceding album. Each option shall be automatically exercised by Company unless it gives written notice to the contrary prior to the date the then current period would expire. All productions, recordings, masters and videos made hereunder shall be as a work for hire for Company and Company shall own all sound recording and visual copyrights therein (whether released or unreleased), and shall have the right to exploit same in any and all media or configuration without restriction.

2. Territory: The universe.

3. Income Split/Distribution Of Income:
   a. For exploitation of albums, individual tracks or videos recorded hereunder in any configuration or media, Artist shall receive a royalty of 15% of the retail sales price (or the wholesale of PPD equivalent);
   b. For third party master use licenses fees received by Company on ancillary exploitation of individual tracks or videos recorded hereunder (e.g., film, tv, commercials, video games, ring tones), master use net income shall be split as follows: Artist – 50%, Company – 50%.
   c. Artist's royalty or "net" share is inclusive of mechanical royalties.
   d. Income to Artist shall be subject to standard industry deductions for packaging, free goods, reserves, foreign sales, internet/new media, etc, and shall not be paid until after recoupable costs are deducted as set forth in Exhibit A attached hereto from this or any other agreement between Artist and Company.

4. Recording Fund/Budget: For any master, album or video recorded hereunder, Company shall pay all recording/production costs pursuant to budget(s) prepared and approved by Company.

5. Accounting: For all monies due Artist hereunder, Company shall account to Artist 2 times a year, within 90 days of periods ending 6/30 and 12/31.

6. Mechanical License: Each song written, owned or controlled, in whole or in part, by Artist is called a "Controlled Composition." Each Controlled Composition embodied in a Master recorded or delivered to Company hereunder is hereby licensed to Company for the purposes of this agreement. For sake of clarity, the inclusion of any Controlled Composition in any video hereunder shall be on a gratis "synch" license, and the royalty in section 3 is inclusive of the mechanical royalty.

7. Creative Controls: All creative issues (selection of studio, producer, material to be recorded, final mixes, album artwork, etc) shall be approved by Company with input from Artist.

8. Distribution: Artist hereby acknowledges that Company may enter into an agreement with any person, firm or corporation for the distribution, manufacture and sale of albums embodying Artists performances recorded during the term. Company shall have the right to enter into and execute any such agreement on terms and conditions determined solely by Company and Artist agrees that such agreement may modify certain terms and

conditions hereunder and that Artist will comply with such modifications and consider them an amendment to this agreement so long as it does not reduce the royalty and extend the term (with Artist to receive a copy of such third party agreement as it pertains to the applicable modified terms). In connection with each such agreement, Artist hereby agrees to execute and deliver to Company promptly upon its request any and all documents that Company reasonably deems necessary or desirable in connection with its entering into, executing and implementing fully each such agreement, including, without limitation, any so-called "inducement letters" required to be executed by Artist. In the event that Artist fails to execute such necessary document(s) within 10 days of Company's request, Company shall have a limited power of attorney to execute such document(s) on Artist's behalf.

9. Re-recording Restriction: For any song recorded by Artist hereunder, there shall be a 5 year re-recording restriction from time of commercial release whereby Artist cannot record that song(s) for any other third party.

10. Name and Likeness: For any product or associated advertising/promotion hereunder, Artist grants to Company rights to use Artist's name, likeness and bio.

11. Assignment: Company shall have the right, at its election, to assign or sublicense this agreement, or any of Company's rights hereunder.

12. Unique Services: Artist's services are unique and extraordinary, and the loss thereof cannot be adequately compensated in damages. Company shall be entitled to seek injunctive relief to enforce the provisions of this agreement.

13. Mediation; Arbitration. New York laws and forum control. If a dispute arises under this Agreement, the parties agree to first try to resolve the dispute with the assistance of a mutually-agreed upon mediator in New York City, NY. Any costs and fees other than attorney fees shall be shared equally by the parties. If it proves impossible to arrive at a mutually satisfactory solution, prior to going to court, the parties agree to submit the dispute to non-binding arbitration in the same city or region, conducted on a confidential basis pursuant to the Commercial Arbitration Rules of the American Arbitration Association. The non-prevailing party in any arbitration, mediation or court adjudication shall pay the prevailing party's attorney's fees. There shall be a 30 day cure period from time of notice hereunder before any party can seek legal redress.

14. Indemnification. Artist hereby indemnifies, saves, and holds Company harmless from any and all damages, liabilities, costs, losses and expenses (including legal costs and attorneys' fees reasonably incurred) arising out of or connected with any claim, demand or action by any party related to Artist's entertainment activities hereunder. Artist warrants that it has the exclusive rights to use the name "_____" for the purposes of this agreement. In the event that the name "_____" has any trademark or service mark conflicts, Artist agrees to record and perform under an alternative name instead, selected with prior input from Company.

15. Suspension: If for any reason (except Company's refusal without cause to allow Artist to perform), Artist fails to timely fulfill the minimum recording commitment hereunder, Company shall have the option, exercisable by notice to Artist: (i) to either suspend the expiration date of the then current period (and Company's obligations to make payment to Artist thereunder), for the period of the default plus such additional time as is necessary so that Company shall have no less than sixty (60) days after completion of Artist's minimum recording commitment within which to exercise its option, if any, for the next following contract period, or (ii) to terminate Artist's services with no further obligation by Company (except for the payment of royalties on recordings theretofore delivered to and accepted by Company).

16. Website: Company shall have the right to own, operate and maintain an Artist Website and/or Myspace to promote the records recorded hereunder. Company shall have the right to run advertising on such Website.

17. Promotion: Artist agrees to be reasonably available to promote the Album(s) released hereunder (interviews, photo shoots, TV, promotion trips, etc). In particular, Artist agrees to perform at least _____ live concerts/shows at various venues per year. Company

shall have the option to terminate this agreement if Artist fails to comply with this provision.

By signing below, Artist hereby acknowledges that there is good and valuable consideration and that Artist is legally bound to Company for recording and related rights and have had an opportunity for legal review of this agreement prior to their signing. This agreement shall remain in effect until amended or superseded in writing by all parties.

Company:

By _____

Artist:

_____

Name: _____

Tax ID/or other ID #: _____

Tax ID/or other ID #: _____

"EXHIBIT A" - RECOUPMENT POLICY

Artist understands and acknowledges by signing below that <u>no royalties shall be due and payable hereunder</u> until such time as all of the following recoupable costs are reimbursed to Company:

1. 100% of all recording costs and advances incurred by Company in connection with the production of recordings under this agreement consistent with the approved budget therefore.

2. 100% of all other amounts representing direct expenses paid by Company incurred in connection with the recording and release of Masters hereunder (including, without limitation, travel, rehearsal, and equipment rental and cartage expenses, costs incurred in connection with remixing and/or "sweetening," advances to individual producers/mixers, transportation costs, hotel and living expenses approved by Company, all studio and engineering charges, all

mastering costs, all costs necessary to prepare Masters for release on digital media, rehearsal time and space, voice and/or dance lessons, etc).

3. 100% of all costs paid or incurred by Company in connection with the production of and/or the acquisition of rights in, audiovisual works embodying the Artist's performances.

4. 100% of all direct expenses paid or incurred by Company in connection with independent promotion or marketing of recordings of the Artist's performances (i.e., promotion or marketing by persons other than regular employees of Company). Promotional costs shall also include posters, photo shoots, mailings expenses.

5. 100% of all costs paid or incurred by Company with respect to any trademark search, or registration in connection with any trademark search, or registration with any name now or hereafter used or proposed to be used by the Artist under this agreement.

6. 100% of all monies paid by Company to Artist or Artist's producer/mixer, other than royalties, shall constitute advances unless otherwise agreed to in writing by an authorized officer of Company. Each payment made during the term (except such royalties) made by Company during the term to another person on behalf of Artist shall also constitute an advance if it is made with the consent of Artist, if it is required by law, or if it is made by Company to satisfy an obligation incurred by Artist in connection with the subject matter of this agreement.

7. 100% of all monies paid by Company in deficit tour support for tour(s) undertaken by Artist, and approved by Company, to promote Artist's Albums recorded hereunder.

8. Notwithstanding anything to the contrary contained herein, any costs or expenditures, which are payable by Artist or chargeable against Artist's royalties, which are applicable to joint or coupled recordings released by Company shall be computed by pro-rata apportionment.

9. 100% of any and all costs and/or expenses paid, incurred or sustained as a result of samples embodied in the masters.

10. The recoupable costs specified hereunder can be recouped under this and/or any other agreement between Company, or any of Company's sister companies, and Artist.

ACKNOWLEDGED AND AGREED TO BY ARTIST: _____

Appendix I

ASSIGNMENT AND ADMINISTRATION
OF INCOME RIGHTS

FOR AND IN CONSIDERATION of the sum of _____ ($_____) and other good and valuable consideration, the receipt of which is hereby acknowledged by the undersigned, effective as of _____ (the "Effective Date"), _____ whose address is _____ (the "Seller"), hereby assigns, transfers, sets over and conveys to _____ whose address is _____ and its successors and assigns ("Purchaser"), Seller's right, title and interest in and to the following:

PRO INCOME – WRITER'S SHARE OF PUBLIC PERFORMANCE

(i)   _____ percent (___%) of all Seller's worldwide songwriter's share of public performance fees in connection with the musical compositions listed on Schedule A (the "Compositions") attached hereto, and incorporated by reference herein, ("Seller's PRO Royalties").

(ii)   Seller has directed BMI and shall direct any other PRO with which Seller is or may become affiliated, to pay directly to Purchaser's administrator, The Royalty Exchange, Inc. ("REI") such Seller's PRO Royalties, and REI shall collect such Seller's PRO Royalties. Seller has executed the [ROYALTY ASSIGNMENT VERIFICATION FORM] ("the PRO Form") attached as Schedule B (and shall execute any such other form as Seller's or any other PRO may require) and same shall remain in full effect, and Seller shall not attempt to modify the terms of the PRO Form, or notify the performing rights society that Seller's PRO Royalties should no longer be directed to REI.

(iii)   The term of this assignment shall be for [the full term of copyright in the respective Compositions, throughout the universe and including any extensions and renewals thereof] – [a period of ___ (__) years beginning on _____ and ending on _____].

(iv)   This assignment is a grant of the right to receive income only, and shall not be deemed or interpreted as a grant of ownership or control of, or over, the copyright or any other intellectual property or other rights (in whole or in part) in the Composition(s). This assignment is subject to the terms and conditions of Seller's affiliation agreement (to which Seller hereby grants no third party beneficiary rights therein) with Seller's performing rights society and the rules and regulations of the Seller's performing rights society to which the Compositions are registered.

Purchaser's administrator, The Royalty Exchange, Inc. (REI) shall collect one hundred percent of the income referenced above from all sources regardless of when earned, all income of any nature, in respect of Seller's PRO Royalties above is payable to The Royalty Exchange, Inc., 3724 Congeniality Way, Raleigh, NC 27613.

All statements, checks and correspondence relevant to the foregoing Seller's PRO Royalties are to be directed to The Royalty Exchange, Inc., 3724 Congeniality Way, Raleigh, NC 27613.

This assignment of income rights has been executed pursuant to a written (i) Purchase Agreement between Seller and Purchaser dated _____ 2012, and a (ii) Administration Agreement between Purchaser and the Royalty Exchange, Inc. dated _____ _____ 2012, and is subject to all terms and provisions thereof.

(v)   In the event that REI is adjudicated as bankrupt or insolvent, or if the REI shareholders shall resolve to dissolve and liquidate REI, or if REI is otherwise unable to collect monies in respect of the Copyrighted Works, and, if Purchaser at the time of such adjudication, resolution, or inability of REI to collect monies in respect of the Copyrighted Works on Purchaser's behalf, is in full compliance with its obligations under the Purchaser's Agreement, then Purchaser shall have the power to collect any and all royalty payments due and payable to Purchaser, directly from the PRO agencies on its own accord.

(vi)   Any monies collected by REI on behalf of Purchaser shall be reduced by two point five percent (2.5%) (i.e. the percentage of the gross amount paid by Purchaser that REI shall be entitled to collect and retain as its management fee).

(vii)   Purchaser hereby agrees to accept all royalty payments and statements rendered by The Royalty Exchange as the accurate and complete accounting of all monies owed to Purchaser in connection with this agreement. Purchaser hereby also waives and/or disclaims any and all rights to bring a legal cause of action or claim against The Royalty Exchange, Seller or other related third party, or to demand or require The Royalty Exchange, Seller or other third party to institute a legal cause of action or claim, including without limitation, an audit proceeding , related to, arising out of, or otherwise in connection with a claim for the receipt of insufficient funds/royalty payments, inaccurate accounting, or any other payment related claims. For the avoidance of doubt, as between Seller and Purchaser, Seller has the exclusive right to institute and control any proceeding, including without limitation, an audit proceeding, related to the collection of royalty payments. Without limiting the generality of the foregoing, if in connection with a valid, legal proceeding brought by Seller, before a court of law or other entity with appropriate jurisdiction over the applicable matter, it is determined that Purchaser is entitled to additional royalty payments, Seller shall remit such payments to The Royalty Exchange, less any legal and accounting expenses, including without limitation, reasonable attorneys' fees and court costs, and The Royalty Exchange shall remit payment to Purchaser in accordance with the terms of this agreement.
(viii)   Without limiting the generality of the foregoing, Notwithstanding anything to the contrary set forth herein, including, without limitation, the limitation of liability set forth in paragraph 3 below, The Royalty Exchange shall defend, indemnify and hold Seller harmless from and in connection with only those liabilities, claims, actions, damages, expenses, losses, and costs of any kind (including attorneys' fees and costs) arising from or in connection with any error or omission or alleged error or omission on the part of The Royalty Exchange in connection with The Royalty Exchange's royalty collection and accounting obligations under this Agreement. For
(ix)   the avoidance of doubt, The Royalty Exchange does not represent, warrant, or otherwise guarantee that Purchaser shall be entitled to receive any specific amount of money or any money at all. The Royalty Exchange's sole obligation is to remit to Purchaser all royalty payments actually received by The Royalty Exchange on behalf of Purchaser (less any applicable fees, including without limitation, the Royalty Collection Fee) with an accurate, detailed statement of all funds received from the applicable collecting agency no more than thirty business days after receipt.
(x)   If the Purchaser wishes to remove The Royalty Exchange from collection of royalties, they can request, in writing, a release of this contract regard to Royalty Collection only. It is at the sole discretion of The Royalty Exchange to release the Purchaser.
(xi)   If the Purchaser wishes to transfer or sell any share of their royalties, they are allowed to do so in accordance with this agreement. To transfer the royalties to another party, The Royalty Exchange needs to be notified in writing with the new owner's information and what items or percentages are being transferred.

Executed this _____ day of _____

_____
("Seller")

_____
("Purchaser")

State of _____

County of _____

On _____ before me _____,

personally appeared _____,

_____.

who proved to me on the basis of satisfactory evidence to be the person(s) whose name(s) is/are subscribed to the within instrument and acknowledged to me that he/she/they executed the same in his/her/their authorized capacity(ies), and that by his/her/their signature(s) on the instrument the person(s), or the entity upon behalf of which the person(s) acted, executed the instrument.

I certify under PENALTY OF PERJURY under the laws of the State of _____ that the foregoing paragraph is true and correct.

WITNESS my hand and official seal.

Signature _____

Index

Books from Allworth Press

Allworth Press is an imprint of Skyhorse Publishing, Inc. Selected titles are listed below.

Booking Performance Tours
By Tony Micocci (6 x 9, 304 pages, paperback, $24.95)

The Business of Being an Artist
By Daniel Grant (6 x 9, 448 pages, paperback, $27.50)

Creative Careers in Music
By Josquin Des Pres (6 x 9, 240 pages, paperback, $22.95)

Gigging: A Practical Guide for Musicians
By Patricia Shih (6 x 9, 256 pages, paperback, $19.95)

Making and Marketing Music: The Musician's Guide to Financing, Distributing, and Promoting Albums
By Jodi Summers (6 x 9, 240 pages, paperback, $19.95)

Managing Artists in Pop Music, Second Edition: What Every Artist and Manager Must Know to Succeed
By Mitch Weiss and Perri Gaffney (6 x 9, 288 pages, paperback, $19.95)

The Profitable Artist: A Handbook for All Artists in the Performing, Literary, and Visual Arts
By Artspire (6 x 9, 240 pages, paperback, $24.95)

The Quotable Musician: From Bach to Tupac
By Sheila E. Anderson (7 ½ x 7 ½, 224 pages, paperback, $16.95)

The Radio Producer's Handbook
By Rick Kaempfer (6 x 9, 256 pages, paperback, $19.95)

The Songwriter's and Musician's Guide to Nashville
By Sherry Bond (6 x 9, 256 pages, paperback, $19.95)

Starting Your Career as a Musician
By Neil Tortorella (6 x 9, 240 pages, paperback, $19.95)

To see our complete catalog or to order online, please visit *www.allworth.com*.